# Peripheral Vi

## Inside the Game Boy's Accessories & Add-ons

Daniel S. Baxter

ISBN: 9798374167351
Independently published

# Acknowledgments

First and foremost, I'd like to thank my parents for believing in me and letting me pursue my dreams. This book would not have been possible without their support, especially dad's photography or mom's cooking. My sister has also been a constant source of artistic inspiration and companionship. The entire family has shown me nothing but patience and love while I was busy writing and editing.

Although much of the knowledge needed for this project came from first-hand experience, I could not have done it without the fine efforts of numerous others from the game preservation and emulation scene. EchelonPrime has been my "partner in crime" for years now, sharing all sorts of useful information that I'd otherwise have completely missed. Vojtěch "sCZther" Straka has also been another person whom I relied upon greatly for all sorts of data and tidbits. The Reverse Engineering Open Network (REON) Dev Team has been a phenomenal resource on all things related to the Mobile Adapter GB, composed of some of the best experts on the subject. Thanks goes out to Lior Halphon (aka LIJI32) and Joonas Javanainen
(aka gekkio) for their extensive Game Boy documentation. Last but not least, endrift, the author of the prominent emulator mGBA helped immensely with this work. Her emulator allowed me to capture a lot of tricky gameplay screenshots, particularly the e-Reader and GBA Link Cable. We also collaborated on researching the Battle Chip Gate hardware a few years ago, which was an exciting experience I remember fondly.

A general shout-out goes to the Emulation and Game Boy communities on Reddit. I probably wouldn't be interested in writing a book like this if I hadn't dabbled with posting articles on emulation. Mad props to MAME, groups like No-Intro and Redump, and all of their contributors for caring so much about video game preservation. Good vibes to everyone else who supported me throughout this long but fulfilling process.

And not to be forgotten, thank you, the reader, for purchasing *Peripheral Vision*! I mean, you did buy it... right?

## *Acknowledgments*

In loving memory of Spyro Baxter
The best cat and secretary there ever was


In remembrance of Aunt Lynne
A great woman whom we lost all too soon


In honor of Near aka Byuu
Rest easy, you legend

From the very beginning, the Nintendo Game Boy was more than just a simple handheld gaming console. As soon as it was introduced to markets around the globe, secondary accessories emerged: the Game Link Cable, carrying cases, and headphones. Although the earliest of these were fairly tame, others soon came along that proved more ambitious. Over the years, the Game Boy acquired a vast, impressive set of products. From barcode scanners to real-time clocks, memory cards, sonar devices, mobile phone adapters, music recorders, interactive toys, and even sewing machines, the Game Boy could almost do anything and everything.

The world of Game Boy hardware is quite large, yet it still remains relatively unknown by most. People may recognize some of the more common ones such as the Game Boy Camera, the Game Boy Printer, or those big rumble cartridges used for certain titles like *Pokémon Pinball*, but that's hardly as exotic as it gets. The hole goes far deeper than many realize. These add-ons have been around us for decades in numerous cases, yet even today we find our knowledge incomplete. Both fans and scholars alike are greeted with a surprising lack of in-depth and detailed information. As an unfortunate result, it seems these fascinating bits of gaming history have been left in the shadows.

I took an avid interest in Game Boy odds and ends in May 2017 after purchasing a game I'd never heard of – *Barcode Taisen Bardigun* – along with a barcode reader and some cards it could scan. At the time, there was little if any material about it online, so I tasked myself with figuring out how everything worked. The goal was to document and preserve that unique combination of software and hardware, to shed some measure of light on a subject that had been neglected for years. After that, however, I became aware of just how many other mysterious and obscure devices like it there were for the Game Boy. While all of the *Pokémon*, *Mario*, and *Zelda* games grabbed everyone's attention, the rarer stuff was left untouched, like an artifact buried by the ancients.

Since then, I've tracked down various Game Boy-related hardware, one by one, poking and probing them to reveal their secrets, their stories. Thanks to this research, the efforts of other programmers and developers, and the support of the online Game Boy community, a wealth of data about these products is readily available. Now with proper emulation of these devices, gamers can digitally recreate and experience them long after the original hardware ultimately disappears. Even so, it is not enough to merely catalog and record such things. While we must ensure that these peripherals are not lost to time, we also need to contextualize their impact and significance. We have to understand these devices not only in relation to the Game Boy, but across the entire video game industry. This book is meant to address that gap.

As a fair warning, however, I should mention what this book is not. While plenty of weird and wacky accessories were designed for the Game Boy, such as the terrifying Booster Boy by Saitek and the convoluted Handy Boy by STD, those examples are not covered in these pages. Instead, the focus here lies exclusively with hardware that games were specifically programmed to use, hardware that changed what code the Game Boy actually ran. As great and innovative as the above pieces were, they had no impact on the software itself. This book aims to show people how hardware made a difference to overall gameplay. Some games unlocked wild and crazy bonus material with their accessories, and others weren't even playable without having these extras plugged in. The power to change, add, or enhance whole features of a game is a key distinction that makes such products extraordinary.

This book does not touch upon the dozens and dozens of unofficial items created over the years. Unfortunately, while using a Game Boy Advance as a diagnostic tool for your car or turning a Game Boy into a dial-up e-mail client with the Shark MX are amazing feats, they happened outside of Nintendo's endorsement. Regrettably, there are just too many out there to reasonably fit alongside the licensed entries. To reduce and refine the scope of this work, I want to tell the story of all the insane things that Nintendo really did allow, all of the "out-there" ideas that they said were okay for commercial sale on their handheld.

Last but not least, I'll have to exclude things such as the Super Game Boy and Game Boy Player. While they're essentially Game Boys fused onto other Nintendo consoles, those are best classified as SNES and GameCube accessories, respectively. Perhaps one day I'll write about them in another volume dedicated solely to those systems. Some accessories, such as the GameCube-to-Game Boy Advance Cable (DOL-011) which still technically classifies as a GameCube item, are mentioned briefly in certain sections due to their relevance.

While this book is not all-encompassing given these omissions, the final section delves into the previously unexplored realm of canceled peripherals. Had they made it to retail, they would have no doubt found a place among these pages. Somewhere along their journey from Research & Development to store shelves, however, they were scrapped, canned, and shutdown. Despite never seeing a real release, this potential hardware left behind trace evidence: remnants of code tucked away inside games, screenshots and snippets from magazines, and in a few cases actual prototypes. Every chapter represents ideas that failed to have their fair chance on the market. Nevertheless, in examining them, perhaps they will at last get the recognition they were once denied.

Diving into this hardware is above all an integral part of studying video games and the larger industry behind them. It provides another piece of the puzzle, without which we cannot fully comprehend the history of electronic entertainment. The list of things companies made the Game Boy do is not a short one at all. These devices run the gamut of wondrous, bizarre, baffling, exciting, ingenious, laughable, laudable, and everything in between. Nonetheless, in each of them we see how the business evolved, how it overcame limitations, and how it advanced gameplay concepts over several decades. For too long, however, accessories have never been the center of our attention, lying just beyond the edge of our sight. It's time we turned our heads and took notice of what's always been sitting within our peripheral vision.

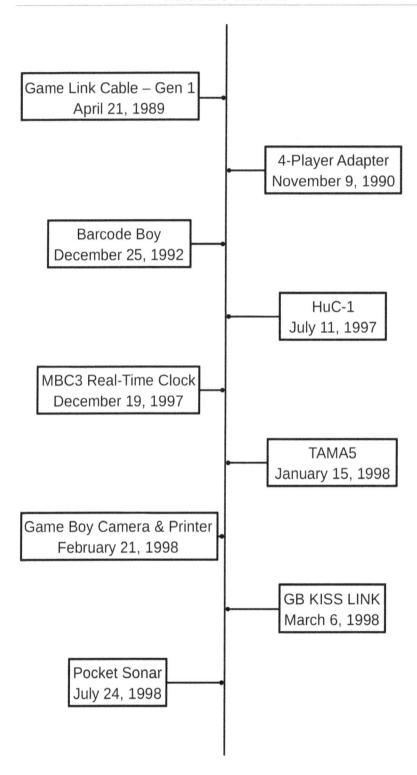

Game Link Cable – Gen 1
April 21, 1989

4-Player Adapter
November 9, 1990

Barcode Boy
December 25, 1992

HuC-1
July 11, 1997

MBC3 Real-Time Clock
December 19, 1997

TAMA5
January 15, 1998

Game Boy Camera & Printer
February 21, 1998

GB KISS LINK
March 6, 1998

Pocket Sonar
July 24, 1998

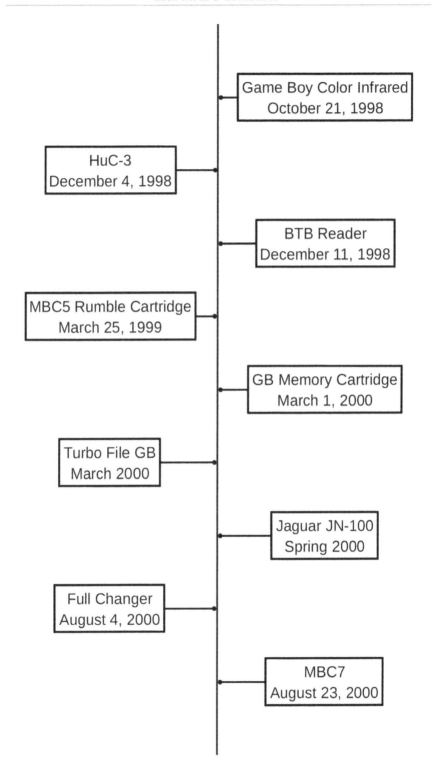

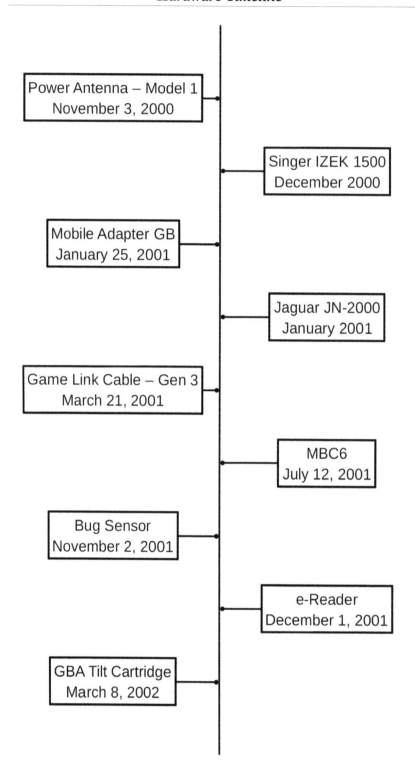

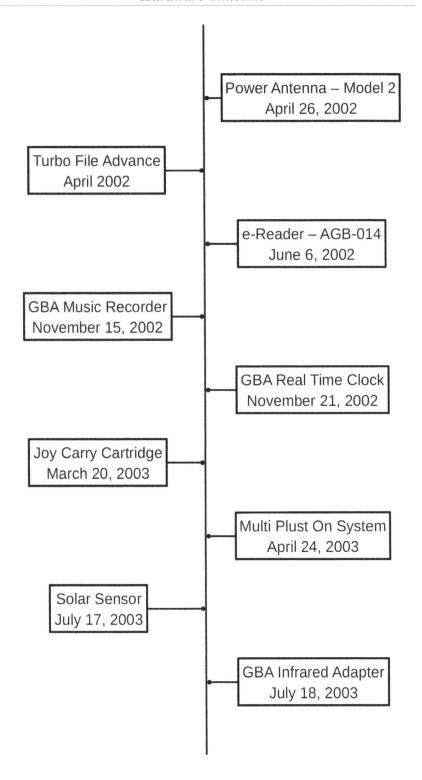

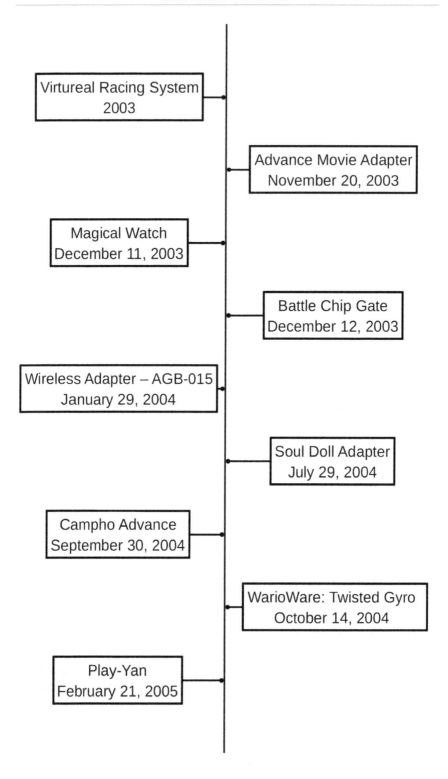

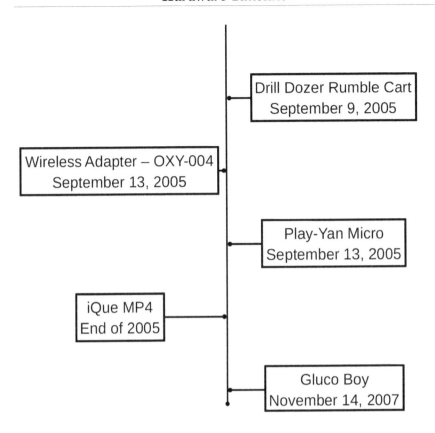

# Table of Contents

# Table of Contents

# Table of Contents

# Table of Contents

From April 21, 1989 until March 21, 2001, the original Game Boy and its upgraded models ruled the handheld video game market. During this time, Nintendo's products managed to fend off more technologically advanced rivals that touted better graphics, bigger screens, clearer sound, and faster processors. The Game Boy became a juggernaut within the industry, knowing nothing of defeat. It was perhaps due to this sheer dominance that a great deal of new and exciting hardware was created for the platform. Given the Game Boy's popularity and global audience, accessories and add-ons could easily capture the attention of many consumers.

This era of Game Boy hardware breaks down into three key categories. Most prominent of them all is the use of specialized game cartridges known as "mappers". These mappers often gave the Game Boy abilities that it ordinarily lacked. Though they frequently contained complex circuitry, mappers were an elegant method of expanding the Game Boy's roles. For the most part, all of the fancy and difficult bits were handled by the mapper itself, with input and output abstracted to a simple interface that Game Boy software could easily manipulate.

The mappers have several common themes. Real-time clocks allowed games to simulate a player's local time. Alarms were also present in a few, generating sound from the cartridge even when the Game Boy was powered off. Long lasting and persistent storage was also introduced through some mappers, saving data in flash ROM or EEPROM as opposed to battery-backed SRAM, a practice that would later spread on the Game Boy Advance. Towards the end of this period, mappers also promoted sensory immersion through the use of rumble for force-feedback and accelerometers for motion controls.

In the second category, devices that used the Link Cable to communicate with the Game Boy offered unprecedented innovation. As these items were external and not constrained to cartridges, they were often large in size. In some cases, they matched the dimensions of the Game Boy, and in some examples they dwarfed it several times. The Link Cable allowed the hardware to be designed and implemented independently from the Game Boy. As long as the two sides could talk to one another, everything would work out. As a result, these kinds of accessories brought the Game Boy into areas that were outside of its traditional domain.

Here, a handful of themes exist as well. Card scanners were able to process barcodes quickly and transmit that data serially over the Link Cable. Several sewing machines were completely driven by the Game Boy, accepting instructions for different patterns directly over the cable. Since the handheld could basically plug into anything, it started encroaching on territory typically reserved for bigger home consoles, such as the use of memory cards. The Link Cable also saw the Game Boy Color go online, becoming Nintendo's most extensive push into internet gaming until the Wii and DS.

Lastly, this span of time marks one of the most prolific uses of infrared communication. Although some of these achievements overlap with the specialty cartridges mentioned previously, they represent a category of their own here given how widespread the technology became. Third-party developers were able to bring some internet connectivity to the Game Boy in the mid '90s thanks to infrared, allowing players to download messages and minigames. When infrared hardware became standard on the Game Boy Color, a number of games adopted it, eventually paving the way for wireless data transfers that are common today on the Nintendo Switch. Beyond that, however, infrared was used in a variety of unique ways, from harvesting light from lamps, to intercepting signals from a TV remote, to communicating with Tamagotchi-like toys and Furby dolls, to registering movement from proto-Wii Remote-like gadgets.

Even with such a multifaceted array of accessories, one central idea ties all of them together. While the Game Boy's humble specifications presented some limits on what could be done, developers found ways to overcome these obstacles. The hardware featured in this section all demonstrate the ingenuity of their makers, taking advantage of the open-ended nature of cartridges, the Link Cable, and the infrared port to give the Game Boy powers that were normally out of reach. Each product stands as a testament to how far the Game Boy could be pushed. Ultimately, the handheld exceeded its initial scope of a mere gaming machine, cultivating a rich and diverse ecosystem that few others have ever come close to matching.

**Release Date:**
April 21, 1989

**Maker:**
Nintendo

**Legacy:**
Launched multiplayer on the Game Boy and became the standard communication method for later accessories.

Released on the same day as the Game Boy, the original Nintendo Game Link Cable was the very first accessory that expanded the handheld's capabilities. Every Game Boy came with a built-in communications port on the side which allowed games to transfer data between two units. From the start, Nintendo designed their portable console with an eye towards multiplayer. Launch titles such as *Baseball, Tetris, Tennis,* and *Yakuman* instantly took advantage of the Link Cable. Due to its simplicity and utility, the Link Cable became the most widely supported accessory across the Game Boy library, with hundreds of titles using that feature in some capacity.

Multiplayer on the Game Boy differed notably from other consoles such as the SNES or Sega Genesis/Megadrive. Players couldn't simply add another controller to join a game. Instead, each player brought their own system and their own copy of a game, and at least one of them had to provide a Link Cable to connect everything. Despite taking so much hardware to get multiplayer running, the Link Cable remained popular during the lifetime of the original monochrome Game Boy and its successor, the Game Boy Color. Best-selling titles such as *Pokémon*, which heavily promoted linking games for trading and battling, further cemented the Link Cable as an essential Game Boy product.

As a result of its early introduction, the cable had an immediate and lasting impact on the way games were designed for the Game Boy. Entire genres such as fighting, racing, and sports soon made 2-player modes a standardized feature. By giving each participant a separate device, multiplayer matches could now finally break free of split-screen conventions found on other consoles. Furthermore, using separate cartridges enabled games to more easily keep track of their own data on a per-player basis, such as Win/Loss statistics.

The Link Cable transferred data serially, sending and receiving one bit at a time. After doing this eight times, a full byte was shifted from one Game Boy to another. While this process may seem slow, serial transfers are quite common in computing even today. Under ideal circumstances, the original Game Boy and Game Boy Pocket could transmit data at a maximum rate of 1KB/s, while the Game Boy Color could reach a maximum of 64KB/s. When a multiplayer session began, both Game Boys needed to decide which unit became *Player 1* and which became *Player 2*. The game software handled this negotiation, often relying on whichever player entered a certain menu or hit a certain button first. On a more technical level, the software

4

then dictated to each Game Boy whether they would act as the leader or a sort of follower for all further transmissions.

Transfers via the Link Cable were bidirectional. Each Game Boy swapped one byte of data with the other at exactly the same time. Only one Game Boy, however, decided when the transfer actually started. This Game Boy took on the role of controlling serial communications with its partner. The principle was reinforced through the hardware itself. Only one Game Boy could effectively supply a clock signal through the Link Cable, which was necessary to move individual bits along the wiring. To synchronize data, both Game Boys used what is known as "hardware interrupts" to alert their software when a transfer had completed. These types of interrupts were triggered by specific operations within the Game Boy, and they could force the game to jump to areas of code programmed to handle certain events. A dedicated interrupt existed just for serial transfers, so games acknowledged sending or receiving bytes in a timely fashion.

1st Generation Link Cables, known as the DMG-04, were sold individually or as part of a boxed bundle for the Game Boy. This iteration of the Link Cable had a larger connector than any of the later ones and only supported the system's original model. 2nd Generation Link Cables appeared later alongside the Game Boy Pocket, Game Boy Light, and Game Boy Color. These connectors were significantly smaller than their predecessors, leading to incompatibilities without the use of several specialized cables or adapters. One such example was the MGB-004, released the same time as the Game Boy Pocket. It fit onto the end of a 1st Generation connector and converted it to the newer 2nd Generation. Very similar in concept, the DMG-014 worked in the opposite direction, converting a 2nd Generation connector into a 1st Generation type.

Eventually, the MGB-010 "Universal Link Cable" came bundled with every Game Boy Printer. This cable had both a 1st and 2nd Generation connector on one side, and a 2nd Generation connector on the other. With the MGB-010, players only needed to select the correct cable rather than convert an existing one. While there were a handful of Link Cable products that smoothed out the various issues of hooking up 1st and 2nd Generation serial ports, at least two standalone 2nd Generation cables were produced. The MGB-008 and CGB-003 debuted with the Game Boy Pocket and Game Boy Color respectively. Even though they carried different model numbers and were marketed for different Game Boys, there were no incompatibilities between the two.

The Link Cable would eventually become a crucial component for a host of first and third-party accessories. As previously noted, the likes of the Game Boy Printer transferred data through the Link Cable. The Barcode Boy was the first to demonstrate such hardware, and afterwards several others copied the concept. In later years, a more common approach was for these accessories to integrate the Link Cable as a non-removable, always attached part. Some even ditched the cable portion entirely and plugged directly into the serial port. The Link Cable and its various forms served as an important bridge between the Game Boy and its many peripherals.

Ultimately, the cable opened up a nearly endless amount of possibilities for the Game Boy. Data sent and received via the Link Cable had no official format. Each game and each piece of software determined for themselves how best to move information back and forth. This gave game developers tremendous freedom to interact with a wide range of external hardware. Eventually, the fledgling handheld would go on to easily work with printers, barcode scanners, sewing machines, cellphones, and much more. So long as developers could imagine it, they could create all sorts of devices compatible with the Game Boy. Although the Link Cable remains one of the oldest accessories, it helped pave the way for many to follow.

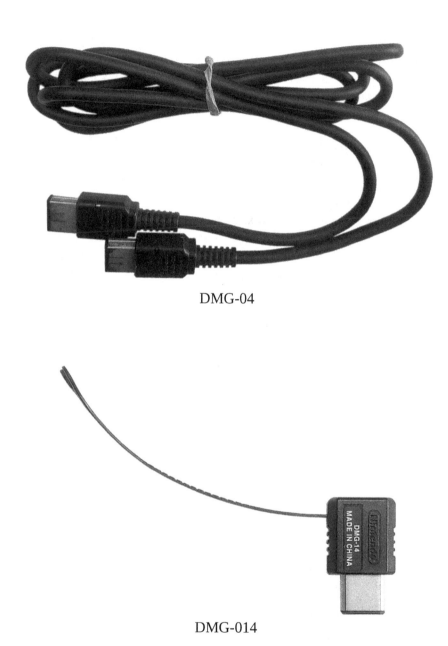

DMG-04

DMG-014

The DMG-04 was the original Link Cable that launched at the same time as the first Game Boy. The DMG-14 was an adapter designed to sit on the end of the MGB-008 or CGB-003.

MGB-004

MGB-008

The MGB-004 was an adapter designed to plug onto the end of the DMG-04. The MGB-008 was the first 2nd Generation Link Cable, allowing two Game Boy Pockets to connect.

8

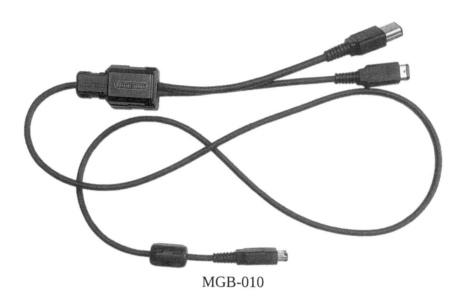

MGB-010

CGB-003

The MGB-010 was known as the Universal Link Cable. It was the ultimate solution, combining 1st and 2nd Generation Link Cables on one end. The CGB-003 was pretty much the same as the MGB-008, except now it came in black.

One of the Game Boy's launch titles, *Tetris*, featured head-to-head competitive play.

Not every game was player-vs-player. *Fortified Zone* paired up two heroes for cooperative action.

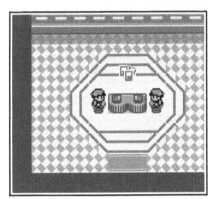

The *Pokémon* games were the very definition of Link Cable gameplay, offering both trades and battles.

Thanks to increased transfer speeds on the Game Boy Color, players could enjoy fast, real-time matches in *Mario Tennis*.

**Release Date:**
  November 9, 1990

**Maker:**
  Nintendo

**Legacy:**
  Brought 4-player action to the original Game Boy, setting the stage for an improved version on the Game Boy Advance over a decade later.

Shortly after the release of the Game Boy and its Link Cable, Nintendo devised a completely new multiplayer mode for their portable system. Rather than the usual two players, now a total of four people could join together for a handheld gaming session. The Japanese company had already dealt with simultaneous 4-player action in arcade hardware via the VS. System in the mid '80s, and in 1989 they brought 4-player software to their home consoles via the NES Satellite. The following year, they released the Game Boy 4-Player Adapter, also known as the DMG-07.

The standard Link Cable that connected Game Boys supported 2-players at most by design. Each participant attached one end of the cable into their respective serial ports, and then the Game Boys started talking back and forth with one another. The general model of communication here was not all that different from hooking up two cans with a piece of string. In order to expand beyond this, Nintendo created a unique cable capable of multi-party transmissions.

The DMG-07 presented itself as a sort of hub, with three exposed slots to receive 1st Generation Link Cables. The top slot had a permanently attached 1st Generation Link Cable of its own. With this setup, only one player needed to provide the DMG-07. Additional players then supplied their own Link Cables and inserted them into the adapter's sides. While it is conceivable that Nintendo could have outfitted all four sides with permanent Link Cables, that might have increased production costs. Alternatively, they may have been trying to boost the overall sales of individual Link Cables.

Each slot was hardwired to associate a Game Boy with a specific player number. Player 1 was always the top slot with the built-in Link Cable, while Players 2 through 4 were consistently identified with the other three slots. When only using two or three players, however, it was possible to have a missing Player 2, Player 3, or Player 4 depending on which slots were empty. Many of the compatible games strictly followed the IDs provided by the DMG-07 instead of using their own numbering. This method vastly simplified programming for the adapter to an extent.

On a low-level, the Game Boy's serial transfer hardware appears to limit itself to two-way bidirectional communication. The Game Boy wrote one byte to a special area of memory and then sent that byte out across the Link Cable. As it pushed out one byte, it also received a byte from the opposite side. No matter what was plugged into its serial port, this was fundamentally how it input and output data. So how did the DMG-07 apply this process to reach more players?

The 4-Player Adapter used a special protocol to handle the task. In the first phase, Player 1's Game Boy activated the DMG-07's "ping" mode. During this stage, the DMG-07 would send a packet of data to each connected Game Boy containing the status of all players. Once a Game Boy sent a response, the DMG-07 acknowledged that player as ready to enter the game. If there was no response from a particular player when the game began, the software assumed there was no active connection and ignored them.

During this time, Player 1's Game Boy also set the transfer speed and transfer size everyone would use by issuing a command to the adapter. Once the game finally began, Player 1 alerted the DMG-07 to switch to a transmission phase. Here, every Game Boy sent their own packets of data to the DMG-07. The adapter internally collected these bytes, and after waiting a while it sequentially returned them to all the Game Boys. Player 1 received everyone else's data, as did Player 2, Player 3, and Player 4. This process repeated as long as necessary for a given game. Finally, once the multiplayer session ended, Player 1's Game Boy could instruct the adapter to reset into "ping mode" and prepare for another round.

The 4-Player Adapter's setup acted very much like a small network, with the DMG-07 taking the role of a server and the Game Boys being its clients. Players only indirectly exchanged data. They had to interface with the accessory, talking exclusively with the DMG-07. However, due to the way the DMG-07 managed all of that information, all sides eventually got copies of what was sent out by others. It was thanks to the adapter's job as an intermediary that four players could race, battle, and compete against themselves.

A rather notable urban myth persists around the 4-Player Adapter to this day. The first-person shooter *Faceball 2000* was long rumored to have a 16-player mode. All anyone needed to do was somehow link together a bunch of DMG-07s and the game would allow additional opponents to enter the arena. For years, many had tried to assemble enough pieces to test whether or not *Faceball 2000* really supported more than four people. There was limited success in a few attempts. The game recognized Player 5 or Player 7 for example, but others would be missing even though they seemed connected.

In truth, the DMG-07 was not meant to link with other DMG-07s. There's nothing inside the hardware that was designed to take advantage of five or more players. However, *Faceball 2000* did indeed have a 16-player mode buried in its ROM. During its initial development, a different, customized Link Cable was created. This cable acted as a "daisy-chain", a circular method of transferring data across all connected devices. When one Game Boy sent a byte, it traveled across every other Game Boy like a ring.

The original plan was to package this custom cable with every copy of *Faceball 2000*. However, once the developers learned of the DMG-07, they opted to use that instead, but with a reduced number of players per match. The code for the original cable was never removed from the game. As a result, *Faceball 2000* supported the 4-Player Adapter, the standard Link Cable, and its own unreleased accessory. The story behind this cable was largely lost for quite some time until an interview with the main programmer Robert Champagne surfaced in 2005. Even with this information, tales of *Faceball 2000*'s 16-player mode continued a decade later, insistent that the DMG-07 was key to unlocking any secrets.

Some intrepid hackers have since crafted their own versions of the *Faceball 2000* cable and have functionally demonstrated the 16-player mode working with five or six players at least. It is the intent of this book to reinforce a fact that cannot be stressed enough: ***Faceball 2000*'s 16-player mode used a custom cable that was nothing like the 4-Player Adapter.** It started as an innocent misunderstanding due to incomplete knowledge of the game's history. Hopefully now, the idea that the DMG-07 plays any role in this may finally fade away.

Unfortunately, the DMG-07 was not supported for very long. Halfway through the '90s, compatible games stopped appearing. At the beginning, the hardware arrived in stylish fashion in the West, being bundled with *F1 Race* and *Super R.C. Pro-Am*. Other major titles like *Wave Race* and *Faceball 2000* tried to push the utility of the new cable, but few developers made similar efforts. In North American and European markets, the 4-Player Adapter fizzled out among game makers after nearly two years. It lasted longer in Japan with a wider library. Still, it only managed to claim little more than a dozen games in that region.

A couple of factors may have limited its widespread adoption. It demanded a lot of physical components to fully set up: one 4-Player Adapter, three Link Cables, four Game Boys (with 16 AA batteries altogether), four of the same cartridge, and four friends. In contrast to multiplayer on home consoles, which only required extra controllers and a multi-tap device at most, these were tall barriers to overcome.

The lack of notable software also decreased the probability that players or their friends would even own the games necessary to use the DMG-07. Taking advantage of the adapter was a cumbersome and potentially expensive process given all the hardware involved.

Additionally, programming for the DMG-07 was more challenging than the standard Link Cable. As it used a rather complex protocol, most developers may have decided to overlook the accessory altogether. Many of the games that did support the 4-Player Adapter also had support for the regular Link Cable, meaning they technically had to code two different multiplayer modes depending on the cable used. This code could have occupied precious memory space in a cartridge, or it could have placed a strain on the project's budget or deadline.

An updated version of the DMG-07 could have potentially used the 2nd Generation Link Cable, making it natively compatible with Game Boy Pockets and Game Boy Colors. The relative unpopularity of the adapter, however, ensured Nintendo did no such thing. By the time newer Game Boys were sold, the 4-Player Adapter had already been forgotten. Not until the Game Boy Advance debuted did Nintendo attempt to bring four players together again like this.

Ultimately, however, the 4-Player Adapter was not a failure. Despite having only a handful of games to its name, the DMG-07 was fairly advanced for that era. Before wireless or internet functionality dominated handheld multiplayer, other portable systems typically only linked two players at most. Of all the original Game Boy's rivals, only the Atari Lynx supported four or more players. Nintendo eventually learned from their faults with the DMG-07 and later successfully revived 4-person multiplayer on the Game Boy Advance. Thanks to those improvements, programming multiplayer modes became easier, and linking the handhelds together was cheaper, simpler, and more straightforward. The 4-Player Adapter may have had its rough edges, but it gave Nintendo valuable insight on building better connections for its later portable consoles.

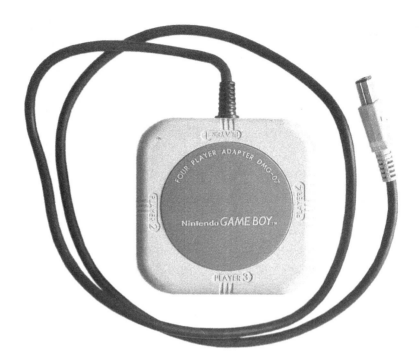

DMG-07 aka 4-Player Adapter

The DMG-07 acted as a hub, with other Link Cables plugging into the sides. Each of these represented a hardwired player number, as shown by the engravings. This peripheral only accepted 1st Generation cables, so newer Game Boys had to use adapters of some sort. Its basic design was similar to the AGB-005, the Game Boy Advance Link Cable, which also allowed 4-player games.

At the time, supporting anything more than two players was quite advanced for a handheld gaming system. Despite such an amazing feat, only about 20 titles supported the DMG-07, a small number in comparison to the standard Link Cable.

The *Downtown Nekketsu* series had a number of spin-offs on the Game Boy, a few of which were competitive 4-player sports.

*Faceball 2000* brought a "family friendly" first-person shooter to the Game Boy, with support for 2-4 players using the DMG-07.

*F1 Race* served as an introduction to 4-player Game Boy titles in the West. It was impressive given its speed and intensity.

*Super R.C. Pro-Am* came bundled with the DMG-07 too and proved linking four Game Boys together could be fast and fun.

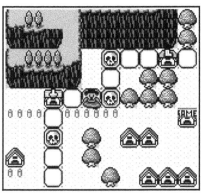

The adapter supported a number of card/board games, such as *Jinsei Game Densetsu* (aka *The Game of Life*).

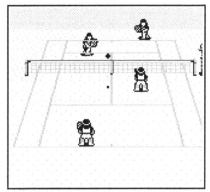

While many titles emphasized head-to-head action, *Top Rank Tennis* featured teamwork in 4-player doubles matches.

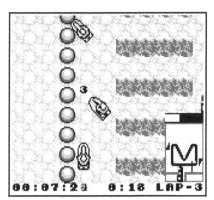

The *Wave Race* franchise began on the Game Boy, and had 4-player races from the very start.

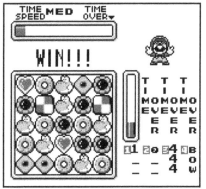

Rare for the DMG-07, *Yoshi's Cookie* featured puzzle-based gameplay with a group of friends vying to best one another.

**Release Date:**
   December 25, 1992

**Maker:**
   Namco

**Legacy:**
   First unique third-party accessory for the Game Boy that added functionality not native to the handheld. First ever card scanner on the Game Boy.

During the early '90s in Japan, scanning barcodes on cards became immensely popular thanks to an LCD-based handheld called the "Barcode Battler" from Epoch Co. It attained such a following that even Nintendo licensed special *Mario* and *Zelda*-themed cards for the Barcode Battler II. Following this trend, Namco decided to bring a similar experience to the original Game Boy.

The Barcode Boy allowed players to swipe and scan cards, and then use the extracted data to alter gameplay. Depending on the card, different characters or items could be generated, often with unique stats or abilities. While Nintendo eventually brought about its e-Reader some years later for the Game Boy Advance, the Barcode Boy marked the earliest form of card scanning on any Game Boy system.

Each Barcode Boy-compatible game came with its own set of cards bundled in the box. The cards themselves featured exactly what the player would receive when scanning them. *Kattobi Road*, for example, showed the type of car along with attributes such as Class, Transmission, Power, Torque, and Weight. Players could then strategically choose which card they needed for a certain race, or perhaps simply experiment with new vehicles.

The cards, however, were not limited to just one specific game. Any cards from *Battle Space*, for example, worked perfectly with *Monster Maker*. In these cases, the game created a random character or item based on the barcode. Furthermore, the Barcode Boy could read any barcode of the proper format, creating endless possibilities outside of the standard cards Namco offered. Players were free to print out their own barcodes or even take them from other sources such as labels on product packaging.

Somewhat embarrassingly, however, a few of the barcodes on the cards were utterly broken. *Family Jockey 2* displayed the ratings of several horses on its cards, showing how strong or weak they were in multiple categories. Out of the eight barcodes for the game, only three correctly generated horses with the listed ratings. The rest were either off by a little or made the horse unfit for competition. Who would race a horse with various attributes rated 0/10? Could someone even race a horse with zero stamina? It appears to have been an oversight that didn't get noticed before production.

Two types of Barcode Boy games were made: those that required the accessory in order to play and those that optionally used it to enhance play with additional content. Only *Battle Space* and *Monster Maker* fell into the first group. If they did not detect a

Barcode Boy linked to the Game Boy, both games failed to move past a few initial menus. Constantly scanning numerous characters from cards was a central element of these games, thus making the Barcode Boy an essential component.

While the original Game Boy needed four AA batteries to run, the Barcode Boy used two AA batteries by itself, making this accessory particularly expensive to power up. It had an ON/OFF switch along with an LED indicating its status. When turned on, the Barcode Boy was always active, waiting for incoming barcodes and consequently draining its power source at any given moment. The actual scanning process was fairly fast and simple, so players were advised to turn off the unit when the game didn't use it.

A very short 1st Generation Link Cable connected the Barcode Boy to the Game Boy. It should be noted that the Barcode Boy was not only the first card scanner for Nintendo's handheld platform, it was also the first major third-party hardware of its kind that relied on the serial port to provide extended functionality. When a barcode was processed, the Barcode Boy communicated the results to the Game Boy through the cable. It was also the first piece of hardware that used the Link Cable for purposes other than multiplayer.

The Barcode Boy attached to the top of the original Game Boy, locking on tightly and snapping into place. Although newer Game Boys were capable of working with the Barcode Boy if the proper cables were used, due to their different sizes they did not align correctly with the scanner's plastic shell. When using a Game Boy Pocket, for instance, the Barcode Boy would have to sit off to the side awkwardly, reducing the overall portability of both the handheld and accessory. Namco designed the peripheral long before any other smaller Game Boy models ever existed, so naturally they could not anticipate this shortcoming.

As for the protocol between the Game Boy and the Barcode Boy, software would first exchange a brief handshake with the card scanner. If the handshake was successful, the Game Boy knew a Barcode Boy was hooked up and the game could proceed normally. Otherwise, if the handshake returned an error code, the games would show a message indicating the problem. After this stage, the games waited until the Barcode Boy captured a valid barcode. The hardware's internal camera positioned inside the card slot monitored any changes from light to dark that represented barcode segments. Once it was finished processing a full strip, the Barcode Boy converted the results into a series of 13 bytes. These values were the

EAN-13 format of the barcode encoded as 8-bit ASCII characters, specifically numbers ranging from 0 to 9. For the final stage, those numbers were sent back to the Game Boy, where the software interpreted what they meant for the game. Overall, no actions were necessary from the Game Boy aside from reading data whenever the Barcode Boy transferred it.

Although the Barcode Boy was quite innovative for its time, it did not become widespread. Only five compatible games in total were released. Within the span of a single year, Namco stopped making any additional titles that supported their new accessory. As the Barcode Boy was Namco's project alone, no other developers created software for it, licensed or unlicensed. The Barcode Boy's impact on the market would never reach the same heights as other devices such as the Barcode Battler. What's more, the Barcode Boy remained a Japanese exclusive, perhaps due to the smaller appeal of barcode scanning in the West.

Even so, today the Barcode Boy stands as a historically significant product. With a total of 34 cards released, it proved that barcode scanning could be done on the Game Boy. Despite supporting only a handful of games, it showed that there was an audience for add-ons with unusual features. Likewise, Namco demonstrated to future developers how the Game Boy was capable of broadening itself through specialized hardware and how the games themselves should adapt. While Namco's experiment did not gain universal fame or attention, it successfully established a path forward that others would eventually build and improve upon. In many ways, the Barcode Boy was fundamentally the beginning of a long tradition of extraordinary Game Boy accessories.

Barcode Boy attached to a DMG-01 Game Boy.

The Barcode Boy slipped over the top of the handheld and snapped in place. It was only designed for the original Game Boy, so it wouldn't fit newer models. A short Link Cable connected the Barcode Boy and Game Boy. Cards were swiped at the top of the unit.

Despite appearances, the Barcode Boy itself was fairly light, so stacking it on top of a Game Boy didn't cause it to feel unbalanced when playing.

Barcode Boy Box Set #2 Front

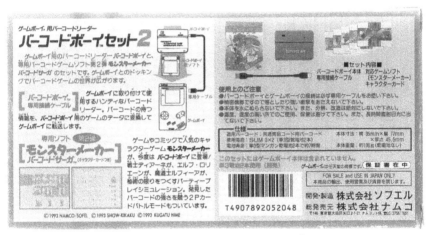

Barcode Boy Box Set #2 Back

Barcode Boy Box Set #2 Side

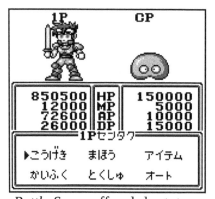

*Battle Space* offered short, turn-based RPG battles using characters scanned from cards.

The barcode generated different stats such as Hit Points, Magic Points, Attack Points, and Defense Points.

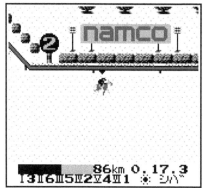

*Family Jockey 2*, a horse racing game, had players running around the track, managing the horse's position and stamina.

The horse's abilities were governed by the barcode that was scanned.

*Monster Maker: Barcode Saga* was a turn-based strategy RPG involving many fantasy-inspired characters.

The barcode determined how well the character performed in certain categories. Players were encouraged to make their own barcodes too.

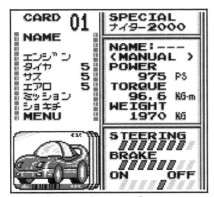

*Kattobi Road*, a top-down racer, used barcodes to make cars with different steering, braking, and horsepower.

*Famista 3* was a traditional baseball game, but players with specific athletic traits could be obtained through barcodes.

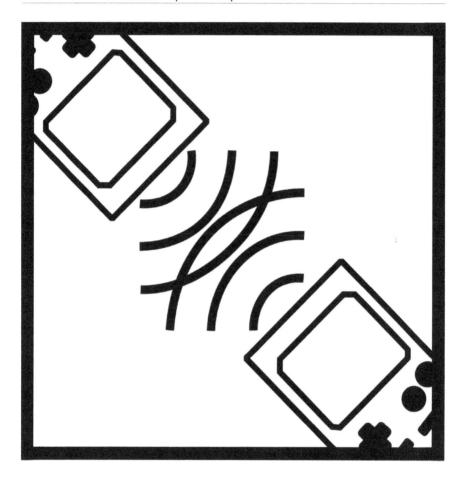

**Release Dates**

|  |  |
|---|---|
| HuC-1: | July 11, 1997 |
| GB KISS LINK: | March 6, 1998 |
| HuC-3: | December 4, 1998 |

**Maker:**

Hudson

**Legacy:**

First use of infrared communication on the Game Boy. First instance of Game Boy-to-PC connectivity for downloadable content. Began the trend of adding new hardware directly to the cartridge itself.

The infrared communication port remains one of the many unique and prominent features of the Game Boy Color. However, when it was released, Nintendo wasn't the only one experimenting with the technology. Rather, wireless data transfers on the Game Boy had already been achieved by another company. Thanks to Hudson's HuC-1, a specialized cartridge with infrared diodes built into the PCB, the third-party developer established their own brand of compatible games. Dubbed "GB KISS", these titles predated Nintendo's own efforts by over a year. While Hudson set the way for others to later tread, they were more ambitious than merely letting players link up without cables. During a brief few years, Hudson would go on the bring the Game Boy its first PC and internet connectivity along with the earliest forms of downloadable content on the platform.

The HuC-1 made its initial appearance in the summer of 1997 with the game *Super B-Daman*. In this somewhat spin-off franchise of *Bomberman*, players battled opponents by strategically shooting different marbles or "B-Damans". The HuC-1 allowed players to trade various B-Damans with one another via the GB KISS function. Despite its playful name, the infrared transfers required both Game Boys to face each other in close proximity, to the point where they were touching, or perhaps even "kissing". Internally, HuC-1 cartridges came with two separate diodes, one for receiving signals and one for sending them. Situated at the top of the board, these diodes aimed at the cartridge's translucent plastic shell. Even though all HuC-1 cartridges appeared black, they did in fact allow infrared light to pass through.

In most regards, the HuC-1 looked just like an ordinary Game Boy cartridge, maintaining the same style and dimensions as standard games. Aside from its dark coloring, nothing outwardly set it apart from others. On a lower level, it shared many technical similarities with the MBC1 mapper regarding ROM bank management and SRAM handling. The only exotic components were its integrated infrared hardware. To control transmissions, the HuC-1 had a dedicated infrared mode, making SRAM temporarily inaccessible and replacing it with input and output for the diodes. Here the Game Boy sent or received signals.

Hudson also introduced a system whereby players could exchange messages with others through GB KISS. It became a staple for nearly all the supported HuC-1 and HuC-3 cartridges, with some exceptions. By using GB KISS, even two distinct games from completely different franchises could swap e-mails. It also worked with a limited range of files, allowing players to distribute digital items such as custom maps and levels. The interface remained consistent throughout Hudson's software. It would later serve as the primary method of interacting with another of the company's peripherals that brought desktop computers and the Game Boy closer than ever before.

Formally known as the HC-749, the GB KISS LINK attached to a PC via parallel port. Once connected, it ran on a software package that translated data from the computer into infrared signals. These beams of light, in turn, were received by a Game Boy equipped with Hudson's HuC cartridges. The GB KISS LINK thus bridged the gap between PC and Game Boy, permitting both sides to transfer arbitrary amounts of information. Included with every purchase were two floppy disks containing Windows 95 hardware drivers and a total of 29 minigames that could be sent to the *GB KISS Minigames* cartridge. The GB KISS LINK had an exposed PCB, so it also came with a plastic pouch to protect it from dust. Additionally, it needed a 9V battery as a power source. The unit lacked an ON/OFF switch, operating whenever the computer issued commands. It sold in relatively small numbers, being exclusively available through mail orders to ASCII Corporation.

Through the PC's internet modem, users could download online data and use the GB KISS LINK software to pass it to their Game Boys. This was the first time the Game Boy ever communicated with any sort of external network and the first instance of DLC becoming available on the system. The material, provided through Hudson's website, could then be saved in the cartridge's backup RAM. As an example, *Pocket Family*, a social simulation game featuring a robotic landlord, had a downloadable photo event. Users obtained a special "GBF" file from the site. Once that was transmitted through the GB KISS LINK, players could take a photo of their current family and even print it with the Game Boy Printer. Additionally, users could download a custom jingle for the game's alarm. Even though this internet connectivity was somewhat primitive – but in some ways more advanced compared to consoles such as the Tiger Game.com – it was an evolutionary step forward for the Game Boy.

As the first examples of infrared communication on the Game Boy, Hudson's cartridges put that feature to good use in nearly all of their GB KISS games. *Pocket Bomberman* let players create and trade custom-made stages. *Daikaijuu Monogatari: Miracle of the Zone* enabled card trading between players. *Pocket Family* offered marriage matchmaking, exchanging residents, and visiting another player's house. *Chousoku Spinner* had a head-to-head battle mode where two players tested their yo-yo skills. It also provided a 10-player contest, making it the largest multiplayer experience on the Game Boy at the time. *Nectaris GB*, a turn-based war strategy game, could save and send custom maps. Using the map editor for the PC version of *Nectaris*, the GB KISS LINK could convert those files and send them to the Game Boy as well. With the infrared hardware, the *Robopon* games let players swap multiple characters, and quite innovative for the time, receiving random signals (such as from a TV remote) would cause their robot's stats to increase. While most Game Boy fans may not realize it, the Japanese version of *Pokémon Trading Card Game* used the HuC-1 instead of the Game Boy Color's infrared port. The features were the same, such as Card Pop and trading individual cards.

As the end of 1998 approached, Hudson produced one last specialty cartridge for the Game Boy. Known as the HuC-3, not only did it come with built-in infrared diodes, it had a real-time clock and built-in speaker. The hardware design may well have taken inspiration from Bandai's TAMA5 cartridge released earlier that year, which also had a clock and speaker. Similarly, the HuC-3 had an oversized PCB, prominently sticking out of the Game Boy's cartridge slot. This new version granted players the ability to keep track of timed in-game events. Often, when certain situations required the player's attention, the speaker would generate a tune, even when the game was turned off. In *Robopon*, for example it informed players when the Illusion Village made its daily appearance. In *Pocket Family*, it was used for urgent family matters or phone calls. Thanks to a CR2025 battery, the clock ran constantly, triggering the speaker according to a schedule.

When the HuC-3 had finally released, however, the Game Boy Color was already retailing in stores. Nintendo's handheld now had its own infrared port that was available to every developer. The HuC-1 and HuC-3, however, were exclusive to Hudson's own games or ones that they helped develop, restricting their use to a mere dozen titles altogether. The Game Boy Color's infrared port saw far greater adoption, eventually surpassing Hudson's efforts in just a few years. The HuC-3's infrared abilities were undercut the moment it hit the market, but Hudson's approach still offered some advantages.

On older Game Boy models such as the original DMG-01, Pocket, and even Super Game Boy, infrared communications were possible using the HuC-1 or HuC-3. A game like *Pocket Family*, for example, was compatible with all Game Boys and didn't require a new system. The HuC-1 and HuC-3 were also surprisingly future-proof. The Game Boy Color was only around for a few years before its successor arrived and the native infrared port disappeared. However, up until the Nintendo DS and Game Boy Micro were introduced, Hudson's hardware played on just about anything. Since the electronic components were built directly into the cartridge, the infrared functions were independent from the rest of the game console.

Even so, the HuC-3 ultimately dropped infrared support in one particular Game Boy Color-only game, removing the diodes in *Pocket Family 2*. In their place, the official infrared port was used, consequently making it one of the few HuC cartridges that had nothing to do with GB KISS. The HuC-3 remains a bit of a curiosity for collectors given it was the only time such an exotic cartridge came to the West. While all other HuC games were Japan-only, *Robopon Sun Version* released in North America late in the Game Boy Color's lifespan. The unusual shape and features of the cartridge continue to draw attention to this day.

Like other mappers, the HuC-3 granted access to its hardware by reading and writing certain addresses typically reserved for the cartridge's ROM and RAM. By writing to specific regions, the Game Boy switched the cartridge into a mode that could manipulate the real-time clock, set the piezoelectric alarm, or deal with infrared transmissions. The clock counted time in terms of minutes and days, opting not to have dedicated values for things such as seconds or hours. In that respect, the HuC-3 was somewhat less sophisticated than earlier real-time clocks on the Game Boy. Internally, the HuC-3 calculated the number of seconds passed thanks to its 32,768Hz crystal oscillator, however, it simply did not provide this information to the Game Boy. The software had to divide the number of minutes passed in a given day to get the current hour. The HuC-3's alarm could be turned on or off, and the exact time it would ring could also be specified. Finally, the infrared worked as it did in the HuC-1, simply turning the signal ON or OFF at set intervals and reading incoming pulses.

Throughout video game history, Nintendo is often seen as one of the chief innovators within the industry, leading the charge with new and daring concepts. In this particular instance, however, the company was bested not once but twice on their own console. Hudson managed to not only bring infrared to the Game Boy, but also the internet in some capacity. Nintendo would eventually explore these areas for themselves with the Game Boy Color and the Mobile Adapter GB, becoming more successful than Hudson in the process. Given the differences in funding and assets between the two developers, it wasn't unexpected for Nintendo to outcompete anyone else making hardware for their systems. Nevertheless, it was rare for someone to beat Nintendo like this on two fronts, at least for a short while.

Hudson was the first to see that Game Boy cartridges could include hardware that extended the console's capabilities. What started here was a trend that would last well into the later years of the Nintendo DS. After the HuC-1, the Game Boy would have many new functions added in a similar fashion, from sonar devices, motion controls, rumble support, card scanners, music and video players, and even camera phones. The only restrictions on creativity were cost and space, and even then some companies ignored that. It was a bold but effective method of overcoming the Game Boy's limited processing power and resources, proving popular with consumers and developers alike over the years. Ultimately, Hudson's HuC cartridges and GB KISS LINK were true trailblazers, carving out a small niche for features that would later be widely adopted and adapted by others.

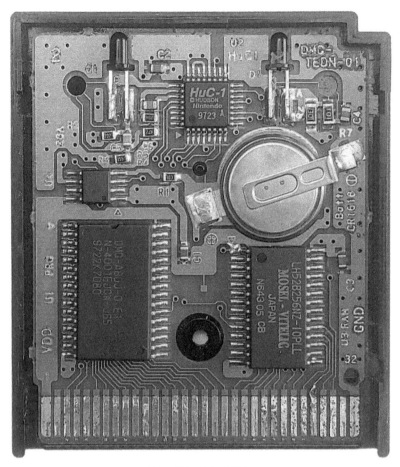

The HuC-1 PCB

The HuC-1 was the first Game Boy cartridge to make use of hardware not related to mapping ROM or RAM. It had two infrared diodes, one for sending a signal (featured on the right) and one for receiving signals (featured on the left).

All HuC-1 cartridges were black, however, they were actually translucent at the very top, allowing infrared signals to pass in and out. It's noteworthy that these black cartridges were released well before the Game Boy Color arrived, which also used black cartridges to distinguish compatibility with both new and old Game Boy models.

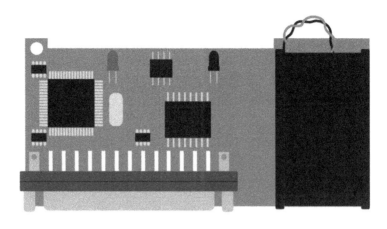

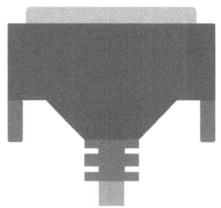

A simple illustration of the GB KISS LINK

The GB KISS LINK, also known as the HC-749, is one of the rarest Game Boy accessories, as it was not mass produced and sold at retail. It allowed the Game Boy and PC to interface with one another via infrared, thus making it possible to pull data from the internet. This was the first instance of downloadable content becoming available on the Game Boy, something that wouldn't happen again until the Mobile Adapter GB was released.

HuC-3 Cartridge

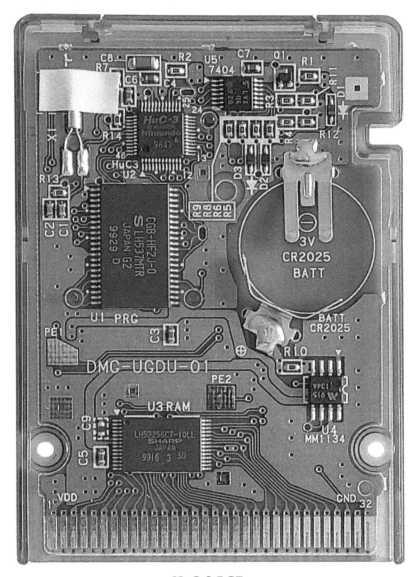

HuC-3 PCB

The HuC-3 featured a speaker, real-time clock, and infrared diodes. Those diodes were removed in *Pocket Family 2*, however. A single CR2025 battery powered the speaker, clock, and game saves as well.

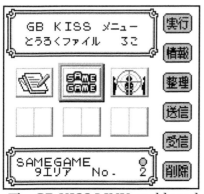

The GB KISS LINK could send data files over infrared, including minigames.

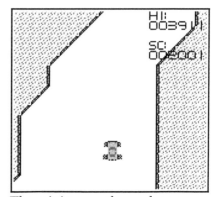

The minigames themselves were basic, such as this one where players raced until they crashed into an obstacle.

Both Game Boys had to aim at each other very closely in order to start the transmission.

*Super B-Daman* was the first HuC-1 game Hudson made. The GB KISS feature allowed players to swap items without cables.

The Japanese version of *Pocket Bomberman* used GB KISS. It came with a built-in monster fighting sub-game, allowing for wireless battles.

The HuC-3 introduced real-time clock functionality. *Robopon Sun*, for example, made extensive use of time and dates.

Another new feature of the HuC-3 was its speaker, alerting players when certain events happened according to the cartridge's real-time clock.

*Pocket Family* used the infrared capabilities of the HuC-3 to compete against other players or download events like new jingles or a family photo mode.

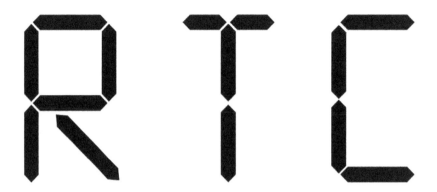

**Release Date:**
December 19, 1997

**Maker:**
Nintendo

**Legacy:**
First example of real-time clocks in a handheld console. Helped to legitimize using real-time clocks in general for gaming.

Game developers often turn to many tricks and techniques to increase the player's engagement with their virtual worlds. As these methods grow more detailed and believable, players are further drawn into this illusion. Recreating the passage of time is perhaps one of the simplest but most effective means of doing so. By having a game's events unfold as they would in real life, the simulation becomes stronger and richer. By the mid 1990s, however, few video game consoles took advantage of any sort of system clock. Only a handful of examples existed, such as the Sega Saturn itself, or SNES cartridges with specific enhancement chips. On the Game Boy, however, a new cartridge mapper arrived that would bring time-based gameplay to the forefront of the industry.

On December 19, 1997, a Game Boy version of *Harvest Moon* released in Japan. This was the first commercial game to use the MBC3 Real-Time Clock cartridge. The mapper was functionally identical to normal MBC3 boards commonly used then, however, it featured one key difference: a 32,768Hz crystal oscillator. That component ran constantly thanks to a CR2025 battery, therefore it could be used for accurate time keeping even when the Game Boy was powered down. The clock incremented various counters for seconds, minutes, hours, and days. Game Boy software looked up these values by reading specific memory addresses within the cartridge. On previous mappers, these areas were typically associated with configuring ROM or backup RAM, but here they could be repurposed for the real-time clock.

The addition of a clock allowed developers to create settings and scenarios that were always changing, even when players were away. In *Harvest Moon GB*, certain events required gamers to wait a specified amount of real-time versus in-game time. Upgrading the "Hoe" item, for example, took an actual 24 hours. Other titles such as *Cardcaptor Sakura* or *Keitei Denjuu Telefang* used the clock to cycle through morning, day, and night phases depending on the player's local time. Other less exciting uses found in *Mary-Kate and Ashley – Pocket Planner* turned the Game Boy into a PDA-like device complete with dates and calendars.

Perhaps the most prominent and noteworthy demonstration of the real-time clock's power came from the second generation of *Pokémon* games. *Gold*, *Silver*, and *Crystal* versions not only featured three distinct times of day with monsters specific to each, they also used a 7-day week. Bug-catching contests, cruise ships, various non-playable characters, and even special Pokémon were only available on certain days, forcing players to maintain a real schedule if they wanted to experience everything. Thanks to the sheer popularity of the franchise, it was the first time many people were exposed to real-time clocks in gaming, pushing the concept into the mainstream.

Unfortunately, the MBC3 Real-Time Clock had one design flaw. The same battery it used to keep the clock ticking was also the same battery used to maintain backup game data. If the cartridge's battery was completely drained, not only would the clock stop or malfunction, any saves would be completely erased. The situation was compounded by the fact that the clock ran continuously, consuming small amounts of power even when sitting on a shelf. In a way, playing a game like *Pokémon Crystal* was effectively a time bomb waiting to go off. Although there were some technical means to prevent this fate, most average folks simply suffered this dreaded deletion.

Even with this shortcoming, the MBC3 Real-Time Clock helped pioneer a new approach to creating games and made the Game Boy the first handheld of its kind to support clock-based activities. Its rivals soon adopted similar tactics, with Bandai's WonderSwan adding crystal oscillators to their own cartridges, and SNK's Neo Geo Pocket making the clock part of the system itself. Other mappers on the Game Boy, the TAMA5 and the HuC-3, would also appear later, adding their own versions of real-time clocks. Afterwards, the Game Boy Advance supported a few titles that included such clocks, though not nearly as numerous as its predecessor. The end result of this MBC3 variant, however, was the eventual integration of clocks into platforms such as the Pokémon Mini and the DS. Ever since then, the real-time clock has been a persistent presence on Nintendo's portables.

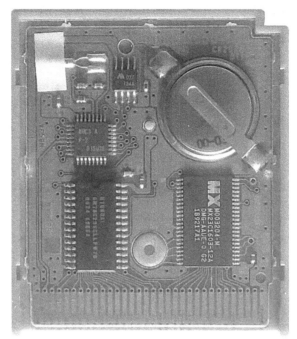

The MBC3 Real-Time Clock

The crystal oscillator, the main component that drove the clock

Pokémon Gold, Silver, and Crystal all took advantage of the real-time clock for various events on certain weekdays.

The clock played a big role in *Cardcaptor Sakura: Itsumo Sakura-chan to Issho*. Some events did not happen until a specific time.

*Keitai Denjuu Telefang* implemented morning, day, and night cycles based on the player's local time.

In *Harvest Moon GB*, certain events required real-life hours to pass by. Harvest Sprites could only be used once every 24 hours.

The addition of a clock made it possible to transform the Game Boy into a PDA-like device, such as in *Mary-Kate & Ashley: Pocket Planner*.

*Tottoko Hamutarou: Tomodachi Daisakusen Dechu* was essentially a non-interactive real-time hamster simulator.

In *Itsudemo! Nyan to Wonderful*, players raised virtual pets. At night, they'd fall asleep.

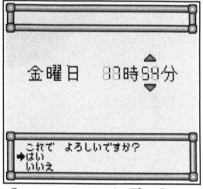

Some opponents in *The Great Pocket Battle* were only available on certain weekdays.

**Release Date:**
    January 15, 1998

**Maker:**
    Bandai

**Legacy:**
    The second ever Game Boy cartridge to feature a real-time
    clock. First ever Game Boy cartridge with a built-in speaker.
    Helped establish clock-based mechanics in games alongside
    the MBC3.

In the middle of the 1990s, "virtual pet" games and devices rapidly became popular. Of all the brands, Bandai's Tamagotchi was perhaps the most sought after. In addition to making egg-shaped keychain Tamagotchis, Bandai brought the franchise over to the Game Boy. In the span of only six months, they released three titles for the system. This software was a digital recreation of the physical hardware, allowing players to raise their own Tamagotchi by feeding and playing with the creature. However, for their third and final game – *Game de Hakken!! Tamagotchi Osucchi to Mesucchi*, or more commonly called *Tamagotchi 3* – Bandai created an entirely new cartridge mapper, one with several unique capabilities.

Known as the TAMA5, this tall, light-blue cartridge came with a real-time clock as well as a small piezoelectric speaker. Nintendo may have been the first company to bring real-time clocks to the Game Boy, but they were hardly alone in this endeavor. The TAMA5 launched barely a month after the first specialty MBC3 mapper reached retail. It was likely developed simultaneously, albeit separately from Nintendo's official cartridge. Bandai's latest work was a logical step forward for their video games. The keychain Tamagotchi models all had internal clocks of their own. These constantly measured how much time had passed in order to calculate when the Tamagotchi needed food, when it needed sleep, or when it should grow. Earlier Game Boy versions, however, had to make do by simulating time. One real-life minute might equal several in-game minutes, for example. When the TAMA5 was introduced, however, Game Boy players could finally experience raising a Tamagotchi as if it were the real thing.

Despite being beaten to the market by the MBC3, Bandai's TAMA5 featured a more advanced clock. While both could keep track of seconds, minutes, hours, and days, only the TAMA5 tracked months and years. It relied on a slim CR2016 coin cell battery to run. Unlike the MBC3 cartridges, the TAMA5's battery was only responsible for maintaining the clock's crystal oscillator. If it died or needed a replacement, the player's progress wouldn't be erased. This was thanks to the TAMA5's use of EEPROM to store game data, which required no power to retain information. This was the first officially licensed Game Boy cartridge ever to utilize EEPROM, which wouldn't appear in other games until the MBC7 mapper arrived in 2000. Incredibly, *Tamagotchi 3* used only 32 bytes when backing up user data.

The miniature embedded speaker distinguished the TAMA5 from any other previously made cartridge. Naturally, its purpose was to mimic functionality present in keychain Tamagotchis. On those models, the creatures could "call" out to their owners via a series of beeps, even when the device itself was in standby. This alerted caretakers to tend to their Tamagotchi's needs, such as more food, more playtime, or some measure of disciplinary action. The original Game Boy, however, was incapable of going into any sort of genuine sleep mode, nor could it spontaneously wake up and start generating sounds. Since the handheld itself was not suitable for this task, Bandai chose to have the cartridge assume this role instead. As a result, the TAMA5 operated independently, triggering a brief jingle even when the Game Boy was shut off or when the cartridge was completely removed from the system. An ON/OFF switch could physically shut the speaker off, in case players didn't want to be disturbed by their Tamagotchi.

When raising pets in *Tamagotchi 3*, players had to choose between two modes: "Tamagotchi Time" and "Real Time". The former functioned like the previous Tamagotchi games, while the latter worked with the TAMA5's new clock. When using the Real Time Mode, players first entered in the current date, setting the year, month, day, hour, and minute. After selecting an egg and watching it hatch, the game began recording changes in time. The Tamagotchi would evolve on a set schedule, such as moving from the Baby to Teen phase after 24 hours. The Tamagotchi needed nurturing at set intervals depending on its current stage of life. When the player wanted to quit, the game not only updated the save data, it also issued commands to the TAMA5 that instructed it when to activate the cartridge's speaker. The player had to deal with their Tamagotchi quickly or else the creature's development would be negatively affected. In extreme cases of neglect, the digital pet even died. Aside from tracking the overall growth of the Tamagotchi, the real-time clock was also used to "step out" between the hours of 9:00 AM to 6:00 PM, allowing the Tamagotchi to visit new places briefly for a change of scenery.

Like many other mappers on the Game Boy, the TAMA5 read from and wrote to areas of memory typically reserved for cartridge data. The TAMA5 only used two bytes that were normally dedicated to cartridge RAM, however, here they were repurposed to send a command along with data as a parameter. The commands generally involved either changing ROM banks so the Game Boy could read any data necessary to run the software, latching and reading data from the real-time clock, and saving or loading user data. Among the Game Boy's many mappers, its operation was one of the most intricate and convoluted. Only very recently have all of its features been documented by outside researchers.

In terms of size, the TAMA5 was quite an oddity for its time. For a short while, it was the largest Game Boy cartridge available. Also notable was the fact that a special plastic clamshell case was produced just for the TAMA5. It was included with the game to protect against dust and damage. Despite being taller than every other game, the TAMA5 managed to fit in a standard Japanese Game Boy box. Additionally, *Tamagotchi 3* was compatible with the Super Game Boy, creating a rather impressive sight when slotted inside the SNES accessory. In the same year the TAMA5 was released, however, its height was promptly surpassed by Nintendo's Game Boy Camera. Later, Bandai's own Pocket Sonar, another blue-colored cartridge of gargantuan proportions, would become the biggest one ever sold.

Although the TAMA5 could not claim to be the first example of real-time clocks on the Game Boy, it still entered gaming history at nearly the same moment. Like its MBC3 counterpart, Bandai's mapper marked the beginning of a new trend, allowing games to unfold and progress at a natural rate, one in sync with everyday life. More so than others, *Tamagotchi 3* pushed the idea of a game world that persisted, even after the console itself was turned off. By letting players actively hear their Tamagotchi from the cartridge, it furthered the illusion that their pet was somehow alive. The TAMA5 unfortunately never left Japan and was only ever used in *Tamagotchi 3*. Nevertheless, it served as a prime example of the real-time clock's use for later games. In many ways, it also became the foundation for other mappers, such as Hudson's HuC-3, which bore a similar shape and many of the same functions. Ultimately, Bandai's TAMA5 cannot be trivialized as an odd "one and done" affair thanks to the influence it had on future hardware and software design.

The TAMA5 Cartridge

At the time, it was the largest officially licensed Game Boy cartridge available. It would only wear this crown for less than a week before the Game Boy Camera appeared. The TAMA5 was also something of a rarity given its light blue shell. Only a handful of Game Boy titles had unique colors, and even fewer had special hardware inside.

The TAMA5 PCB

The cartridge had several components, such as the TAMA6 (the MCU) and TAMA7 (the ROM). TAMA5 was the actual mapper, and thus the hardware is commonly called by that name. It had a crystal oscillator like other real-time clock hardware. The battery was only used for the clock. Game saves were stored on EEPROM instead of SRAM.

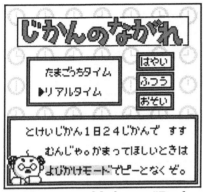

Players could choose "Real Time" or "Tamagotchi Time" when they raised a new pet.

Afterwards, the exact time and date would be set, including the year, month, and day.

The real-time clock allowed players to experience raising Tamagotchis in a manner that mirrored the original toys.

From 9:00 AM to 6:00 PM, players could take their Tamagotchi to different locations outside.

There were four areas to visit. However, each area could only be visited once a day.

After saving data, it expected players to turn the Game Boy off. The clock was still running, and the speaker would alert players at specific intervals.

When saving or loading, players were reminded of whether they chose "Real Time" or "Tamagotchi Time".

BEWARE! Failing to properly nurture a Tamagotchi had serious consequences!

**Release Date:**
    February 21, 1998

**Maker:**
    Nintendo

**Legacy:**
    Smallest digital camera at the time of its release. Exemplified
    Nintendo's philosophy of making fun products outside of
    traditional video games.

In the eyes of many today, Nintendo is most well-known as a maker of video game hardware and software. The company, however, has a deep and rich history outside the electronic entertainment industry. From hanafuda cards in the 1800s to children's toys like the Ultra Hand in the 1960s, Nintendo has always pursued products that were interesting, innovative, and above all fun. Their decision to make a working camera for the Game Boy may initially seem bizarre and baffling, yet it perfectly aligns with their ethos.

Released simultaneously alongside the Game Boy Printer in 1998, the Game Boy Camera let players capture snapshots using a specially designed cartridge. It featured a single, large camera head that rotated horizontally 180 degrees, allowing people to aim forwards and backwards. Long before "selfies" became a common term, the Game Boy Camera actively encouraged players to take photos of their own faces. The lens itself also rotated 180 degrees so that shots could be taken at various angles as well. Inside the cartridge lay a Mitsubishi M64282FP CMOS image sensor. Known as the "Artificial Retina", it was capable of detecting shapes and edges in real-time and dynamically processing them. Its job was to ultimately produce a 128x128 pixel image in four colors, and later reduce that to 128x112.

The Game Boy Camera was the most advanced cartridge mapper of its kind when it launched. While previous mappers such as the HuC-1 used infrared communication, or real-time clocks in certain MBC3 boards, and even buzzers on the TAMA5, none of those quite compared to the Game Boy Camera's ability to record pictures. Arguably, only the Pocket Sonar was more complex when it sold some four months later. Although the Game Boy Camera was not the most sophisticated digital camera of that era, it was still an engineering wonder for being the smallest of its kind. Additionally, it became one of the cheapest and most accessible entry points for digital photography, putting an emerging technology within reach of children.

Despite having a goofy and kid-friendly interface, the Game Boy Camera offered a wide range of options when taking shots. Players could adjust settings such as the contrast, brightness, palette, and amount of dithering. A variety of so-called "trick lenses" could be applied, allowing special effects such as mirrored shots or 2x2 panel shots. Perhaps most surprisingly, the Game Boy Camera helped users take vertical and horizontal panoramas. It would even display the edges of the previous photo to help align the next shot. Since the camera's 128x112 images did not use the Game Boy's full resolution, a border could be selected for each photo. Last but not least, the software also came with a countdown timer.

The Game Boy Camera provided many creative editing tools as well. Users could manipulate images in their album via Paint or Stamp modes. Paint mode presented several different pens that drew pixels directly onto a photo. The pen's color as well as the speed of the cursor could also change. Stamp mode placed several predefined pictures or letters over a photo, making this a great way to insert Mario, Luigi, or even text. The Game Boy Camera also added small amounts of metadata to photos in the form of short comments. Interactive buttons called "Hot Spots" could be embedded in album shots, triggering sounds or jumping to another image when selected. It was possible to combine separate photos via tiling or fusion for more unusual and artistic results.

While largely famous for photography, the Game Boy Camera also dabbled with video, to a certain degree. In Animation mode, users created brief clips using photos from their album as individual frames. Up to 47 frames were available. The overall timing of the animation could be controlled along with whether or not the animation looped. Although these clips hardly qualified as movies on their own, the camera's manual suggested using the Super Game Boy and SNES to display the finished animations. From there, users could record their works on VHS.

As a bonus, several minigames and activities came packaged with the software. *Ball* focused on catching falling balls in a somewhat *Game & Watch* fashion, while *Space Fever II* was a top-down UFO shooter. A *DJ* mode turned the Game Boy into a chip-tune machine, with extensive options to create custom rhythms using the handheld's sound capabilities. A secret minigame called *Run! Run! Run!* could be unlocked from *Space Fever II*; here the player raced against a bird and a mole. All of these extra modes could take images of the user's face and turn them into characters, echoing some of the later design concepts behind *Face Raiders* on the 3DS.

Nintendo did not limit the Game Boy Camera to its own world; instead they added compatibility for it across other products. The Super Game Boy let users change an additional border as well as further manipulate the palette. More importantly, however, the Game Boy Printer turned users' digital photos into physical ones. With that accessory, an entire album could be saved permanently on paper. On the Nintendo 64DD, *Mario Artist Paint Studio* imported Game Boy Camera photos through the Transfer Pak. Users could then edit the images with a comprehensive and powerful software suite. The classic Nintendo 64 first-person shooter *Perfect Dark* also had plans to utilize the Transfer Pak. It would have pulled data from the Game Boy Camera to superimpose players' faces on enemies. The idea was scrapped before the final version was released, however.

The Game Boy Camera mapper greatly simplified the process of taking shots. Although similar to the MBC3 mapper on many levels, the Game Boy Camera included additional input and output related to the image sensor. The software controlled the camera by writing to a handful of memory addresses that configured specific parameters such as the unit's capture status, what kind of dithering and contrast to apply, exposure time, and edge enhancement ratios.

Typically, the Game Boy Camera's software would adjust these settings accordingly before manually triggering the image capture process. Afterwards, it needed to wait a bit for the camera's hardware to convert everything into a format that the Game Boy's VRAM could handle. This data was initially stored in the cartridge's SRAM, but it could be directly copied to video memory to display to the user. Most of the heavy lifting was taken care of by the M64282FP and other components such as the MAC-GDB. The seemingly complicated task of taking pictures with a Game Boy was reduced to merely reading and writing a few values here and there, as far as the software was concerned.

Despite having a few minigames buried in its ROM, the camera fell short of what many define as a video game. In fact, categorizing it as such may actually ignore the intention behind Nintendo's invention. The Game Boy Camera was a demonstration of the company's commitment to "the art of play", making and selling items that were both fun and enjoyable. Regardless of its reputation as a premier game maker, here Nintendo showed the world that its focus on play needn't always take the form of something traditional. This desire to simply make useful and entertaining products would later help expand the Game Boy beyond mere games and travel into other realms such as sonar devices, sewing machines, and multimedia playback. In many ways, the Game Boy Camera marks the realization of some of the handheld's full potential.

Although the Game Boy Camera remains a popular, recognizable, and even iconic bit of hardware, it never received a genuine upgrade. Even as the Game Boy Color and Game Boy Advance arrived, the camera itself was left behind. A special *Hello Kitty* themed version of the Game Boy Camera was later planned, complete with unique graphics, sounds, and minigames. Sadly, it was ultimately canceled. Nintendo started working on a proper successor called the Game Eye sometime around 2002. Had it been released, that accessory would have brought multicolor photography to their latest handheld. For whatever reasons, however, that device quickly vanished after being demonstrated to the public. Instead, only a handful of unofficial third-party offerings made their way onto the Game Boy Advance. It wasn't until the Campho Advance came about that cameras returned to the Game Boy in a licensed but limited capacity. Nevertheless, Nintendo's pocket-sized product set off a sort of chain reaction of events.

Not only did the Game Boy Camera impact the eventual evolution of other exotic hardware and accessories, it had an enduring effect on culture. The *DJ* mode arguably served as an inspiration for many current chip-tune efforts. Today, numerous people carry around cameras hundreds of times more powerful than this cartridge. Prior to 1998, however, portable digital photography that fit in one's pocket was an uncommon phenomenon. Thanks to Nintendo, an entire generation was exposed to a new means of self-expression and creative content that might not have been possible until years later. While the camera itself may have been low resolution, it established a distinctive artistic legacy that continues to endure years later.

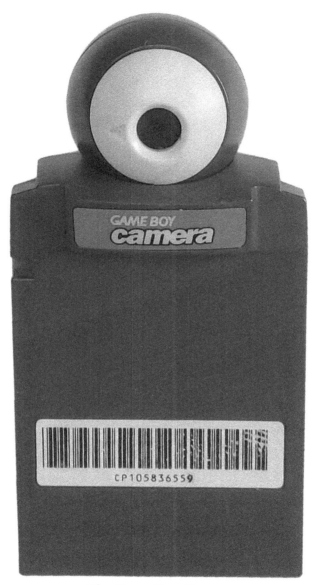

The Game Boy Camera

It came in five standard colors (Red, Blue, Green, Yellow, Atomic Purple). Two special editions were released as limited promotions, one for Coro Coro Comics and one for Nintendo Power, the latter of which was golden.

An internal look at the Game Boy Camera

When it was released, the Game Boy Camera was technically the most sophisticated cartridge for the system. As a mapper, it showed that the Game Boy's true potential was unlimited.

59

The software had an overall goofy, weird, and experimental vibe. Users were presented with a dancing Mario as soon as they turned it on.

Basic controls such as brightness and contrast were available when taking shots.

Stamp mode let users paste pre-defined graphics on top of their photos. Nintendo themed stickers featuring Mario, Luigi, and Pokémon characters were also available.

Paint mode let users draw lines over their shots. The color and type of brush used could be changed.

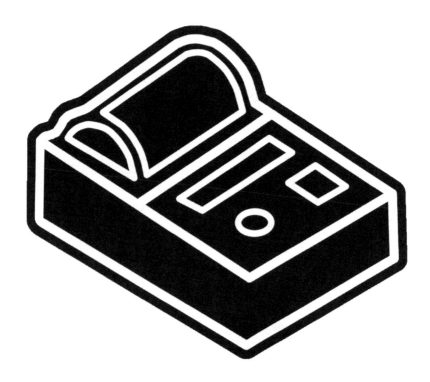

**Release Date:**
  February 21, 1998

**Maker:**
  Nintendo

**Legacy:**
  Further increased the Game Boy's non-video game roles.
  Established a path forward for later accessories that used the
  Link Cable.

In early 1998, Nintendo began selling what could be described as its most novel Game Boy accessory since the handheld's launch. The Game Boy Printer served as the logical counterpart to the new Game Boy Camera, producing monochromatic pictures on physical paper. Both devices were released on the same date, and together they formed a cohesive package that was unlike anything else on the market. On its own, however, the Game Boy Printer would move far past the camera and expand its presence to dozens of other games. For the first time ever, Game Boy fans could print out items, designs, lists, messages, and high-scores right from the system itself.

The premise behind the Game Boy Printer was fairly straightforward. It used thermal printing instead of ink or toner. Here, the paper had a special coating that reacted to heat. By targeting which areas were heated as the paper passed through, individual dots were drawn, which in turn formed words or images. Technologically speaking, the Game Boy Printer closely resembled the same printers used at retail checkouts for receipts, albeit in a portable and miniaturized fashion. Thanks to this printing technique, all the Game Boy Printer needed to function were six AA batteries and a roll of paper.

A large number of titles eventually supported the printer, offering a wide range of bonus content. *Pokémon Yellow, Gold, Silver,* and *Crystal* allowed players to print out specific Pokédex entries along with diplomas. *Donkey Kong Country* and *Link's Awakening DX* had various detailed portraits available to print once unlocked in their respective games. *Super Mario Bros. Deluxe* printed long banners, fortune-tellings, calendars, stickers, character icons, and other artwork. Many games predictably used the Game Boy Printer for top scores, letting players prove on paper just how good they were.

Supported software used the Link Cable to transfer information to and from the Game Boy Printer. The unit had a Link Cable port of its own, although it only worked with 2nd Generation cables designed for the Game Boy Pocket and later models. As a sizable amount of original Game Boys with the 1st Generation Link Cable port were still in circulation, Nintendo decided to release the so-called "Universal Link Cable" as a pack-in with every Game Boy Printer. This special cable had a split end on one side that plugged into either a 1st or 2nd Generation port. As a result, Nintendo ensured that any Game Boy model at that time could readily use the printer without any additional hassles. The Universal Link Cable was only ever bundled with the Game Boy Printer.

To actually put anything onto paper, Game Boy software had to follow a packet-based protocol when communicating with the printer. The packet itself consisted of a sync signal, a specific command for the printer, an option for data compression, the length of the data, the data itself, and a checksum for the data. For the most part, as the Game Boy sent data, the printer simply responded with its status once it completely received the packet. The game focused primarily on providing the information necessary for printing.

There were four known commands. INIT began the printing process by clearing any previous settings and data. DATA stored an array of bytes into an 8KB internal buffer used for images. PRINT activated the thermal head and used the aforementioned buffer for the printing process. STATUS simply pinged the Game Boy Printer for its current operational state and any errors that may have occurred recently. Typically, games would work with 160x144 pixel segments, starting with an INIT command, multiple DATA commands for the image, and finally a PRINT command. Afterwards the STATUS command was constantly sent to see whether the printer had finished its job and was ready for more tasks.

The pixel data transferred to the Game Boy Printer used the exact same format as the background graphics found in various Game Boy titles. This made the process of supporting the printer straightforward for developers, as they could use their existing tools to create the appropriate information. Images for the printer were broken down into 8x8 pixel sections called tiles, with each tile containing four shades of gray at most. Uncompressed, each tile used 2-bits per pixel, or a total of 16 bytes. Thankfully, the Game Boy Printer supported a type of run-length encoding compression which could save space by marking bytes that repeated. Even so, the amount of time needed to transfer a complete image could take a while depending on the game.

Each DATA command filled up 160x16 pixels in the printer's image buffer, and this size was consequently the minimum of any given print. The hardware could generate prints of an unlimited length – as long as there was paper – by continuously chaining 160x144 sections together. The Game Boy Printer could also apply margins to the beginning and ends of prints, and by setting both to zero, it produced long, seamless images.

As it relates to the world of Game Boy peripherals, the Game Boy Printer had a fairly significant impact. Prior to this, only one other major accessory for the Game Boy existed: the Barcode Boy. In all the years following the Barcode Boy's release in 1992, no other company had successfully tried to expand the Game Boy's utility or functionality via the Link Cable. Most efforts were instead focused on making several mappers that incorporated concepts such as infrared transceivers or real-time clocks directly into the game cartridges. The Game Boy Printer, however, once again highlighted how external accessories could enhance the player's experiences.

The Game Boy Printer managed to attract a host of compatible titles, more so than any other piece of hardware before it besides the Link Cable. In general, peripherals of this sort tend to see low uptake, however the Game Boy Printer was a relative success with over 100 games using it in some form. It proved that there was a viable space for complex devices that simply connected to the Game Boy through a small cable. Indeed, after the Game Boy Printer, many other innovations soon followed. Memory cards, cellphone adapters, and sewing machines hit the Game Boy Color. Later, the Game Boy Advance received toys-to-life figurines, racecars, and digital watches. While the Barcode Boy broke new ground, showing the world how to use the Link Cable to bring fresh ideas to Nintendo's handheld, it was the Game Boy Printer that demonstrated developers should continue exploring these possibilities.

As an add-on, the small printer challenged what most people conventionally thought a video game system ought to do, especially a portable one. Yet it was this willingness to go against the norm that eventually gave rise to a myriad of other wild creations on the Game Boy. Although the Game Boy Printer wasn't the first to tread this path, in many ways it set expectations for hardware that would come later. From here on out, through the Game Boy Advance and into the Nintendo DS and 3DS eras, Nintendo's handheld platforms became a source of constant creativity and eagerness to push the boundaries of video gaming via accessories.

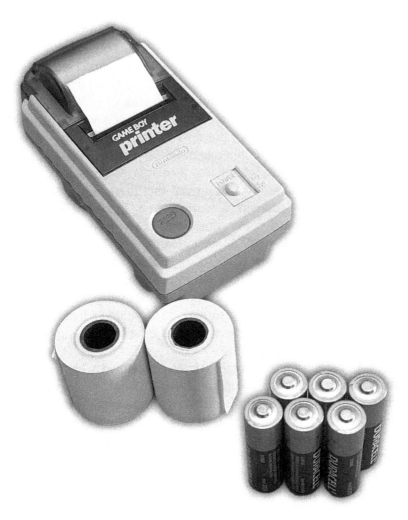

The Game Boy Printer, printer paper, and batteries

The original thermal paper had adhesive backing, peeling away to become a sticker. Stock paper eventually went bad due to chemical breakdowns caused by aging, but modern replacements are available.

When it was released, the Game Boy Printer was the most power-hungry peripheral of its time, needing a staggering six AA batteries.

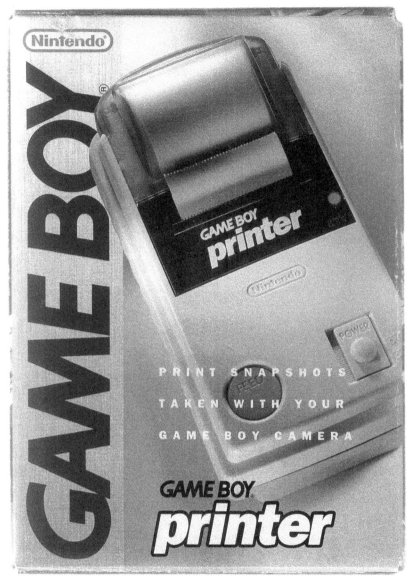

The Game Boy Printer's Box

A special "Pikachu Yellow" version of the printer was also sold. The only differences were its color and design. The *Pokémon* games themselves utilized the printer rather extensively.

66

Games like *Super Mario Bros. Deluxe* offered many printable portraits.

*Donkey Kong Country* had collectible stickers players could trade and print.

The *Pokémon Trading Card Game* allowed prints of individual cards, decks, and a list of all obtained cards.

From *Pokémon Yellow* until *Pokémon Crystal*, the core series had printable Pokédex entries, as well as a diploma for capturing all 151 or 251 Pokémon.

The Game Boy Printer could add borders to photos taken from the Game Boy Camera.

Some games, like *Tony Hawk's Pro Skater 2* unlocked digitized photos to print.

Many titles were fond of printing lists. *NFL Blitz* would print out teams and stats.

Printing out high scores gave players physical proof of their prowess. *Pokémon Pinball* let people show off their scores for bragging rights.

**Release Date:**
July 24, 1998

**Maker:**
Bandai

**Legacy:**
First ever sonar device to use a handheld game console. Part
of the trend to make fishfinders smaller, portable, and
cheaper.

In the spring of 1998, Bandai revealed their latest project for the Game Boy: a portable handheld fishfinder. Originally called the Handy Watcher at the Tokyo Toy Show and Tokyo Game Show, it would later be renamed the Pocket Sonar when it sold that summer. One of the most infamous examples of exotic Game Boy hardware, this specialized cartridge came armed with real sonar functions. Here the Game Boy provided the screen, sound, and user input, while the hardware inside the peripheral separately handled sound pulses. Together, the Game Boy and Pocket Sonar were capable of scanning aquatic objects and terrain.

While it may seem odd to use the Game Boy for anything other than video games, there were plenty of reasons for the Pocket Sonar to exist as it did. In Japan, Game Boys were quite common and relatively cheap. For fishing enthusiasts, they may have already had a Game Boy or knew someone who did. At the time, a decent dedicated fishfinder could have easily exceeded the cost of both a new Game Boy and the Pocket Sonar. Bandai's product thus found a market through modest pricing as well as convenience.

The Pocket Sonar was the largest officially licensed Game Boy cartridge ever made. Sporting a bulky blue plastic body, it extended over the top of the Game Boy. At the end was a cap that twisted off, revealing a 3.5mm jack that connected the underwater microphone. The cable for the microphone measured a lengthy 15 meters; as a result, it came with a spool to loop it around. A yellow foam tube also surrounded the microphone, allowing it to float at or near the surface.

In addition to being the biggest Game Boy cartridge, the Pocket Sonar also required the most batteries. Four AAA batteries were needed to power its sonar features. A simple red LED indicated whether the sonar was on or off when flipping a switch on the side of the cartridge. If the sonar was not enabled, players could still run the software. Other menus and secondary features remained accessible, however, the fishfinder would only show an empty screen.

Curiously, there were some rather strange compatibility issues with the Pocket Sonar. Anything from the Game Boy Color and later simply could not operate the hardware. The only models known to work were the original Game Boys (DMG-001) and Game Boy Pockets (MGB-001). Something changed with the Game Boy Color, something Bandai didn't take into account when designing the Pocket Sonar. In all fairness, however, by the time they'd finished developing and producing the Pocket Sonar, the Game Boy Color hadn't been released yet. While it was not future-proof, Bandai ensured the Pocket Sonar was compatible with every Game Boy available on the market.

The fishfinder portion of the software presented a range of options for users, such as setting the depth of the current body of water, changing the display refresh rate, toggling magnification of the sonar results, and toggling icons that represented fish locations. When activated, the Pocket Sonar would draw an image of the waters below. It could show the surface, open water, debris, and the bottom, assuming it was in range. These images were captured in "frames" that the Pocket Sonar scrolled from left to right. All the while, the software reported the depth detected by the Pocket Sonar at each section. Officially, both the manual and box stated the Pocket Sonar supported probing depths of up to 20 meters. The software, however, offered an option for a whopping 30 meters at maximum. Some Pocket Sonar owners have verified that it did indeed work at that range. Even if 20 meters were the deepest it could reliably check, the Pocket Sonar boasted an incredible reach for a handheld unit of that era.

Internally, the Pocket Sonar used custom circuitry to drive its sonar functionality, including a 200MHz transducer from Honda Electronics. While the PCB used parts of the MBC1 cartridge mapper, it also had quite a few changes that distinguished it from normal MBC1 games like *Super Mario Land*. Contained within the Pocket Sonar's casing were two separate PCBs connected by a few wires. No other original Game Boy cartridge did this, making the Pocket Sonar rather exceptional. The lower PCB largely acted like an ordinary MBC1 mapper, while the upper one dealt with sonar.

Most of the Pocket Sonar's hardware automatically handled all of the complicated bits, such as calculating the response from any pings. The software only needed to perform three actions: turn the sonar on, fire a sonar pulse, and read the results. Once it had the results, the Game Boy could display them on-screen. The process was incredibly simplified from the software's perspective, allowing a mere 8-bit handheld to accomplish an advanced and complex task.

The Pocket Sonar's unique mapper, nicknamed the MBC1-S, exposed three registers that the Game Boy's CPU could read from or write to. By accessing certain memory regions on the cartridge, it manipulated the sonar. After booting the cartridge, the sonar was enabled first. When using the fishfinder, the software periodically issued pulses through a specific register. Later, the Game Boy read another register containing a single byte of sonar information or a flag indicating a fish was found. By continually pulsing and reading data, the Game Boy eventually built an image of what was below the water. The sonar information returned by the MBC1-S was a simple value of 0 to 7. Depending on which values the software received, the Game Boy drew different patterns. Since it used a limited number of values, the Game Boy only had to perform a quick look-up to generate the proper pixels. Altogether, the final output was a 160x96 sonar screen.

It must be noted that the Pocket Sonar was technically a video game and not merely a digital tool designed for a game console. One of the options in its main menu offered a fishing minigame. Fish came from both sides of the screen at various levels, and it was up to the player's fisherman to snag them on his lines before they escaped. Should too many leave the screen, it was Game Over. Although the minigame had a somewhat *Game & Watch* style of play, it was admittedly only a very small part of the Pocket Sonar.

Also embedded in the software was a browsable miniature catalog of fish. Users could search for fish by name, water quality (sea or fresh water), or silhouette. Selected entries then displayed a brief amount of information related to the fish. This feature gets less attention than the sonar itself, but it was quite ingenious at the time. Before smartphones and mobile networks with internet access widely existed, this provided a handy way to determine what type of fish might be in a given area.

While the Pocket Sonar was the first device of its kind, it would not be the last. Less than a year later, the Handy Sonar released for the WonderSwan. In many respects, it was very much identical to the Pocket Sonar, except now it worked on an entirely different handheld. Bandai manufactured WonderSwans and perhaps saw fit to make sure its sonar legacy spread to its own platform in addition to Nintendo's.

Today, the Pocket Sonar remains something of a relic. Current portable sonars are essentially little buoys that can easily sit in the palm of one's hand. They map out depths deeper and more accurately than the Pocket Sonar could ever. Battery usage has been greatly reduced as well. With phones, fishers can access the web almost anywhere to get information about wildlife and habitats. Even so, the Pocket Sonar proved quite revolutionary when released. It was intended to be a relatively inexpensive and approachable handheld sonar, and there it succeeded. In that light, the Pocket Sonar deserves credit in the overall progress of modern fishfinders.

Pocket Sonar Box Front

The Pocket Sonar was not only the largest official Game Boy cartridge, it also had the biggest box, measuring at 28x17.5x9cm.

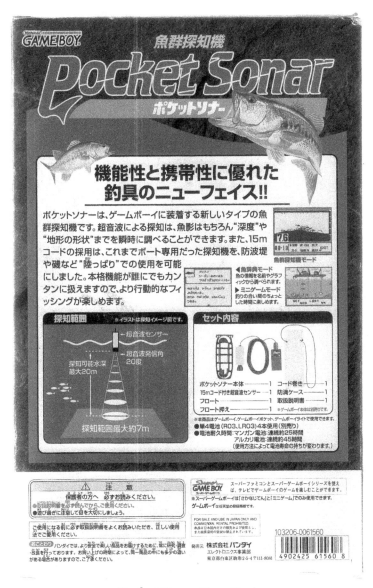

Pocket Sonar Box Back

Although Super Game Boy support was mentioned here, this only applied to the fishing minigame and the fishing encyclopedia. The actual sonar functionality was incompatible. Just as well, given how improbable it would have been to properly setup a Super Famicom/SNES and a TV near a body of water.

The Pocket Sonar and yellow buoy

The top of the cartridge could be unscrewed. Underneath was a microphone jack. The Pocket Sonar came with a very lengthy cable. It was designed to be cast out, sometimes at significant distances from the user. This cable was also how users were supposed to retrieve the sonar, by gently pulling it back towards the shore or boat.

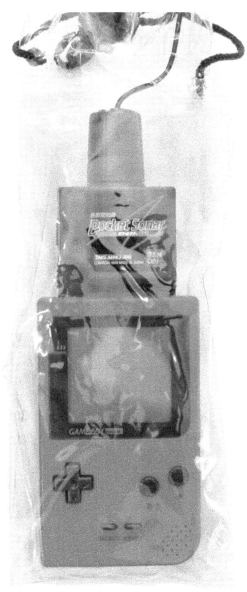

Pocket Sonar and Game Boy Pocket

Each Pocket Sonar came with its own plastic pouch for the Game Boy. This protected the handheld when taking it on a boat, as it might have potentially been exposed to waves, surf, mist, and other water droplets.

The Pocket Sonar's dual PCB design

No other original Game Boy cartridge looked anything like the Pocket Sonar. Inside, it was actually two separate PCBs wired together. This mapper was as unique as it was complicated.

The sonar screen showed a wealth of information, such as the underwater landscape, fish locations, and varying depths.

A "fish dictionary" helped anglers identify their catch. They could search by a number of criteria like name or shape.

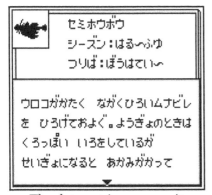

The data entries were quite detailed and thorough.

Although simple in premise, the included fishing minigame could get quite intense.

**Release Date:**
October 21, 1998

**Maker:**
Nintendo

**Legacy:**
Became Nintendo's first widespread use of wireless communication for their handheld systems.

The successor to the original Game Boy came packed with a large array of upgrades. The Game Boy Color doubled its video memory capacity, quadrupled its general purpose RAM, increased its Link Cable transfer speed from 1KB/s to a blistering 64KB/s, doubled the CPU speed, and most importantly allowed games to display new colors onscreen. Introduced alongside all of these changes was a brand new infrared port built right into the system itself. Now, the humble handheld could send and receive signals, paving the way for widespread wireless communication.

While Hudson had been dabbling with infrared for over a year with its HuC-1 cartridge mappers and the GB KISS interface, that technology was confined to one company alone. With the advent of the Game Boy Color, however, any developer could bring infrared capabilities to their software. Furthermore, since infrared was included as part of the console's base hardware, players had no need to purchase any additional products. Nintendo ensured that it could easily and quickly be adopted by both game makers and consumers.

One common misconception lingers around the Game Boy Color's infrared support. Many claim that only a relatively small number of games used it at all. Contrary to that assertion, about 90 different titles featured some form of infrared compatibility. This accounts for nearly 17% of the 530 unique games released during the handheld's lifetime, an impressive amount compared to the few dozen most ordinarily cite. This disparity is perhaps explained by the fact that very few games touted their infrared options, so just a handful of well-known titles are recognized today. A large portion of these games were only released in Japan, which may have given American and European audiences the wrong impression regarding developer uptake. At any rate, the Game Boy Color saw infrared reach a wide variety of its software library.

Games implemented infrared functions to achieve different goals. Swapping small amounts of information was common, such as brief messages, "e-mails" between two friends for example, or things such as virtual cards, stamps, pictures, profiles, or high-score lists. More advanced forms of trading transferred complete characters along with their levels and stats. On the other end of the spectrum, infrared was used as a key for unlocking hidden stages or bonus material. The most famous were the "Ubi Key" games from Ubisoft. Finding a special key in one game would allow players to open "Ubi Key" content in other games, nearly all of which granted access to secret areas. More uncommon, a couple of games used the infrared port for true wireless multiplayer sessions in turn-based battles.

A fourth category took the Game Boy Color into new territory by utilizing infrared signals from a secondary device, one that was not another Game Boy. As discussed later in this book, the motion controls of the Full Changer from *Zok Zok Heroes* were powered by infrared. In another notable example, *Chee Chai Alien*, players had to harness everyday light sources such as lamps in order to capture tiny creatures called Chaliens. The game even came packaged with a plastic tool that snapped onto the Game Boy Color to better filter and concentrate infrared light into the port.

Even more bizarre was *Dancing Furby*, a somewhat *Dance Dance Revolution*-esque rhythm game where players timed their input to get a Furby to move with the music. Once the dance was complete, the Game Boy Color sent infrared beams to a real, physical Furby Doll. Depending on the player's dance performance, the Game Boy would program the Furby to react accordingly. *Mission Impossible* could record output from a TV remote, thereby learning commands such as adjusting the volume and changing the channel. The software allowed players to transform their handheld gaming device into a full-fledged universal remote. Both versions of *Bomberman Max* encouraged using TV remotes to generate random bonus stages. Titles like *Kaijin Zona* and *GB Harobots* also accepted infrared signals from any source to generate random puzzles or spare robot parts, respectively.

Perhaps the most memorable of these types of external infrared devices were the Tamagotchi-like Pokémon Pikachu 2 and Pocket Sakura. The Pokémon Pikachu 2 was the colorized sequel to the original Pocket Pikachu. Players could interact with their very own Pikachu, playing games, observing its behavior, and becoming friends by giving it Watts. The unit had a built-in pedometer, and walking a given amount of steps produced new Watts. These Watts could be exchanged via infrared for items when using the Mystery Gift functions in *Pokémon Gold*, *Silver*, and *Crystal*. Although it required some effort, it was possible to generate an unlimited supply of Rare Candies through the Pokémon Pikachu 2, making it an invaluable tool for Pokémon Masters at the time.

The Pocket Sakura was very similar to the Pokémon Pikachu 2 in terms of size and shape. Aside from a change in color schemes, the two devices were near copies of each other. Released as a special package for *Sakura Taisen GB*, the Pocket Sakura allowed players to watch the main character travel around Imperial City and other locations, having conversations with several people from the game. At times, Sakura even addressed the players directly. The unit's pedometer converted steps into points, which could then be transferred back to the Game Boy Color. These points unlocked different extras in *Sakura Taisen GB*.

Operating the infrared port was relatively straightforward for software. The Game Boy Color simply turned the infrared light on or off for different lengths of time. Often, games would wait for a short incoming signal and then measure the delay between the next burst. The exact protocol varied for each title, as game developers were given the freedom to choose how they implemented everything.

Several precautions were necessary, however. It was possible for the Game Boy Color to accidentally receive its own infrared signals in some instances, so games had to be careful not to read and transmit at the same time. Another odd quirk was related to a so-called "signal-fade". If the Game Boy Color began receiving an infrared signal, and if that signal continued for a while, the system would eventually ignore it and treat it as having turned off. Even if the original signal was still active, the Game Boy Color erroneously detected it fading. As such, games had to restrict the amount of time they turned on the infrared light, typically using rapid blasts.

Unfortunately, the Game Boy Color's infrared capabilities fell short as a true replacement for the Link Cable. Software had to manually monitor the status of their infrared communications. Unlike the later adapter released for the Game Boy Advance, the Game Boy Color's native infrared port did not use hardware-based interrupts. When the software constantly watched the hardware for signal changes, it had little time to run other areas of code, such as updating the game logic, checking for button input, and handling graphics or sound. Interrupts would have allowed the software to continue normally until a specific event occurred, such as coming across an infrared signal. This factor limited infrared's role in Game Boy Color multiplayer and explains why it was rarely used for real-time transmissions. Instead, games often relied on turn-based actions, where one side could wait indefinitely for the other to finish.

The Game Boy Color's infrared port was also not suited for long distance transfers. At best, it was designed to receive signals from a few inches or centimeters away. Any greater distance increased the chance of lost signals or interference from infrared light in the environment. It was more than capable of sending signals across a large room, for example, but its reception was generally poor after a certain length. Furthermore, the Game Boy Color's sensor did not perform very well outside its line-of-sight. Any incoming signals had to enter directly into the transceiver. Even slight changes in angle or elevation could disrupt communication. In comparison to the HuC-1 and the GB KISS, the Game Boy Color offered better range for infrared, however, it still came with a handful of constraints.

Regardless, the Game Boy Color's infrared functions established Nintendo's dedication to wireless technologies for its handhelds. The company would eventually make the Mobile Adapter GB, which saw Game Boys interact with cellphones and servers. Although infrared connectivity essentially vanished on the Game Boy Advance, the next generation system offered a new radio-based adapter that supported a broad selection of games. From there, the Nintendo DS and 3DS incorporated Wi-Fi directly into their hardware and finally made local wireless and online modes widely available on the company's portable devices. Ultimately, this small seemingly insignificant infrared port began a long evolutionary process. Although the methods changed, the goal of linking two Nintendo systems together without cables can be traced to the Game Boy Color.

The light enhancing plastic accessory used with *Chee Chai Alien*

Despite how it looks, the attachment didn't always work as intended and sometimes failed to help with the game at all. *Chee Chai Alien* was not always sensitive enough to infrared light to begin with. Still, it was quite an ingenious concept.

Pokémon Pikachu 2

Pocket Sakura

Several mainline *Pokémon* games made good use of infrared. Mystery Gift allowed players to receive items and later battle copies of their friend's team.

Trading items or high scores was a frequent theme, such as in *Super Mario Bros. Deluxe.*

A small number of games used infrared for head-to-head gameplay. *Bakuten Shoot Beyblade* and *Game Boy Wars 3* (seen above) were such examples.

Unlocking secrets was also a major theme. Ubi Key games typically offered hidden levels, such as Ubi Cliff in *Rayman.*

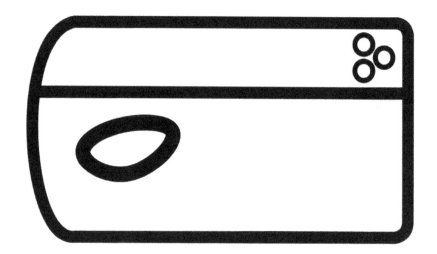

**Release Date:**

December 11, 1998

**Maker:**

Tamsoft

**Legacy:**

Second Game Boy barcode reader, predating the Nintendo e-Reader.

Years after Namco's Barcode Boy arrived, yet another barcode scanner was released for the Game Boy. In late 1998, Tamsoft published a game called *Barcode Taisen Bardigun* as part of a boxed bundle. Included inside were a few starter cards along with a small, purple card reader. Although the barcode craze earlier in the decade was not as prevalent by that time, Tamsoft aimed at another category of games rising in popularity: monster collecting, training, and battling.

*Barcode Taisen Bardigun* (shortened to BTB) followed players raising various creatures called "Bardi" from eggs. The catch here was that hatching them required swiping a barcode through the scanner. In addition to this, the critters could learn new moves through the cards. What might have been a decent if uninspired *Pokémon* look-alike suddenly became an interesting use of Game Boy technology.

The BTB Reader connected to the Game Boy using its hardwired Link Cable. Unlike its predecessor, the BTB Reader was designed to accommodate a wide range of Game Boy models, with the Game Boy Micro being the sole outcast. Although the software was released during the Game Boy Color era, it supported older DMG-01 models with the proper adapter, as well as the Super Game Boy 2, which featured a Link Cable port. As a result, the game retroactively brought its card scanning to past platforms.

Even with its relatively slim body, the BTB Reader required three AAA batteries to operate. Instead of an ON/OFF switch, the reader had a button players pressed to temporarily activate the hardware. This method saved on power as opposed to a "constantly on" mode, however, it called for some coordination on the player's part. The Game Boy had to be set aside while the button was held and the card was moved through the BTB Reader's slot.

Without the cards, the BTB Reader, or cheat codes, the game itself was impossible to start, let alone finish. Players were not given any initial Bardi of their own, and eggs could only be hatched once the correct card data was scanned. As a result, not having any default Bardi prevented the story mode from being selected, and practice battles remained inaccessible as well. Additionally, the Bardi needed cards to gain more attacks and abilities. The accessory was therefore an absolute requirement for the game.

As for the technical details of how the BTB Reader worked, the Game Boy constantly pinged the hardware via the Link Cable. With each transmission, the Game Boy sent a byte to the BTB Reader, and in response it received another byte. It was largely irrelevant whatever the Game Boy sent, as the BTB Reader didn't actually accept any commands or other types of input. Instead the BTB Reader returned what was effectively a data stream of the entire barcode. The Game Boy simply needed to initiate these transfers when appropriate.

So long as the BTB Reader's button was pressed while the player swiped a card, the scanner would eventually return non-zero data, which marked the beginning of barcode data. Unlike other barcode readers that have built-in hardware that automatically calculates any numeric values represented by black-and-white strips, the BTB Reader merely returned the bars themselves. The game had to check the length of each bar and then manually convert those into numerical form for processing.

Whenever a light area of the barcode was detected, the BTB Reader registered a "0". Whenever a dark area of the barcode was detected, the BTB Reader registered a "1". The data sent back to the Game Boy was really just a long series of zeroes and ones alternating in groups. Although only 8-bits of data could be transmitted at a time, the BTB Reader finished its task relatively quickly.

Each group of zeroes or ones indicated a white or black strip. Longer strips had larger groups, while shorter strips had smaller groups. That was enough information for the game to validate a specific barcode. Once the BTB Reader stopped detecting any new strips, the software could then assume all scanning was complete and start verifying the data. The format of the barcodes used in BTB was EAN-13, the same as its predecessor, the Barcode Boy.

Interestingly enough, two revisions of the BTB Reader and game were sold. DMG-ABEJ-JPN was Nintendo's official product code for the original, while DMG-ABEJ-JPN-1 was the later version. The peripheral itself remained unaltered, while the game featured a few minor stylistic updates, including a different Super Game Boy palette. The box was edited slightly, but the manual got a bigger overhaul. Each of the included cards gained a new look and feel as well, although they were still functionally the same, as the barcodes hadn't changed at all. Finally, the game's title text shifted from blue to gold and yellow. Both revisions, however, utilized the BTB Reader in exactly the same manner, so no incompatibilities appeared between either cartridge.

Despite being impressive for its time, the BTB Reader didn't become an overnight success. A few factors likely held it from reaching a wider audience. The genre Tamsoft entered in was fairly crowded, especially in Japan. *Pokémon Yellow,* for example, had only been released a few months prior to the company's efforts. Nintendo and Game Freak's established heavyweight likely reduced overall interest for other lesser-known games that followed a similar formula.

Furthermore, the BTB Reader only worked with a single game. Unlike the Barcode Boy, which at least supported a handful of titles, this miniature scanner was strictly tied to one piece of software, thereby limiting its value to buyers. When the BTB boxed set cost more than an average game, price-minded players may have well looked elsewhere when shopping for new software.

Lastly, players could only use BTB cards with specific barcodes printed on them. This stood in contrast to the Barcode Boy, which could accept any EAN-13 barcode and generate randomized characters and items. Without a full set of cards, the game itself was constrained, allowing players to train just a small subset of Bardi. Of course, players were expected to go out and collect more, but it added yet another barrier to making the most out of the hardware and software, especially when the boxed edition only came with just three starter Bardi.

As a result of these circumstances, the game and the barcode scanner have fallen into relative obscurity, seemingly forgotten even in its country of origin. Although Tamsoft didn't create a sensational new franchise, they were willing to prove that card scanning on the Game Boy could be an attractive element of gameplay. While only Nintendo's e-Reader would eventually reach mass appeal in multiple markets, the BTB Reader served as an early model for some of the same concepts.

*Barcode Taisen Bardigun* Box Front

*Barcode Taisen Bardigun* Box Back

*Barcode Taisen Bardigun* Reader Top View

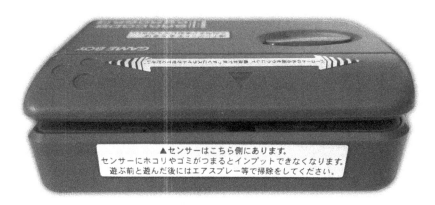

*Barcode Taisen Bardigun* Reader Side View

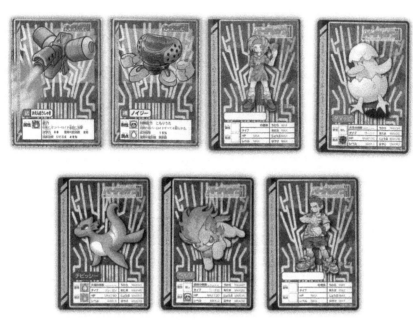

*Barcode Taisen Bardigun* Cards—Front

*Barcode Taisen Bardigun* Cards—Back

Bardi came from eggs. By swiping a card, they would hatch into new critters ready to fight.

Players could scan cards to give Bardi new abilities or help them grow.

Different opponents could be fought in 3-on-3 matches.

Battles were viewed from a side-on perspective as each team attacked the other.

**Release Date:**
   March 25, 1999

**Maker:**
   Nintendo

**Legacy:**
   Introduced haptic feedback for handheld consoles.

With the advent of 5th Generation game consoles, a new level of immersion was offered to players. In April of 1997, the Nintendo 64 Rumble Pak launched, followed by the DualShock PlayStation 1 controller in November of that same year. From that moment onward, video games would vibrate, shaking and quaking in everyone's hands as they blasted aliens, revved up turbo-charged engines, or smashed their way through fistfights. Today, it's almost impossible to imagine any standard controller from Sony, Microsoft, or Nintendo lacking rumble support. While this trend gradually became universal among traditional game consoles, it was largely absent from handhelds. Nintendo, however, was willing to bring haptic technology to the humble Game Boy.

In 1999, several unique Game Boy cartridges started appearing on the market. The first of these was *Top Gear Pocket*, hitting retail stores in North America on March 25. Soon, classics such as *Pokémon Pinball* began selling the following month. These games introduced a new type of mapper. Under the hood, their components were essentially the same MBC5 design used for numerous Game Boy Color titles. They featured one critical difference, however: an oversized plastic shell that housed an electrically powered motor. The so-called "Rumble Carts" used a single AAA battery to drive the motor, rapidly rotating it on command. The motion was fast enough to cause both the cartridge and the Game Boy itself to vibrate.

It was a technical achievement for Nintendo and other developers, as previously no other handheld had ever supported this kind of rumble functionality. Rivals such as the Game Gear, Lynx, Neo Geo Pocket Color, and WonderSwan for example, never released any comparable experience. Although natively the Game Boy had no way of vibrating, adding that ability inside the cartridge completely bypassed this limitation. Like other Game Boy hardware tied to mappers, the cartridge became a means of expanding what the handheld could do.

The programming behind Rumble Carts was quite simple. Games only needed to set a specific bit to "0" or "1" when configuring the cartridge's SRAM bank. Rather than affecting backup data, that bit controlled the motor's ON or OFF state. Depending on the length of time the motor was turned ON and the intervals between ON/OFF transitions, games could produce different types of rumble. Light, moderate, heavy, ramping up, or ramping down were some of the most common effects. While the Rumble Carts lacked some of the fine tuned options found in modern controllers, such as generating sine and triangle rumble patterns, they nevertheless provided handheld games with a sense of depth that was unheard of at the time.

Despite being the first to popularize portable force-feedback, Rumble Carts only appeared in a limited amount of games due to several constraints. Since rumble support was part of the actual cartridge, this incurred higher production costs as opposed to normal MBC5 hardware. Additionally, rumble support had to work well with the overall gameplay; it couldn't merely be an afterthought or poorly integrated. As a result, only 23 Rumble Carts in all were sold. The majority consisted of racing, pinball, and various sports (bowling, fishing, golfing). A handful of action games made up the small remainder. In terms of raw numbers, the Game Boy's Rumble Cart fell far short in comparison to the Nintendo 64 or PlayStation 1.

This disparity was likely due to how the Rumble Carts were designed. Since they were heavily dependent on the cartridge and its associated price, not every developer could readily add rumble to their games. In contrast to this, the Nintendo DS Rumble Pak was an optional accessory, one that developers could support merely by changing a few pieces of code here and there. It required players to invest in the necessary hardware rather than the makers of the game. The DS add-on eventually supported over 50 titles during its time, thus validating a different approach to handheld rumble.

Although the Rumble Carts were never adopted as extensively as their home console predecessors, they paved the way forward for Nintendo's later portable systems. The Game Boy Advance likewise resorted to specialized cartridges for rumble in select titles, and a handful also used the Game Boy Player in conjunction with GameCube controllers. At the same time, rumble came as part of the default hardware in the Pokémon Mini. The DS' Rumble Pak seamlessly incorporated vibration via the unit's Slot-2 port. Ultimately, "HD Rumble" came to the Nintendo Switch where countless games now support haptic feedback. The Rumble Carts marked the start of a slow transformation, and today they remain one of the most visible examples of using cartridge-based techniques to broaden the Game Boy's functionality.

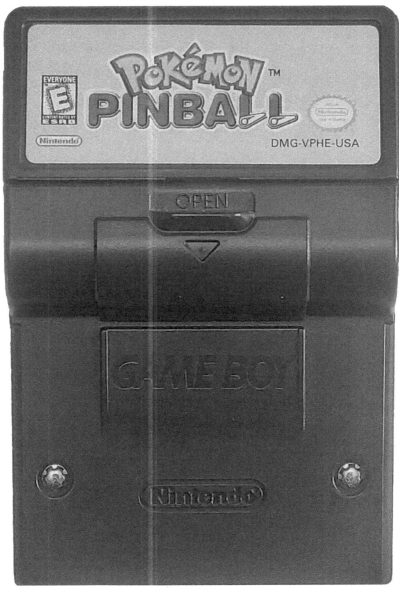

The MBC5 Rumble Cartridge

Due to its unusual shape, these rumble cartridges are often a hassle for collectors. They'll either have to find the original box (which can be expensive these days) or make a solution of their own.

98

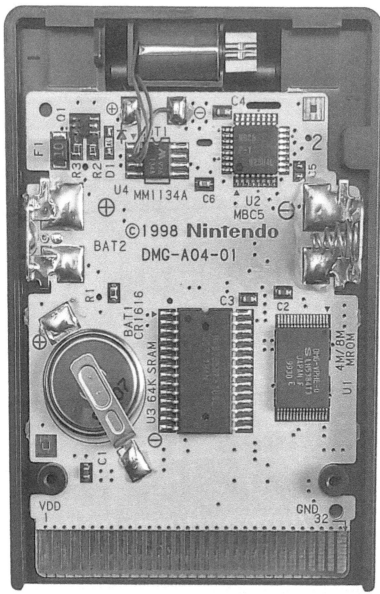

The MBC5 Rumble Cartridge PCB

Despite the small size of the motor, in comparison to its counterparts on the Sony PlayStation and Nintendo 64, the Game Boy's rumble features still managed to pack a punch.

*Pokémon Pinball* was one of the earliest rumble cartridge games and helped popularize the feature.

Many games offered options to turn off rumbling.

Racing, pinball, and sports games made up the vast majority of supported titles.

A tiny handful of action games took advantage of rumble. Both the Nintendo 64 and Game Boy Color versions of *Perfect Dark* used it.

**Release Date:**
>March 1, 2000

**Maker:**
>Nintendo

**Legacy:**
>First official Game Boy cartridge that utilized flash memory.
>Helped establish Nintendo's digital distribution methods for
>handhelds.

After Nintendo sold their Famicom Disk System in 1986, the company began a service that allowed customers to rewrite the game data on their disks. For a fraction of the typical price of new games, players could buy different titles from a simple kiosk. Famicom Disk Writers became quite popular in Japan and were supported by the company until 2003. Having seen the immense value of rewritable storage media, Nintendo then built a similar service for the Super Famicom in 1996. Using flash memory, the Nintendo Power Cartridge was able to store multiple 16-bit games written by a kiosk. Following the success of these two efforts, the same concept eventually came to the Game Boy.

In March of 2000, the GB Memory Cartridge launched. With the aid of special Nintendo Power copier machines that operated out of Lawson convenience stores, the cartridge could hold a total of seven games at once. To fit them all, the GB Memory Cartridge came equipped with 1MB of flash RAM, an impressive amount of space for that era. Additionally, it used 128KB of SRAM for game saves, the largest size available for the Game Boy. With so much onboard memory, the cartridge could maintain multiple games by giving each one its own separate area. As a consequence of requiring large quantities of memory components, however, the GB Memory Cartridge was actually delayed by five months when the "921" earthquake in Taiwan caused a global shortage in RAM.

Nintendo Power copiers were custom devices that accepted SF Cassettes and later GB Memory Cartridges. Customers would select which games they wanted from a Loppi Ticket Machine and then give the printed "application ticket" to a Lawson store clerk. From there, the clerks instructed the copier to transfer the necessary games. The GB Memory Cartridge had a unique mapper that accepted a series of flash commands for reading and writing bytes. Like most mappers, such features were accessed through specific regions of memory normally dedicated to the cartridge's ROM or RAM. In the case of the GB Memory Cartridge, flash commands and parameters were sent by writing to a handful of memory addresses reserved for the Nintendo logo and other metadata in the cartridge header.

The 1MB of flash RAM present on the cartridge was divided into eight distinct blocks of 128KB. A small menu program occupied the first block. It allowed the player to browse through the available games written to the GB Memory Cartridge, listing the names of the software. Once one was selected, the menu sent a brief command to the mapper, causing it to load the game while forcing the Game Boy itself to reset. Afterwards, the game started up as if it were on an original cartridge. The menu was also used to display information and updates in a news ticker-like manner. Nintendo Power copiers were responsible for writing this data directly onto the GB Memory Cartridge.

The GB Memory Cartridge was compatible with a wide range of other mappers. Across the Game Boy library, different games ended up using different mappers depending on when they were released and what kind of memory they needed. A cartridge designed to hold various games therefore needed to support a number of these. The GB Memory Cartridge could run titles that used the MBC1, MBC2, MBC3, and MBC5 mappers. More exotic mappers, however, were left out. Beyond mappers, there were additional restrictions on ROM and RAM sizes. While a single game could use all eight blocks of flash memory (sacrificing the menu program in the process), none could exceed a total of 1MB. Furthermore, each game could use at most 32KB of SRAM. Despite these limitations, over 130 games were sold for the GB Memory Cartridge.

With the aim of the giving players access to games at cheaper and more affordable rates, many of the titles promoted through the Nintendo Power copier service averaged 1,050 yen. The low and high ends spanned from just 630 yen to 1,575 yen. Meanwhile, the GB Memory Cartridge itself sold for an agreeable 2,500 yen. New Game Boy Color software, in contrast, frequently sold for 3,800 yen. On the whole, it was a great deal for consumers. Players were encouraged to keep records of their purchases, presumably so they wouldn't be charged again if they wanted to rewrite games they'd bought in the past. The cartridge's flash memory provided a long-term storage solution, assuring players that their games and their investments would remain intact for years to come.

Sadly, the Game Boy portion of the Nintendo Power copier service was relatively short and abbreviated. At the end of August in 2001, customers could no longer purchase GB Memory Cartridges at Lawson stores, nor could they download anything to existing cartridges. The service was partially kept alive at the start of September. Nintendo would receive any GB Memory Cartridges sent directly to them and write the games themselves before shipping them back. Although it was still possible to put new titles on the cartridge, it was not nearly as easy or convenient as before. Finally, on February 28, 2007, the Nintendo Power copier service was permanently put to rest.

The GB Memory Cartridge may have been yet another victim of bad timing, arriving scarcely more than a year before the Game Boy Advance released. With a new system to tend to, Nintendo likely focused their efforts elsewhere, so the GB Memory Cartridge and the copier service were quickly relegated to a quieter role. No comparable product was ever released on the Game Boy Advance, possibly due to memory constraints. The newer handheld's games were larger in size compared to earlier eras, often dwarfing them by several times. A Game Boy Advance equivalent would have needed close to 32MB of flash memory to comfortably store several titles, an expensive proposition for the early 2000s.

On its own, the GB Memory Cartridge did not revolutionize digital distribution on Nintendo's platforms. Instead, it served as an important step towards the modern model that many enjoy today. In the end, downloadable Game Boy software would eventually return on Nintendo's 3DS via the eShop nearly a decade later in 2011. The GB Memory Cartridge carved a path towards this future by offering older titles at a discount and making a large catalog from various publishers and developers available to the public digitally. The cartridge, like the SF Cassette before it, also reckoned with the fact that better, longer lasting memory solutions were necessary for such models to truly succeed. Even though the GB Memory Cartridge was itself a physical item, in many respects it heralded an era free of plastic Game Paks, CD-ROMs, or DVDs. Nintendo's first and only official "flash cart" for the original Game Boy and Game Boy Color may not have been around for very long, but it certainly helped pave the way for the online storefronts of later generations.

GB Memory Cartridge

Internal view of the GB Memory Cartridge

GB Memory Cartridge Box Front

The menu program of the GB Memory Cartridge when playing on the Game Boy or Game Boy Pocket.

The menu program of the GB Memory Cartridge when playing on the Game Boy Color or Game Boy Advance.

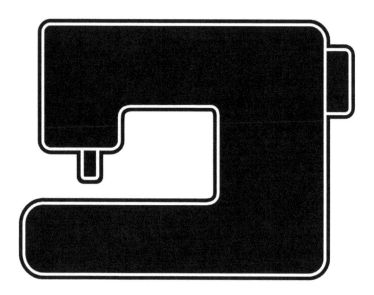

**Release Dates:**

| | |
|---|---|
| JN-100: | Spring 2000 |
| IZEK 1500: | December 2000 |
| JN-2000: | 2001 (February 1st at the latest) |

**Makers:**

Jaguar International Corporation
Singer Corporation

**Legacy:**

First computerized sewing machine controlled by a handheld video game console. Made computerized home sewing more accessible using the Game Boy as its interface.

The Game Boy is often viewed strictly as a gaming device, being one of Nintendo's most popular and well-known products. Despite this reputation, the Game Boy was essentially just another computer. It had a CPU to process instructions, used RAM to hold data, output audio and video, and took input in the form of buttons. Previous hardware such as the Game Boy Camera and the Pocket Sonar pushed the idea that the humble handheld could do much more than virtual entertainment. They showed that the Game Boy was in fact a versatile, multifaceted electronic tool. Given the right combination of additional parts, the Game Boy could handle almost any application.

Nothing better demonstrated how far the Game Boy could extend itself than the handful of sewing machines that appeared shortly after the new millennium. In the spring of 2000, Jaguar International Corporation unveiled the Jaguar JN-100, also known as the Nu-yell. This computerized sewing machine sported a built-in 2nd Generation Link Cable, allowing it to connect directly to a Game Boy. The cartridge bundled with the unit, *Raku x Raku Mishin*, had dedicated software for operating the machine, containing instructions for over 300 different stitching patterns such as lines, zig-zags, flowers, swans, stars, letters, and kana. It even let users create their own designs. Once plugged in, the Game Boy simply transferred the patterns, and the machine was ready to start sewing.

It was the first sewing machine to interface with any sort of gaming system. In short order, the JN-100 managed to capture 10% of the Japanese market for computerized sewing. Although it was a sophisticated and complex device, the JN-100 proved relatively easy to use when linked with a Game Boy. A total of six variants were launched, each offering a different color for its translucent plastic body. The sleek, curved aesthetics moved away from the somewhat boxy and rigid forms of other machines from the last few decades. The JN-100 stylistically evoked a sense of newness and modernity in an old and established market.

The JN-100 would not be the last Game Boy-compatible sewing machine. As the JN-100 was being developed in 1999, Singer Corporation also agreed to manufacture a similar machine. While the JN-100 hit Japan first, followed by Europe some time later, Singer targeted North American audiences. The company worked on the IZEK 1500, a tribute to their founder and a celebration of their 150th anniversary. It sold in select stores before Christmas of 2000. After a trade show in Chicago the following January, the IZEK 1500 reached wider retail availability. For all intents and purposes, it was an exact copy of the JN-100 with minor visible changes, such as the power cable. Unlike its eastern counterpart, the IZEK 1500 came in a single shade of blue.

Jaguar would go on to make yet another sewing machine that utilized the Game Boy. Some time before February of 2001, they introduced the JN-2000, also known as the Nuotto. This new machine used a different body than either the JN-100 or the IZEK 1500. In addition to its improved stitching speed, the JN-2000 handled multicolor embroidery. To accomplish this, Jaguar made the EM-2000, an embroidery arm that plugged into a slot at the base of the JN-2000. The embroidery package also came with new software titles: *Raku x Raku Moji* and *Raku x Raku Cut Shuu*. The former worked with kanji, while the latter had 32 embroidery patterns such as rocket ships, dolphins, cats, and flowers.

Perhaps the most famous and well publicized software for the JN-2000 was *Mario Family*. Released almost immediately after Nintendo's Space World 2001 event, the cartridge held 32 embroidery patterns of classic Super Mario characters and items. Everyone from Mario himself, Luigi, Peach, Wario, Yoshi, Koopas, and Bloopers were included. Oddly enough, Bowser was missing. It was the last piece of software made for these sewing machines and today remains a contender for one of the rarest Game Boy Color titles.

Although the JN-100 initially sold well, the JN-2000 fell below expectations. Two more titles planned to take advantage of the JN-2000's embroidery but were ultimately canceled. *Kanji Shishuu* was to be similar to *Raku x Raku Moji* except with hundreds of more characters. *Kirby Family* would have been analogous to *Mario Family*, with 32 patterns that stitched Kirby, Waddle Dee, and others from the franchise. Supposedly, software with a *Pokémon* theme was also considered. *Kanji Shishuu* and *Kirby Family* were basically completed projects but remained unreleased due to low sales from the JN-2000. In 2020, however, builds for both were leaked online, giving a glimpse at the history that was lost.

On the other side of the world, the IZEK 1500 failed to capitalize on its premise of drawing in younger customers. While Singer wanted to bring over a model similar to the JN-2000, the product simply couldn't be justified in light of the IZEK 1500's performance. As a result, the western market was restricted to either the JN-100 or the IZEK 1500. Neither would ever gain the type of embroidery that defined the JN-2000's library.

All three sewing machines were compatible with the base software. In Japan this was the *Raku x Raku Mishin* cartridge, while in the West it was the *Sewing Machine Operating Software* cartridge. These titles issued identical instructions to each machine. They were both effectively the same program, with the only difference being a change in menus and a different selection of which characters to stitch. It was therefore possible to use the Japanese version with the IZEK 1500 and the North American or European versions with the JN-100 and JN-2000. Contrary to many misconceptions, neither the IZEK 1500 nor the JN-100 were compatible with any of the other cartridges that targeted the JN-2000. The machines lacked the necessary port to accept an EM-2000, and the software explicitly checked to see if the embroidery arm was present. Failing the test prevented the machine from receiving any embroidery patterns.

Communication between the Game Boy and the sewing machines centered on individual packets of data. In general, the handheld sent coordinates that determined where the machine had to make its next stitch. Once all of that data was transferred, the machine continuously reported its current state, such as whether the foot pedal was active or if any errors occurred. Each packet began with a header that specified where or how the first few stitches should be placed. For normal stitching, this started the pattern. After receiving further horizontal and vertical coordinates, the needle could only shift left, right, up, or down a few millimeters or so, enough to make elaborate designs constrained to a narrow column.

For embroidery, the header declared an initial offset. The machine could more or less stitch freely once it received horizontal and vertical coordinates, shifting in all directions indefinitely until it met the edge of the embroidery hoop. Additionally, the EM-2000 allowed the machine to halt stitching in one area and jump to a completely different area. This non-contiguous stitching was required for certain patterns, such as when outlining two parts that were not connected at all, for example, Luigi's eyebrows or the ridges of his gloves. Because many embroidery designs used multiple colors, the software broke up stitching into separate phases, pausing to let the user swap threads as needed, or letting them skip sections entirely.

The rise of Jaguar and Singer's machines was fairly short-lived. By late 2001, development of further software had ceased, ending any hope of updated content. After *Mario Family* was released, all three products were on their way to becoming novelties as Nintendo pivoted to focus on the Game Boy Advance and

GameCube. Still, in that time, these machines made a number of achievements. Not only were they the first sewing machines to link to a game console, currently they're the only ones that ever have. To date, they are the largest and heaviest officially licensed Game Boy peripherals. They also marked the only instance where Nintendo's characters were formally given embroidery designs that anyone could use themselves.

These machines did make one key contribution to the sewing industry: bringing better accessibility to digitized sewing. Although they were not the first machines to download stitching data from an external computer, the JN-100, IZEK 1500, and JN-2000 were each groundbreaking in their approach. The Game Boy itself offered a simple to use interface, having only a handful of inputs. It was intuitive to pick up and manipulate even for non-gamers. The included software featured things such as built-in setup tutorials and detailed error screens that pinpointed exactly what the problem was. With the power of the Game Boy, users could start sewing amazing patterns with the mere push of a button.

While some may dismiss sewing machines with Game Boy support as just a gimmick, the overall package worked quite well in practice. Modern machines have since moved to USB-to-PC connections, providing a similar but more advanced experience to what Jaguar and Singer delivered. A few sewing machines even have full-color touchscreens of their own. The machines examined here were part of a long trend from the 1990s that revitalized the home sewing market with computerized components. Although they were only relevant for a brief period, they left a legacy that showed how the Game Boy could transform itself into something more than a gaming device. Nintendo's handheld was, in fact, a mobile platform that all sorts of applications could be developed for.

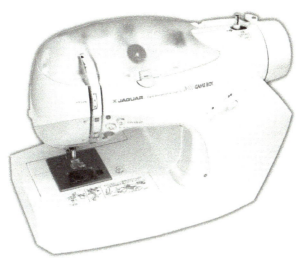

The Jaguar JN-100

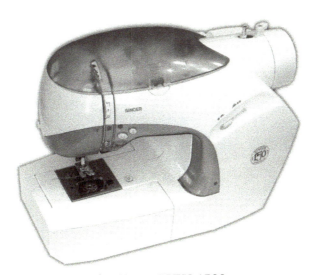

The Singer IZEK 1500

The Jaguar JN was sold in six different colors: Pink, Pale Green, Blue, Violet, Orange, and Clear. The IZEK 1500, however, only came in Blue. Both sewing machines were virtually identical in all respects.

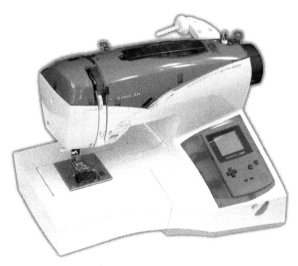

The Jaguar JN-2000

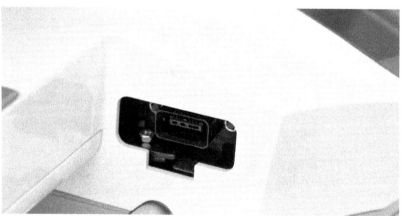

The slot where the EM-2000 plugged into the JN-2000

Contrary to common misconceptions, only the Jaguar JN-2000 was compatible with software such as *Mario Family*. The JN-100 and IZEK 1500 had no slot where an embroidery arm could be inserted.

The JN-2000 closely resembled later Singer Futura models.

A digital representation of Princess Peach's full embroidery pattern

A digital representation of Wario's full embroidery pattern

Digital representations of Mario and Kirby embroidery patterns

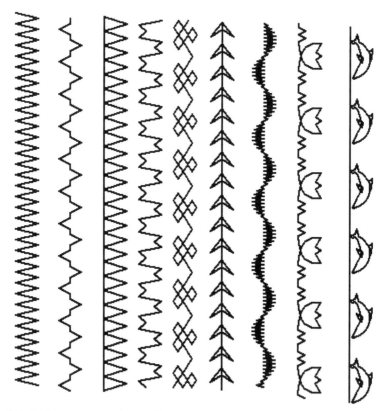

Digital representations of various available stitching patterns

The first cartridges came with dozens of stitching patterns. They could be mirrored and adjusted for width and height.

Individual characters could be stitched as well. The Japanese version used kana.

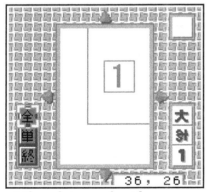

When doing embroidery, users could plot where exactly the design would stitch on the material.

Embroidery designs were designated as "Large" or "Small" depending on how much space they required.

**Release Dates:**

| Turbo File GB: | March 2000 |
| Turbo File Advance: | April 2002 |

**Makers:**

ASCII Corporation

Sammy Corporation

**Legacy:**

First use of memory cards on a Nintendo handheld, predating the rise of SD cards for save data.

Throughout the 1990s and into the early 2000s, one particular accessory became an essential for video games. Many systems gradually began to rely on optical discs. As such, they could no longer store user data on game cartridges with dedicated backup RAM. Memory cards provided a clear solution to the format shift happening across various home consoles. The handheld market, meanwhile, experienced no such change. For numerous Game Boy titles, the saves were exclusively tied to the physical cart. Memory cards simply belonged to a different domain of gaming.

In early 2000, ASCII Corporation altered this equation by releasing its Turbo File GB. The device acted as external storage for the Game Boy Color. Connected via a built-in Link Cable, the Turbo File GB allowed games with specific programming to read and write up to 1MB of data to the unit itself. This was eight times as large as the maximum typically permitted for Game Boy Color software. Additional memory cards could double the overall capacity, once slotted inside.

The Turbo File GB had a long lineage behind its hardware, as this was not the first time ASCII had created something of this nature. On the Famicom, the original Turbo File and Turbo File II performed similar functions, giving games a way to save data externally. ASCII later released a Turbo File Adapter which made the two earlier items compatible with the Super Famicom. The following Turbo File Twin was native to the Super Famicom and greatly updated the amount of available backup RAM. The Turbo File GB was the last such product made by ASCII and brought the end of a legacy that began in 1986.

Unfortunately, the Turbo File GB did not work with every game. In fact, only two compatible games existed: *RPG Tsukuru GB* and *Uchuu Nin Tanaka Tarou De RPG Tsukuru GB2*. Both were part of ASCII's *RPG Maker* franchise where players used a handful of tools to create their own role-playing adventure, customizing the storyline, cutscenes, and dialog. Each game used a massive amount of data, so much so that only one "file" could be saved to the cartridge at a time. Making a new RPG required the old one to be deleted, unless the Turbo File GB was used.

While memory cards on the Game Boy may sound bizarre in concept, it worked in the case of the *RPG Tsukuru GB* games. The idea was to not only let players save dozens of RPGs they'd made but also share them and collaborate with others. Players could, for example, use the same Turbo File GB to distribute an RPG widely among friends. They could also work together by downloading an

RPG from the Turbo File, editing it, then reuploading the new version. While memory cards didn't make sense for a number of portable games, in ASCII's case, it fit the vision they had.

Both *RPG Tsukuru* titles had menus to access the Turbo File GB. From there, players could copy RPGs to and from the device as well as completely erase entries. Each RPG appeared as an actual file with a user-created name to identify itself. The software helpfully showed players the remaining free space in terms of 8KB blocks. A glitch in both *RPG Tsukuru* games regrettably prevented them from using all of the blocks. When a memory card was inserted, the menu would prompt players to choose between the card or the onboard flash memory.

Physically, the Turbo File GB somewhat resembled USB models of Zip drives. It used four AA batteries to run. Thankfully it did not require the batteries for save data to remain persistent. A handy switch enabled a Write-Protect mode, essentially setting all data on the Turbo File GB to Read-Only. This eliminated any chance of accidentally overwriting important information. A small, red LED indicated read and write activity when in use.

The Game Boy communicated with the Turbo File GB through a specialized protocol. It was for this reason that ordinary games could not take advantage of the hardware to gain more saves. The software had to implement a series of commands sent through multiple data packets. First, the Game Boy and the Turbo File GB established a sort of handshake with each other, known as a sync signal. The software sent out a single byte and waited for the hardware to respond with a predetermined value. Once that value was received, the Turbo File GB was ready to accept a packet containing a command and any parameters it needed. Afterwards, the Game Boy issued a brief one-byte checksum for the Turbo File GB to verify the integrity of the transmission. Finally, a second sync signal was sent to mark the end of communications. After the Game Boy sent a command, the Turbo File GB eventually returned a packet of its own, generally with any data requested by the game.

This process repeated for however many commands were needed for a given task. Commands ranged from starting and finishing all data operations, setting read and write banks, reading and writing data, and getting the Turbo File GB's current status. The Game Boy never directly touched the internal flash memory or memory cards. It interfaced with the Turbo File GB through these commands, which in turn were interpreted by additional components inside the

accessory. All of that was obscured from the perspective of the software, and completely transparent to the player.

As previously mentioned, both instances of *RPG Tsukuru* on the Game Boy Color shared a programming error that stopped them from utilizing the full 1MB of storage space on either the Turbo File GB or the expansion memory cards. Thanks to an "off-by-one" counting bug, the last few blocks were inaccessible to the software. While the data was in fact available to use, the code mistakenly assumed there wasn't enough space to write anything. When completely empty, there were 128 free blocks on the Turbo File GB or its memory card. The software, however, only counted 127 blocks. As a result, players had access to slightly less memory than advertised.

Eventually, ASCII ceased producing the Turbo File line. Development of the next piece of hardware fell to Sammy Corporation, which released the Turbo File Advance in April of 2002. A subsidiary of ASCII, Enterbrain Inc., published the games that would use the peripheral. Although the names of its makers changed, the Turbo File Advance was essentially a continuation of the Turbo File family. In truth, very little was modified for the new model. Aside from supporting the Game Boy Advance and altering the color scheme, the Turbo File Advance was an exact copy of the Turbo File GB. Even the lettering on the PCB still read "TURBO FILE GB", as if nothing at all had been updated. The protocol was a 1:1 match, with the only observable difference being an extra command not used on the Turbo File GB.

Once again, only two compatible games were launched: *RPG Tsukuru Advance* and *Derby Stallion Advance*. Both series had a long history of support for previous Turbo File products, and these portable versions were no exception. Like earlier entries, *RPG Tsukuru Advance* allowed players to save unique, hand-crafted adventures to external storage. The improved capabilities of the Game Boy Advance enabled better graphics and sound and made some of the game-creation tools easier to manipulate. Thankfully, unlike their predecessors, both games could read and write to the entire memory space offered by the Turbo File Advance.

*Derby Stallion Advance* revolved around the extensive and intricate world of horse breeding and racing. Players could take a horse and micromanage many layers of its development over weeks, months, and years. The game used the Turbo File Advance to save the horse and its various stats. Thanks to this, an entire stable of different foals could be raised and entered into competition. The data for each horse was surprisingly small in comparison to every other Turbo File game, taking up just one 8KB block.

The Turbo File GB and Turbo File Advance only retailed in Japan, where both devices saw a shockingly low amount of supported games, all of which came from ASCII or Enterbrain. It isn't surprising that the *RPG Tsukuru* games never released worldwide or overseas. Each one had a great deal of text and menus to translate. Only in recent years has the *RPG Maker* series consistently sold console versions with English counterparts. The vast majority of the older library remains Japanese-only, including the Turbo File compatible titles.

Although the Turbo File products on the Game Boy accomplished something new, they filled a very small niche. The reality was that most handheld software at the time did not benefit from memory cards or external storage solutions. While the Turbo File satisfied the needs of *RPG Tsukuru* and *Derby Stallion*, it offered less functionality to others, specifically those that required only small amounts of save data. In the end, far fewer games utilized the Turbo File GB and Turbo File Advance than the previous Turbo Files on the Famicom and Super Famicom.

The failure of these two accessories to make a larger impact stemmed from the fundamental differences between handhelds and home consoles. By design, the Game Boy was a portable gaming system, something players carried around from place to place. Adding the Turbo File made it less mobile, or at least more of a burden to move. Instead, saving data to the cartridge let players take the most advantage of the Game Boy's ability to roam.

Home consoles, on the other hand, were intended to remain fixtures in front of a TV or display. Whether or not a memory card was attached made little difference how people used the console. Once plugged in, these saving devices could safely be forgotten, and many times they were left alone permanently. The Turbo Files on the Game Boy simply could not replicate this ease of use, requiring constant interaction such as connecting/disconnecting the cable, turning the units on/off, and maintaining the batteries.

These problems arose because there was no way to fully integrate the Turbo Files into a Game Boy. Handheld systems eventually did come to rely on memory cards, such as the Memory Sticks on the PSP and SD cards on the 3DS. At that point however, such cards could be inserted directly into the system without needing bulky, third-party tools wired into one of its ports. If the Turbo Files had somehow found a way to become more embedded into the Game Boys, perhaps they would have seen wider adoption.

However, it is inappropriate to view the Turbo File GB and Turbo File Advance as ultimately having been unsuccessful. The goal behind them was most likely not to be revolutionary new items that would enhance the way every single Game Boy game was made and played. It's best to examine them as limited add-ons intended only for a scant handful of games. Rather than looking to dominate the world, the devices were essentially tailored specifically for the likes of *RPG Tsukuru*. To that end, they served their purpose quite well.

Given the small scope with which they affected the market, the Turbo File GB and Turbo File Advance are certainly curiosities to say the least. Memory cards were foreign ideas to handhelds at the time, yet ASCII and Sammy showed that it was possible to implement them. The Turbo Files did not cause any sort of changes to the video game landscape, yet today they stand as examples of ways companies constantly pushed the limits of what was possible on the modest Game Boy.

Turbo File GB Box Front

Turbo File GB Box Back

Turbo File Advance Box Front

Turbo File Advance Box Back

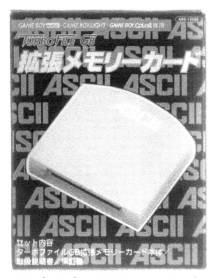

Turbo File GB Memory Card
Box Front

Turbo File GB Memory Card
Box Back

Turbo File Advance Memory
Card Box Front

Turbo File Advance Memory
Card

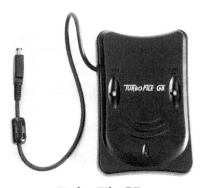

Turbo File GB

Turbo File GB Memory Card

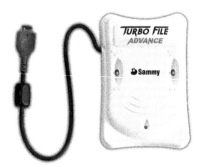

Turbo File Advance

Turbo File Advance Memory
Card

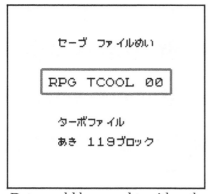

Data could be saved to either the Turbo File itself or an inserted memory card. Game saves were measured in "blocks".

Naturally, saves could be retrieved as well, loading an entire RPG from the Turbo File.

The file format for the Turbo File Advance allowed for longer filenames.

The Turbo File Advance let players save a lot of horse-related data. A LOT.

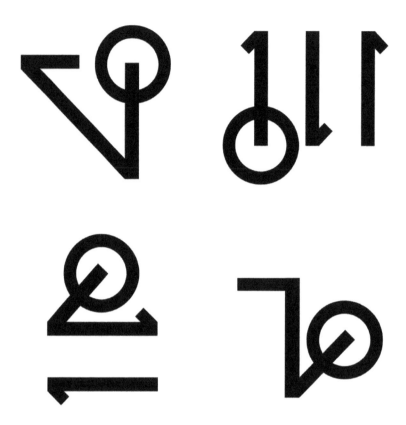

**Release Date:**
August 4, 2000

**Maker:**
Media Factory

**Legacy:**
First use of motion controls on the Game Boy.

With the advent of the Game Boy Color, infrared communication was now a standard component of the handheld's hardware. The built-in transceiver allowed a host of new devices to connect with the Game Boy without having to rely on the serial port. The wireless nature of the infrared port enabled game developers to create products that were previously unthinkable. This idea was perhaps most evident in *Zok Zok Heroes'* add-on: the Full Changer.

Towards the tail end of the Game Boy Color era, Media Factory released a quirky role-playing game in Japan. The player assumed the task of becoming a hero to defend people against various evil and bizarre villains. Ordinarily, the player was a regular little boy or girl, but once they performed a special series of movements, they transformed into a "Bright Hero". These movements weren't just automated cutscenes or screens; the player had to physically do them in real life using the accessory.

There were 70 different heroes the player could transform into, with corresponding strengths, weaknesses, and abilities. Each hero was represented by a "Cosmic Character", a pattern of straight lines. Players shifted the Full Changer according to the pattern to activate the accessory. Once it was ready, the bottom of the Full Changer was pressed against the Game Boy Color's infrared receiver. After the game analyzed the signals sent from the Full Changer, it allowed the transformation, complete with a unique animation sequence.

The Full Changer itself was a rather blocky accessory with an ovular faceplate. It came with an adjustable strap so players could hold it properly as they swung it through the air. On the top, three LEDs indicated the number of movements successfully registered. Each Cosmic Character involved three distinct motions. The Full Changer turned on an LED and beeped as a particular pattern was correctly followed. When the Cosmic Character was complete, infrared pulses were sent from a small section located at the base of the Full Changer.

Only two buttons were present on the peripheral. The larger one on top started recording motions for the Cosmic Character. All three LEDs would flash for approximately five seconds; during that period the players swiped the Full Changer through the air, otherwise it would reset to a neutral state. The bottom button was triggered when the Full Changer and Game Boy Color made contact. At that point, the Full Changer was positioned directly over the Game Boy Color's infrared port and began to emit light.

Although many today may associate motion-based controls as something that caught on during the Nintendo Wii era, it was technically achievable on even the simple Game Boy Color and third-party hardware. The Full Changer detected spatial changes via four Hall effect sensors. They measured differences in voltage when placed in an electromagnetic field, enabling them to sense position, velocity, and direction of movement when used appropriately. With these components, the Full Changer determined which way the player was moving it, even diagonally, and if the movement was long or short.

During battles, all of which were one-on-one fights, the default form of the boy or girl character had fairly weak attacks. In order to defeat foes, they had to change into a Bright Hero. The game allowed the player to change once per turn. If that option was selected, *Zok Zok Heroes* switched to a static screen, waiting for the player to use the Full Changer or press the B button to cancel. The game showed a brief scene of the Bright Hero when it received the correct infrared signals, and the player gained new moves, stats, and elemental attributes.

Not every Cosmic Character was immediately available. Players had to locate them scattered throughout the game's world, often in strange and unexpected places or items, such as a cup in the kitchen or a toy car. Only once the Cosmic Characters were found did they unlock their associated Bright Hero. *Zok Zok Heroes* helpfully included a menu that showed the exact movements for the Full Changer for all of the player's Cosmic Characters. It wasn't possible to cheat by looking up movements for Cosmic Characters not in the player's current index. The game checked the list and displayed an error message in that case.

Each Bright Hero was rather cartoonish and imaginative. They spanned the likes of a robo-battery man, a bipedal tiger-businessman hybrid on a cellphone, and an anthropomorphic skateboard. Their names took on a range of similarly wacky ideas such as Zoom Laser, Gorilla Killa, and Nobel Brain. Some of the names were playful puns based on the Japanese language as well. More importantly each Cosmic Character was paired with a specific character of Japanese kana such as "あ"or "か".

The infrared communication protocol was basic but sufficient. The Full Changer sent a total of 18 light pulses to the Game Boy Color. The first and last signals identified the start and stop of transmissions. *Zok Zok Heroes* used the other 16 pulses to determine which Bright Hero the Full Changer was sending. Depending on whether the pulse was long or short, it was interpreted as a "0" or a "1" in the game's code. The end result was a binary number that could be checked against an internal database. This number consisted of two 8-bit parts: an ID for the Bright Hero and a checksum value.

This hardware marked the first time motion-based controls were used in a Game Boy game. It predated *Koro Koro Kirby* (aka *Kirby Tilt 'n' Tumble*) by several weeks. Although it was very different in concept from the special cartridges that Nintendo built, it became a distinctive interactive experience later seen in such controllers as the Wii Remote and PlayStation Move. Players could now use their body to perform actions that directly affected their gameplay.

Although the Full Changer was only used for limited portions of battles, it was actually required to play *Zok Zok Heroes* in any capacity. While in theory it would have been possible to level up the player's default form and try to advance through the game without resorting to Bright Heroes or Cosmic Characters, the first battle of the game functioned as a brief tutorial for the Full Changer. If the device wasn't used, the battle halted and waited indefinitely for infrared signals. Without using the Full Changer or cheats, the game was virtually unbeatable and could not be completed.

Ultimately, *Zok Zok Heroes* may have been too zany for its own good. The game and accessory remained a Japanese exclusive and was never introduced in the West. Localization may have been a bit difficult to attempt, given the nature of the Cosmic Characters being tied so heavily to the Japanese language. Additionally, bringing any type of new hardware overseas always carries a financial risk due to different demographics of the market. There was no guarantee that a North American or European gamer would have seen the appeal of the Full Changer, thus affecting sales. As such, these barriers prevented the game from reaching a wider audience.

The true era of motion-based controls was still years away, but the Full Changer offered a glimpse at its many possibilities, especially in regards to handheld gaming. Instead of dedicated external hardware, however, the trend for portable consoles would later involve gyroscopes or accelerometers built into the system itself or their game cartridges. Even so, *Zok Zok Heroes* pioneered a new method of interacting with the Game Boy. While it may be easy to write off the Full Changer because of its obscurity and niche nature, it helped to further establish a control scheme that was relatively underdeveloped and unexplored.

*Zok Zok Heroes* Box Front

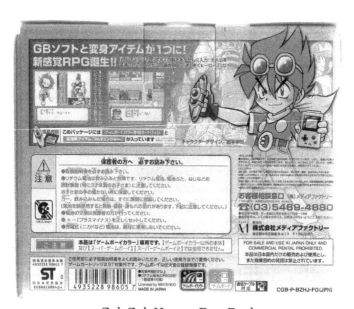

*Zok Zok Heroes* Box Back

The Full Changer came packaged with the game in a special box set (a rarity for Game Boy titles of the time). It even featured a little plastic strap on top to carry it around.

*Zok Zok Heroes* Box Front          *Zok Zok Heroes* Box Back

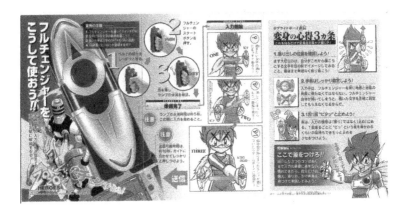

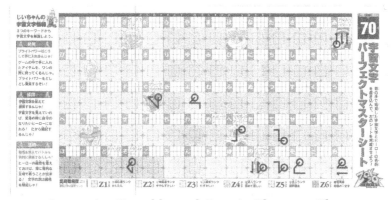

Instruction Pamphlet and Cosmic Character Chart

The Full Changer

The device came with a velcro strap so players could grip and move it around. Cosmic Characters were always made up of three distinct motions. The Full Changer was designed to recognize them and light up and beep when the player was successful. A small infrared transmitter was situated at the bottom.

*Zok Zok Heroes* would patiently wait for infrared signals from the Full Changer.

Once the correct signals were processed, players transformed into Bright Heroes.

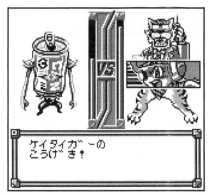

Battles were one-on-one. Players fought against an army of bizarre foes, such as this evil soda can.

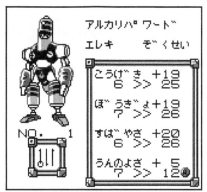

After acquiring a Bright Hero, the game helpfully kept track of the Full Changer movements for that transformation.

**Release Date:**

> August 23, 2000

**Maker:**

> Nintendo

**Legacy:**

> Marked Nintendo's first major and extensive use of accelerometers for motion control. Set the foundation for later generations.

135

Long before the Wii became synonymous with motion controls, Nintendo dabbled with the technology on the Game Boy Color. Although not quite as advanced as the hardware later found in the Wii Remote, the accelerometer built into the MBC7 mapper was more than capable of handling itself. Towards the end of August 2000, the company released *Koro Koro Kirby* in Japan, the title that would eventually become *Kirby Tilt 'n' Tumble* in western markets. The translucent pink cartridge featured the latest mapper for the 8-bit system, one that measured how far it was rotated in four directions.

Using an integrated circuit known as the ADXL202JQC, the MBC7 could constantly report its tilt status to the game. The component only dealt with the X and Y axes, detecting movement for left, right, up, and down. With this, players were tasked with rolling Kirby around various stages, carefully maneuvering him to avoid obstacles, traps, and enemies. Because the mapper had detailed sensors as input, this became the first time a Game Boy title took advantage of analog controls. As long as the MBC7 was calibrated by holding the cartridge flat, players could make precise movements that were all but impossible on a regular directional pad. The mapper was accurate enough to detect sudden changes, such as flicking the Game Boy upright quickly. The game used this trick to make Kirby bounce up high into the air. Although simple in concept, it was in fact an early demonstration of applying gestures in gameplay, something Nintendo would come to master in the future.

Another game utilizing the MBC7, *Command Master*, arrived in November. Here, players transformed into various superheroes by performing a series of timed movements, angling the Game Boy Color in sync with colored bars that scrolled across the screen. Special attacks required tilting in specific directions, and finishing moves involved a rapid frenzy of back-to-back shaking to charge up power. The one-on-one RPG shared quite a few similarities with *Zok Zok Heroes*, however, it more actively incorporated motion controls into each and every battle.

Less well known about the MBC7 was that it took a major step towards improving the reliability of game save data on the Game Boy. It was the second mapper to use EEPROM instead of SRAM. These game saves were no longer dependent on a battery, which could die after prolonged use and erase the player's progress. The lifespan of the save file was in theory longer with EEPROM given normal usage. EEPROM would eventually find a place in many Game Boy Advance cartridges as well. The only drawback on the MBC7 was the measly size of the EEPROM, a mere 256 bytes! For reference, this entire paragraph is only 688 characters long, and the MBC7 would only be able to store about a third of that.

Like other mappers, the MBC7's special functionality was accessed through certain memory addresses. The area typically dedicated to cartridge SRAM instead returned 16-bit X and Y values from the accelerometer. By reading those, the game determined how far in each direction the system was turned. The software had to "latch" the accelerometer values first, essentially freezing the current results and telling the hardware to only update the values when specifically asked to do so. This area of memory also granted access to the MBC7's EEPROM. As with most EEPROM chips, the software transferred data back and forth serially, bit-by-bit. By issuing certain commands to EEPROM, the game could read bytes, write bytes, or erase different portions of the 256-byte save data.

Despite how impressive the MBC7 was at the time, its compatible games suffered from several issues. The Game Boy Color's neutral position was supposed to be mostly parallel to the ground, held horizontally in the player's hands. This somewhat unusual arrangement often caused problems with lighting and visibility as the Game Boy shifted positions. Unmodified Game Boy Color screens had no backlights whatsoever, making oblique angles difficult to see when using the MBC7. Glares from other light sources such as lamps would further interfere with players. These difficulties only served to distract players from the game itself and the innovation it presented.

Another particular limitation of the MBC7 was the inability to account for different orientations of the cartridge. It was made with the assumption that all cartridges would be loaded from the top. Game Boy Advance SP models loaded cartridges from the bottom, however, inverting some of the tilt axes when playing MBC7 titles. To be fair, this was largely a software-based issue. By the time later iterations of motion-sensing cartridges arrived, they were properly programmed to handle multiple positions. Although game developers initially lacked the foresight to future-proof their work on the MBC7, it served as a lesson going forward.

Lastly, the motion-based gameplay was at times viewed as a basic gimmick. *Kirby Tilt 'n' Tumble* was well designed conceptually, but the rolling mechanism was criticized as unnecessary by some reviewers and frustrating by a handful of others. *Command Master*, on the other hand, somewhat forced motion-controls onto situations where it was unwarranted. The sequences used to transform or launch attacks, for example, could have easily been replaced with an ordinary directional pad. There wasn't even a case to be made where the analog precision of the MBC7 would enhance the game. Perceptions about these shortcomings were not universal, however. In hindsight, perhaps certain parts of the industry then were not quite ready to fully embrace motion controls. At any rate, these faults proved that games needed thoughtful planning if they were to include the player's movements as part of the experience.

The MBC7 came and went swiftly. It appeared at the very last stages of the Game Boy Color's life, right as Nintendo and other developers were preparing to launch the next generation Game Boy Advance. As such it only claimed two titles out of the entire library. The technology behind the MBC7, however, would serve as the basis for other Game Boy Advance games that used tilting and rotation. Those efforts later evolved into the Wii Remote, followed by the 3DS, Wii U gamepad, and Nintendo Switch, all of which had built-in accelerometers. The mapper ultimately represents Nintendo's first, true attempt at motion controls. Though admittedly something of an experiment, the MBC7 laid the groundwork for eventual improvements.

*Kirby Tilt 'n' Tumble* Cartridge

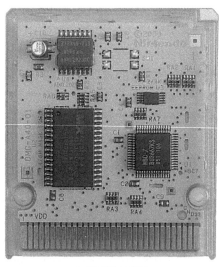

MBC7 PCB

The main component that detects motion, the ADXL202JQC, can be seen in the upper-left corner. The EEPROM is below that and to the right. Both *Kirby Tilt 'n' Tumble* and *Command Master* had specially colored shells (pink and blue, respectively).

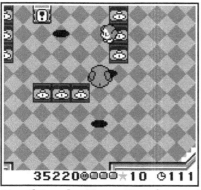

By tilting the Game Boy forward and back quickly, the flick gesture sent Kirby high into the air and flipped over enemies and panels.

Some levels featured brief puzzles, locked doors, and even multi-tiered sections. Here, Kirby needed to flick to get back up.

In *Command Master*, players transformed by tilting the Game Boy accordingly and timing A button presses.

Once transformed, players could launch special attacks with tilt combos.

**Release Dates:**

| | |
|---|---|
| Power Antenna – Model 1 | November 3, 2000 |
| Bug Sensor | November 2, 2001 |
| Power Antenna – Model 2 | April 26, 2002 |

**Maker:**

Smilesoft

**Legacy:**

Helped change the "look and feel" of the Game Boy to match certain items used in the games.

Much of the hardware observed within this book have one thing in common: games were specifically programmed to take advantage of these peripherals. The code explicitly controlled or interacted with the device in question. Another prevalent theme is shared among all of these items: the hardware often added some new and compelling dimension to the game. However, both models of the Power Antenna and the Bug Sensor are a bit of an exception. There's no understating what these accessories were on a fundamental level. Despite their unique and intriguing appearances, they were at best simple LEDs that blinked on and off.

In late 2000, Smilesoft launched its *Telefang* franchise, releasing the game *Keitai Denjuu Telefang* in two separate versions, *Speed* and *Power*. The story followed a young boy named Shigeki as he accidentally arrived in a parallel world ruled by electric beasts known as Denjuu. Using a special cellphone called a D-Shot, it was possible to communicate with Denjuu and befriend them. *Telefang* was in essence a monster collecting and raising turn-based RPG in the same vein of *Pokémon*. In fact, many players may recognize the first *Telefang* game as a translated version that served as the basis for *Pokémon Diamond* and *Pokémon Jade* bootlegs.

Smilesoft decided to include a tiny add-on called the Power Antenna for Limited Editions of both *Telefang* versions. The purpose of the antenna was largely cosmetic. Once pushed into the Game Boy Color's Link Cable port, the handheld then resembled the same D-Shot from the game. The Power Antenna also had another function; whenever the player received an in-game call, the LED flashed accordingly. In conjunction with sounds from the game, this effect was meant to give players the illusion that their Game Boy had now become a working cellphone.

One year later, the company would launch yet another monster-based RPG known as *Network Adventure Bugsite*. Like their previous endeavors, two versions were produced, *Alpha* and *Beta*. Both games took place in the virtual world "Bugsite", which was populated by digital creatures called Bugs. They ordinarily performed various computer-related tasks and were treated as something like pets. A virus running around Bugsite, however, caused Bugs to become aggressive. To stop the chaos, Daichi and his Bug partner Spiral had to fight and capture infected Bugs. Each copy of the games came with a peripheral called a Bug Sensor, named after an in-game item worn by the protagonist. The attachment fit into the Game Boy's Link Cable port just like the Power Antenna. Its role was to flash whenever the player received messages or when a viral Bug approached. In the latter case, the closer the enemy drew, the faster and more intensely the Bug Sensor would switch on and off.

Several months after Smilesoft released the Bug Sensor, they sold a second iteration of the Power Antenna with every copy of *Keitai Denjuu Telefang 2*. As with the prequel, *Telefang 2* came in *Speed* and *Power* versions. Although it differed in shape, the functionality of the second Power Antenna model remained the same; it flashed whenever the player received a call. This model, however, was specifically designed for the Game Boy Advance's Link Cable port, and as such it could not be used on the Game Boy Color. Aside from that one incompatibility, all of the accessories Smilesoft produced were essentially the same device with a different plastic shell. For example, the Bug Sensor could work with *Telefang 1* and *2* as a replacement for the Power Antenna.

In mid 2002, *GachaSta! Dino Device Red* and *Blue* versions hit the market. The pair of games offered more monster raising and collecting, this time in the form of virtual dinosaurs obtained through a gachapon system. During the fights between Dinos, certain attacks would cause the Power Antenna to light up. *Dino Device* was unique among Smilesoft's library in that it was the only title compatible with these accessories that did not come bundled with one of its own. Players would only have access to this little bonus if they had previously purchased the peripheral from other games.

Both Power Antenna models and the Bug Sensor operated exactly the same. The Game Boy only had to toggle a single bit on or off when manipulating data sent over the Link Cable port. The exact procedure varied depending on what type of Game Boy was used. For the Game Boy Color, the software simply transferred one byte. If the first bit of that byte was a "1", the light turned on. To turn the light off, the software just sent a byte that equaled zero. For the Game Boy Advance, it didn't matter what kind of byte was sent. Instead, the software directly set the value of one of the output pins used for the Link Cable port. Changing that pin to "high" or "low" turned the LED on or off respectively.

All three accessories were particularly special in that they were some of the few licensed Link Cable devices known to draw power from the Game Boy Color. Many others, such as the Barcode Boy or Game Boy Printer, used their own batteries, as the handheld itself couldn't provide the necessary energy. The Jaguar sewing machines even came with their own power cable to plug into an outlet. Tiny LEDs, conversely, were quite easy to power on, especially in short bursts. This sort of behavior was seen in unofficial hardware such as the Worm Light, but elsewhere it remained exclusive to Smilesoft's products.

These devices weren't meant to revolutionize the world of gaming, let alone have a huge impact. At their heart, the Power Antenna and Bug Sensor were just playful lights. To be frank, they were merely toys, something to dress up the Game Boy, a decoration. Nevertheless, their purpose was to create a better sense of immersion between the player and the game. By making the Game Boy look and feel like one of the machines from the game, Smilesoft tried to bring their worlds closer to reality. In this regard, these peripherals were a small, inexpensive way to achieve that effect. Although they weren't nearly as extravagant as other add-ons, the Power Antenna and Bug Sensor didn't need to be over-the-top to capture the interest of young gamers. After all, sometimes just looking cool is more than enough.

*Telefang 1 Power* Box Front

*Telefang 1 Power* Box Back

*Bugsite Beta* Box Front

*Bugsite Beta* Box Back

*Telefang 2 Speed* Box Front

*Telefang 2 Speed* Box Back

Power Antenna Model 1 attached to a Game Boy Color

In *Telefang 1*, after players battled Denjuu, they could be called upon for later fights via phone numbers.

At times, these same Denjuu would randomly call the player. The Power Antenna flashed when a call was incoming.

In *Network Adventure Bugsite*, the Bug Sensor increasingly flashed before a battle.

Finally, the enemy revealed themselves, and both sides could now trade attacks.

In *Telefang 2,* Denjuu that the player met would call them from time to time. The Power Antenna flashed here too.

Fortunately, other audiovisual cues alerted the player of a call, making the Power Antenna mostly decoration.

*GachaSta! Dino Device* lit up the Power Antenna when using the gachapon machine to get new Dinos.

Certain attacks would also cause the Power Antenna to turn on.

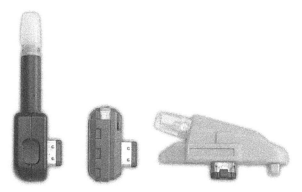

The first Power Antenna, Bug Sensor, and second Power Antenna

**Release Date:**
> January 27, 2001

**Maker:**
> Nintendo

**Legacy:**
> Marked Nintendo's most comprehensive attempt at online gameplay at the time. Eventually pushed the company towards a more modern approach to internet connectivity.

As access to the internet increased during the '80s and '90s, video games gradually expanded into new realms. Through a vast and global network, online players could compete against rivals or cooperate with friends, all at previously unimaginable distances. For home consoles, there were many early but slow attempts to capitalize on this emerging multiplayer medium. Nintendo took the Famicom online in 1988, however, these efforts were fledgling at best. The Super Famicom's Satellaview satellite modem gave the company their most extensive and successful service yet, however, the following efforts on the 64DD failed to match in either quality or quantity. Prior to the DS and Wii era, Nintendo's history with online gaming was marked by this back-and-forth motion, lackluster at one moment then brilliant in the next. After the 64DD, Nintendo pushed the Game Boy online, this time with far greater results.

At Space World 2000, a new accessory for the handheld was unveiled to much fanfare. Introduced on stage was the Mobile Adapter GB, a device that would allow certain models of cellphones to attach to the Game Boy Color. Through that link, the Game Boy could send and receive data wirelessly, thus connecting it to the internet. If everything had gone according to plan, the Mobile Adapter would have released in December to coincide with its flagship title, *Pocket Monsters Crystal Version*. Unfortunately the product and network were delayed by a month and came to stores in late January.

The peripheral sold for 5,800 yen at launch and came in three variants depending on the type of cellphone it worked with. Each sported a different color: blue for PDC phones, yellow for cdmaOne phones, and red for DDI phones. A fourth variant – green for PHS phones – was designed but never sold. The packaging for the variants differed as well, featuring the color of the adapter on the front and a list of compatible phones on the back. Ultimately, the Mobile Adapter was the result of both Nintendo and Mobile21. The latter partner was a joint company owned 50/50 by Nintendo and Konami. Mobile21 would go on to develop a significant portion of games that supported the add-on.

Included with every copy of the Mobile Adapter was a special blue-shelled cartridge called *Mobile Trainer*. It was responsible for setting up the adapter and connecting it to the DION network. Without the configuration process, players could not go online. The software guided users through various steps such as entering their ID, password, and DION-based e-mail address. *Mobile Trainer* also served as an online portal, as it came with a fully usable e-mail client and basic web browser. Users could exchange messages with other players or in some cases characters such as Bowser. The browser supported a limited subset of HTML to display news, events, and updates. It even allowed for small black and white bitmap images.

Players had to mail in registration to DION with their name and address along with a one-time fee of 400 yen. Once they received a reply in the mail, they could then bring their Game Boys online. There were no monthly costs associated with the service. Instead, players were charged 10 yen per minute, along with any other usage fees applied by the phone company. Often these were related specifically to accessing downloadable content. To avoid ending up with a large phone bill, all software created for the Mobile Adapter actively monitored how long the player was connected. They reported the time on-screen in a clear and prominent manner. Additionally, the games always warned players before even attempting to join the network.

Overall, 22 games took advantage of the Mobile Adapter. While the hardware was originally released for the Game Boy Color, it worked just fine on the Game Boy Advance. In fact, the majority of compatible software ran on the newer 32-bit handheld. Only six titles on the Game Boy Color had this online functionality. Given how late the adapter appeared, it isn't surprising that the next generation system saw higher adoption among developers. The additional power provided by the Game Boy Advance's CPU likely made it a more attractive target for managing complex network communications as well. Two games – *beatmaniaGB Net Jam* and *Horse Racing Creating Derby* –  announced support for the adapter but were ultimately canceled.

Like many other accessories, the Mobile Adapter transferred data to and from the Game Boy via the system's Link Cable port. The adapter connected to the Game Boy on one end, while the other plugged into the cellphone, bridging the two devices. In general, the Game Boy sent commands to the adapter, which relayed them to the phone. Once the phone performed a given action, the response was passed back to the Game Boy. The transmission followed a packet-based protocol vaguely similar to the Game Boy Printer. In each packet, the Game Boy defined a specific command along with any necessary data. A brief checksum and acknowledgment signal came at the end. The Game Boy then waited for a reply where the adapter returned a packet of its own following the same format.

The Mobile Adapter featured a wide array of functions. It could initiate or end a telephone call, login or logout of an internet service provider, read or write configuration data stored in the adapter's internal memory, query DNS, and open multiple TCP or UDP connections. Secondary protocols – such as HTTP, POP3, and SMTP – had to be handled via software. The adapter relied on its own firmware to translate incoming and outgoing data between the Game Boy and the cellphone, effectively acting as a sort of middleman for both sides. For each variant of the Mobile Adapter, the actual programming in the firmware was different, as they dealt with separate types of phones.

The Nintendo Mobile System GB, as it was called, ran its data centers through Kyocera Communication Systems Co., Ltd. while the telecom KDDI acted as the ISP. A specific division previously known as Nintendo Network Service Development was responsible for creating the hardware and software necessary for the adapter and its online features. This portion of Nintendo had earlier worked on the Satellaview and would later move on to other areas such as the Wii Shop Channel and 3DS eShop. The servers themselves were hosted at the URL *gameboy.datacenter.ne.jp*. Unfortunately, overall support for the Mobile Adapter was relatively short-lived.

While it lasted, however, the Mobile Adapter proved to be Nintendo's most serious foray into online gaming yet. *Game Boy Wars 3*, a turn-based strategy game, allowed players to download new maps through the service at 30 yen a piece. It also offered several "mercenary units" with increased stats. Once connected to the internet, the player could summon them into battle for the small price of 10 yen. Lastly, the game had a message center where players could receive medals meant to enhance other units. Sadly, the game did not permit players to battle each other via the adapter.

*Mobile Golf* was the sequel to *Mario Golf*'s Game Boy Color port. The new, Japanese-only game used the Mobile Adapter to host online tournaments such as the Nintendo Open. Here, players could register to participate for 50 yen. Over a set timeframe, players from all over Japan would then complete a golf course, and those with the best scores would win. Other competitive areas involving specific challenges were available, such as seeing who could hit the ball closest to the pin and rankings on individual holes. *Mobile Golf* provided a lot of paid downloadable content as well, ranging from new golf courses and minigames to playable characters such as Mario, Peach, Yoshi, and Foreman Spike.

Perhaps the best use of the Mobile Adapter lay with *Pocket Monsters Crystal*. Trainers could battle and trade more or less normally, just as if they were connected via Link Cable. It ran through peer-to-peer networking, directly dialing a friend's phone. Players could store and exchange profile information and contact data to keep track of others. Live battles were limited to three Pokémon for either trainer and generally capped to 10 minutes a day. Helpfully, in the event of a disconnection, the game's AI would assume control over the opponent's Pokémon and let the match continue.

In Goldenrod City, a dedicated building called the Pokémon Communication Center served as a larger hub for additional online activities. It hosted the Trade Corner, an early version of the Global Trade System seen in later games. Trainers could deposit their Pokémon and put them up for trade in exchange for another specific Pokémon. Players could also receive an Odd Egg as part of an event. When it hatched, the Pokémon had a higher chance of being a "Shiny", a rare alternative form with different coloring. The Communication Center displayed news, featured quizzes based on Pokémon trivia, had minigames, and even showed the regional rankings of different players.

With the Mobile Adapter, the Battle Tower in *Pocket Monsters Crystal* unlocked, allowing players to compete in a series of matches. Trainers faced off against seven different AI opponents. Here they could select the level of Pokémon they wished to fight alongside. The rival team consisted of Pokémon previously used by other Trainers connecting online for the Battle Tower, exposing players to a variety of enemies and moves. Based on how well a Trainer performed in battle, they received a rank and potentially appeared on a leaderboard. Last but not least, Trainers could download Battle Data for use with *Pokémon Stadium Gold, Silver, and Crystal*. The Battle Data replayed mobile matches, this time in full 3D with enhanced special effects thanks to the Nintendo 64.

Few Game Boy Advance games provided as many options as *Pocket Monsters Crystal*, however they still made impressive use of the adapter. *Sutakomi* – short for *Star Communicator* – had the player taking care of their own cute, almost Tamagotchi-like animal on a spaceship. Rather than directly feeding or nurturing the creature, players communicated with them and taught them about life. The Mobile Adapter was used for e-mail to exchange messages and information between other players and their virtual pets. As the pets grew, users could arrange a "Star Marriage" where they joined together in matrimony online. Several items could be purchased from a Home Page once connected to the network. News and updates were frequently posted to the Home Page as well.

*Zen-Nihon GT Senshuken*, a professional racing game, let players square off against one another via rankings based on course time completions. The faster the time, the higher players would climb up to the top. The races themselves took place offline, but whenever the player was ready, they could upload their results to the servers. As a nice bonus, special race courses were available for download through the Mobile Adapter as well. Another racing game, the popular *Mario Kart Advance*, had a Mobile Grand Prix mode. Once again, players finished races offline and their completion times were uploaded and used as scoring. Ghost Data could be exchanged online as well. Neither game had a live head-to-head mode, but they made do with other means and still offered a way for players to compete.

Although the list of compatible games was not long, each piece of software pushed Nintendo towards a more modern approach to internet gaming. Their earliest service, the Famicom Network System, was innovative for its time, however it did little to attract gamers by focusing a large portion of software on subjects such as stocks and betting. While the Satellaview let players download an entire library of numerous games and content such as magazines, the service lacked the ability to link two players together directly or via messaging. Randnet on the 64DD had the potential, but with only a small handful of compatible games, its attempt eventually petered out. With the Mobile Adapter GB, Nintendo ensured that the product had decent first and third-party support to push out a number of compelling titles. These games reached a new level of online interactivity that was previously unseen in any of the company's earlier internet adventures.

Tragically, the Mobile Adapter GB's network service lasted less than two full years. On December 14, 2002, any online components that relied on Nintendo's servers became inoperable, with only peer-to-peer connections surviving. Its abrupt end stemmed from several causes. Although the adapter and its games were primarily aimed at children, most kids in Japan at the time did not have their own cellphones. They needed the permission of their parents to use such a device, and it was these adults who ended up paying for any fees. The Mobile Adapter was also not a simple plug-and-play accessory; it required a lengthy multi-step setup. Aside from *Pocket Monsters, Mobile Golf,* and *Mario Kart Advance,* the adapter saw few "killer apps" from popular Nintendo properties, reducing its appeal. Finally, the hardware was rather expensive at launch, costing roughly 2/3 the price of a new Game Boy Color. By the end of March 2001, only 80,000 units had been sold, forcing Nintendo to reduce the price to 3,800 yen in September. Even without the low adoption numbers in Japan, the Mobile Adapter would have been challenging to bring overseas due to weaker wireless infrastructures in countries such as the United States, along with the need for more variants to handle a wider range of phone models.

Despite its brief lifetime, the Mobile Adapter served Nintendo well, giving them a large amount of experience dealing with a real, robust internet gaming service. It advanced Nintendo's network connectivity farther along than any of its previous systems, and even exceeded rivals such as the Tiger Game.com. The games certainly lacked many of the features present in our contemporary understanding of online play, nevertheless the adapter eventually set the stage for more ambitious endeavors. Although their online efforts on the GameCube would falter, losing the momentum the Game Boy had established, Nintendo rebounded in relatively splendid form with their Wi-Fi Connection in the following console generation. Today internet connectivity is standard for their consoles, and the Mobile Adapter was pivotal to reaching such progress.

Mobile Adapter GB Box Front

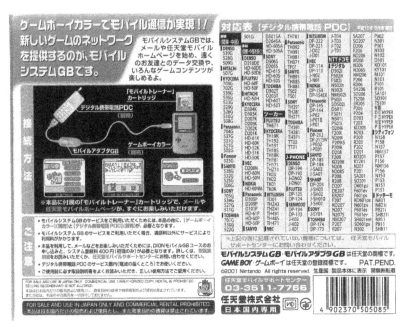

Mobile Adapter GB Box Back

*Mobile Golf* and Mobile Adapter GB Bundle

Rare for Game Boy hardware, the Mobile Adapter GB came as part of a bundle with a game. It included separate boxes for *Mobile Golf* as well as the adapter (seen on the previous page).

157

Mobile Adapter GB

The adapter itself came in three different colors corresponding to the cellphone models it supported. PDC, the most common, used a blue plastic shell.

It connected to a Game Boy via the Link Cable on one end and a compatible cellphone on the other. Inside the plastic shell was a microprocessor that handled exchanging data between the Game Boy and the cellphone.

Thanks to this design, the adapter and phone did most of the low-level networking, allowing the Game Boy to focus on running the game itself. Even though the handheld system didn't natively support internet connectivity, it nevertheless achieved that by relying on additional hardware.

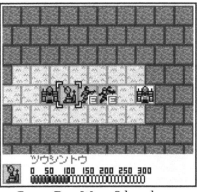

*Game Boy Wars 3* let players download special maps or summon powerful mercenary units. You even had to pay for the soldiers like real mercenaries.

*Hello Kitty no Happy House* allowed users to collect furniture and other items. These could be sent to friends via e-mail.

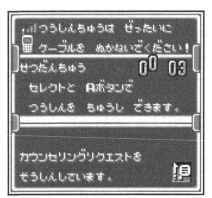

*Mobile Golf* offered a host of DLC, from new characters, courses, to rankings for individual courses or holes. It also had online tourneys.

*Pocket Monsters Crystal* was the first in the series to support online battling and trading. It was the Mobile Adapter's star title.

*Mario Kart Advance* featured an online Mobile GP as well as the ability to exchange ghost data with rivals.

*Sutakomi* gave access to a lot of news surrounding the game as well as downloadable items for virtual pets.

*Zen-Nihon GT Senshuken* could connect online to download new courses and rankings.

*Napoleon*, a strategy game starring the historical French leader, let players download various battle scenarios.

Several sports games featured online rankings and leaderboards.

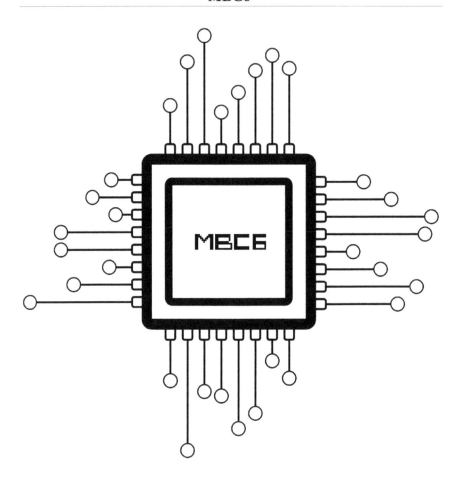

**Release Date:**
 July 12, 2001

**Maker:**
 Nintendo

**Legacy:**
 Provided long-term storage for online downloadable content
 on the Game Boy Color.

Late into both the Game Boy Color and Mobile Adapter GB's lifetimes, Konami released a title known as *Net de Get: Minigame @ 100*. It featured a host of wacky and off-beat minigames. The main appeal, however, was the fact that *Net de Get* allowed players to download 23 additional games through the internet. The new software would have to be stored on the cartridge itself. Unfortunately, the battery-backed SRAM typically used in Game Boy Color cartridges at the time was rather small.

On average, games using the MBC5 cartridge mapper tended to have 32KB of save data, and at most they could come equipped with 128KB. Considering all the code, graphics, and sound necessary for even a scaled-down game, that didn't offer much breathing room, especially when users could potentially download a dozen or more. Furthermore, there was the issue of having a dead battery effectively delete any existing save data, including any downloadable content. This in particular was troublesome given users had to pay to access the minigames. A new cartridge mapper was thus designed to provide long-term storage for large amounts of data: the MBC6.

To solve both of the aforementioned problems, the MBC6 relied on flash memory. With this upgrade, a battery was no longer required to supply a constant charge to keep critical data intact. The MBC6 provided a whopping 1MB worth of flash memory as well, more than enough to save plenty of minigames. *Net de Get* still used battery-backed SRAM, just not for downloading games. Instead, it saved user data such as high scores and records. The MBC6 granted separate interfaces for accessing both flash and SRAM. *Net de Get* used standardized flash commands for reading and writing bytes, as well as erasing entire sectors.

Due to its unique needs, *Net de Get* was the only title to ever use the MBC6. It was the first Game Boy Color game programmed to explicitly take advantage of flash memory for saving data. Later on, several Game Boy Advance games, such as *Pokémon Ruby* and *Sapphire*, would use flash memory as well. Although its primary purpose was expanded memory, the MBC6 mapper deserves special mention in this book. Thanks to its contributions, the Game Boy saw one of the largest pushes for downloaded content yet on Nintendo's handhelds. *Net de Get* served as a pioneer for online video game purchases on mobile platforms, and it was the technology in its cartridge that enabled such efforts.

*Net de Get: Minigame @ 100* Cartridge

MBC6 PCB

The MBC6 was actually released after the MBC7. The numbering likely reflects the point at which they were internally developed rather than when they hit production. The MBC6 wasn't the first officially licensed Game Boy cartridge to use flash memory, but it was just one of two, the second being the GB Memory Cartridge.

Once connected to online servers, *Net de Get* showed a list of available minigames to download.

Each minigame cost 100 yen to download, or about $0.90 in USD at the time.

The download process could take a while, as it worked via cellphone networks in Japan, and it was limited by the Link Cable speed on the Game Boy.

Once downloaded, the minigame would show up in the player's collection. The screen also showed how much available space was left on the MBC6.

On March 21, 2001, Nintendo launched the Game Boy Advance, a portable powerhouse touting a faster CPU, a larger screen, and greatly enhanced graphics and sound. The new handheld ushered in a very different era of add-ons. While its predecessor, the Game Boy Color, made only incremental changes regarding memory, speed, and colors, the Game Boy Advance significantly altered many design aspects. It removed the infrared port, shrunk cartridge sizes, and now provided flexible ways to operate the Link Cable. As a result, certain hardware conventions were left behind. Others, however, remained strong as they adopted new roles.

With the Game Boy Advance's arrival, there was a sharp drop in the number of games that supported infrared communication. Prototypes of the system did indeed have infrared ports, yet this was later scrapped before the console was finalized. Since the platform lacked native infrared capabilities, developers moved away from that feature altogether. Out of the Game Boy Advance's entire library, only a single game supported any sort of infrared interactivity; even then it was only achieved through an accessory. Where the Game Boy Color had overseen one of the most prolific periods of infrared gameplay, the Game Boy Advance effectively killed it overnight.

Despite this tragedy, the Game Boy Advance became a champion of wireless multiplayer via other means. Although the Mobile Adapter GB launched as a device for the Game Boy Color, it was compatible with the Game Boy Advance. The newer system would go on to support more online games than any previous Nintendo console, holding that achievement until the DS and Wii era. Additionally, Nintendo's Wireless Adapter offered players a chance to cut the cord in dozens of titles for local multiplayer. Infrared light pulses were replaced with controlled radio waves, a trend that would culminate in Wi-Fi support for Nintendo's products going forward.

As dimensions of Game Paks grew smaller, they offered less opportunities to fit specialized hardware inside. It was still possible to create larger-than-normal cartridges with complex circuitry inside, but that invariably increased manufacturing costs. Additionally, going too big ran the risk of being physically unwieldy and unstable when running on the Game Boy Advance. Nevertheless, these conditions ultimately did not prevent specialized cartridges from appearing. Card scanners, solar sensors, tilt sensors, haptic feedback, video and music players, and even camera phones were all released. In terms of overall innovation, these kinds of cartridges held steady, however, their total number markedly declined during the Game Boy Advance's lifetime.

Many of these cartridges saw a clear shift towards multimedia. Previously, the older Game Boy's limited audiovisual capabilities made this task mostly infeasible. Thanks to the upgrades present in the Game Boy Advance, however, it could play various movies or sound clips, albeit with some compression. Kemco's Music Recorder let users make their own recordings. The Play-Yan allowed playback of MP3 and MP4 files from an SD card. Lastly, the Advance Movie Adapter cartridge provided anime episodes as well as feature length films squeezed down to a 240x160 resolution. Before smartphones dominated the market, Nintendo's system carved out a small niche for itself as an all-around entertainment device.

The one area of exotic hardware that saw little change was Link Cable accessories. On the Game Boy Advance, they flourished as they previously had. However, a new theme appeared among them, a direction that made them almost toy-like. The Virtureal Racing System dealt exclusively with slot-cars. The Soul Doll Adapter and Multi-Plust On System used collectible figurines. The Battle Chip Gates used plastic chips inserted into a slot. The wearable Magical Watch provided minigames and transferable bonuses. *Cyber Drive Zoids* even featured remote controlled robot dinosaurs. All of the above items engaged players not with gimmicks, but with the thrill of connecting the physical and the digital, bringing the world of the Game Boy closer to reality.

On its surface, the Game Boy Advance's collection of hardware may seem a bit more subdued than the previous generation. No more sewing machines, no more sonar devices, no more printers, and no more alarm clocks built into cartridges. In actuality, the Game Boy Advance continued to host items that were bold, flashy, and groundbreaking for the video game industry. Although the dearth of infrared options was lamentable, the handheld supplied many exciting developments of its own. This same spirit, to explore and experiment with different methods of play through new hardware, carried on beyond the Game Boy Advance. It reached deep into the DS, creating another line of incredible devices. Perhaps that tale too will be written within these pages, one day.

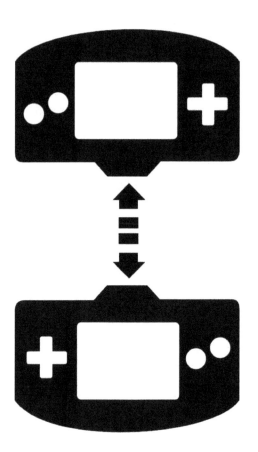

**Release Dates:**

    AGB-005                 March 21, 2001

    OXY-008                 December 17, 2005

**Maker:**

    Nintendo

**Legacy:**

    Massively improved multiplayer options for the Game Boy with built-in 4-player capabilities, downloadable multiplayer sessions, and GameCube connectivity. Allowed other peripherals to communicate more freely with the Game Boy.

The Game Boy Advance was a major evolution from the Game Boy Color in all regards. While the audio and visual upgrades were among the most immediate changes, the multiplayer architecture for the system was completely revamped. For their latest handheld, Nintendo introduced several new paradigms that made games more challenging and entertaining. They increased the maximum number of players, let other Game Boys join sessions even without a cart, and added connectivity with the Nintendo GameCube. Meanwhile, in expanding the capabilities of the Game Boy Advance's Link Cable, the Japanese company also provided developers with a vast array of communication tools, allowing game makers to pursue ideas that were previously impossible a generation ago.

The 3rd Generation Link Cable, the AGB-005, launched alongside the Game Boy Advance itself. In shape and size, it was not much different from the 2nd Generation Link Cable introduced on the Game Boy Pocket. However, this Link Cable now used a 6-pin configuration, whereas previous cables only used 5-pins. With an extra pin, it had more options for transferring data. The Game Boy Advance's Link Cable also featured a small notch at the top to prevent it from accidentally plugging into older Game Boys. While the Game Boy Advance could still use 2nd Generation Link Cables – provided it was running in the DMG/CGB backwards compatibility mode – the 3rd Generation Link Cables were not designed to work with earlier Game Boys at all. Outwardly, the biggest change on the AGB-005 was the hub in the middle of the cable. Here, other Link Cables could attach themselves, allowing up to four people to play and compete simultaneously.

To take full advantage of the Link Cable, the Game Boy Advance had a range of technical modifications to its serial port. The console now supported five distinct modes of operation, each aimed at different uses or needs. Although these modes were not directly a feature of the Link Cable itself, they determined how it was used in various capacities.

First and foremost was "Normal" mode. Rather than implying that the others were strange or obscure, Normal mode was more or less analogous to how 1st and 2nd Generation Link Cables worked. A single value on both sides was transmitted, one bit at a time. Each Game Boy Advance gradually exchanged these bits until they had completely swapped data. Before, only 8-bits could be sent at once, but on the Game Boy Advance this limit was increased to 32-bits. Furthermore, the overall speed of each transmission was greatly boosted. The Game Boy Color theoretically topped out at 64KB/s, meanwhile the Game Boy Advance could hit a maximum rate of 256KB/s. The fastest mode was typically not used by software, however. Instead, most chose a more stable 32KB/s. Normal mode was restricted to 2-players only, but it provided a simple and recognizable interface for developers. Taken altogether, these improvements made large transfers quicker and easier for programmers to manage.

Perhaps the most well-known mode was "Multi-16". This allowed a total of four Game Boy Advances to share data in 16-bit bursts. In many ways, it resembled the 4-Player Adapter released for the original Game Boy. Players were assigned an ID based on where their handhelds were physically connected when chaining together Link Cables. Player 1 always acted as the game's host, while every other player acted as a client. Before the transfer began, each player wrote their own 16-bit value to a specific region of memory. Afterwards, the host initialized the transfer and all connected players would start sharing data. Once that process was complete, each player would have copies of the 16-bit data everyone else sent out.

Overall, the procedure was far more straightforward than the DMG-07. Compared to Nintendo's first attempt, the Game Boy Advance hardware automatically handled many of the inherent complexities of 4-player communication. As a result of how relatively easy Multi-16 mode was, and in conjunction with the "daisy-chain" design of the 3rd Generation Link Cable, 4-player games became increasingly common on the Game Boy. The number of titles that supported Multi-16 quickly surpassed the DMG-07's legacy.

One mode in particular, "JoyBus", spurred quite a lot of innovation in its time. Nintendo developed their own communication protocol called JoyBus during the Nintendo 64 era. It largely served as the basis for controllers to report button input and joystick movement to the console. However, anything plugged into a controller port would use JoyBus to move data back and forth, even non-standard devices like keyboards, mice, or memory cards. JoyBus was carried over to the GameCube as well, and the Game Boy Advance natively provided a new mode to utilize it. The handheld could exchange 32-bits at a time with its home console counterpart, thus enabling GBA-to-GCN connectivity.

By using a special cable, the DOL-011, GameCube games could push data to the Game Boy Advance. The portable system could download minigames, act as a secondary screen for certain scenarios, unlock hidden or bonus content, upload characters or items, or even function as a controller for the GameCube itself. Over in Japan, this feature was called Joy Carry, emphasizing the player's ability to take the downloaded content with them even as they left the GameCube behind. Thanks to a sleep mode, the handheld could rest when not in use, saving on battery life. Unfortunately, Joy Carry data was completely stored in RAM and disappeared once the power was turned off. It's important to note that the Game Boy Advance did not implement the full JoyBus protocol and was narrowly tailored to work with just a handful of commands. Even so, it was Nintendo's most comprehensive effort yet to bind together two separate consoles in such a manner, with dozens of games making use of this feature.

Most of the aforementioned modes let the Game Boy Advance's hardware take care of low-level details on its own. To the programmer, even one working with raw CPU instructions, starting a transfer was as simple as writing the data to send, setting a flag to start the transfer, and waiting for the transfer to complete. Sometimes, however, this was not enough. The "General Purpose" mode offered full control of the signals traveling through the Link Cable's wires. With this, developers could dictate exactly how the Serial Clock, Serial Data, Serial Input, and Serial Output pins were used, giving them free reign to do whatever they wanted.

While this mode was not implemented for any multiplayer setups, it permitted games to openly communicate with specialty hardware that was never intended to interface with the Game Boy Advance. For example, off-the-shelf memory components such as EEPROM chips had no way of talking to any of the other modes unless some sort of intermediary component stepped in to translate. With General Purpose mode, however, the Game Boy Advance could talk directly to other devices using their own protocols, so long as the software could handle the task. As a result, the Game Boy Advance switched to General Purpose mode for many different peripherals such as the Soul Doll Adapter, the Multi-Plust On System, and the Infrared Adapter.

The final mode was "UART", or Universal Asynchronous Receiver/Transmitter. It was a specific method of transferring serial data, particularly useful in that it required just two wires at a minimum to start communication. The Game Boy Advance worked similarly to a typical RS-232 port in this mode. Unlike the previous examples, UART was never actively used in any known commercial software. For game development or debugging, however, it had many applications, such as allowing direct Game Boy-to-PC linking to upload test code. Today, there are many enthusiasts who have created their own USB-to-UART-to-GBA cables, allowing them to send homebrew games to the handheld.

One of the most defining characteristics of the Game Boy Advance's multiplayer was the new Single-Pak option. Thanks to "MultiBoot" – a process where the Game Boy Advance's BIOS waited to download data via the Link Cable – some games were able to share their multiplayer modes as long as at least one player owned the cartridge. As the host, Player 1 transferred code, graphics, and sounds to the other connected Game Boys. The client system's BIOS oversaw the download, and once finished it began executing the program and launched into a multiplayer session. With MultiBoot software, Normal and Multi-16 modes were used for Game Boy-to-Game Boy multiplayer, while JoyBus was used to receive programs from the GameCube.

Like Joy Carry software, MultiBoot apps had to fit within the Game Boy Advance's 256KB of Work RAM. The data received from Player 1 would temporarily be stored in that area, running until the system was turned off or rebooted. As a result of this restriction, some games could not offer a Single-Pak option, since their multiplayer modes used far more data than the limit allowed. These titles remained Multi-Pak only, where every player needed their own copy to play. As a compromise, however, some developers added both Single-Pak and Multi-Pak modes, where the former generally reduced the amount of content available. To illustrate this point, *Mario Kart: Super Circuit*'s Single-Pak mode turned all racers into differently colored Yoshis and had only four racetracks to select. The Multi-Pak mode, on the other hand, unlocked every character and course.

With the release of the Game Boy Micro, Nintendo introduced the 4th Generation Link Cable. In all respects, it was functionally identical to the 3rd Generation save for a redesigned and slimmed down plug specific for the Micro. The OXY-008 cable was sold a few months after the Micro itself launched, hitting stores in December of 2005. Conversely, a Wireless Adapter tailored for the Micro came out on the same day as the revamped handheld. Those wanting a more wired multiplayer experience on the Micro were forced to wait. The 4th Generation Link Cable was physically incompatible with previous generations, however, Nintendo produced a Game Boy Micro Converter Connector (OXY-009) to allow 3rd Generation cables to connect. As the Micro could only play Game Boy Advance titles, any other previous generations of Link Cables remained off-limits. The 4th Generation Link Cable marked the end of such accessories. All future handhelds would make a complete shift to wireless technologies for their multiplayer needs.

These two iterations of Link Cable moved Nintendo's handheld multiplayer forward by leaps and bounds. While 4-player games languished after the DMG-07, the Game Boy Advance brought them back, cementing their place as a standard that was followed well into the DS' lifetime. The idea of allowing multiplayer sessions with only a single cartridge also paved the way for the Download Play function on both the DS and 3DS. Due to the number of options developers could use when programming, particularly General Purpose mode, the Game Boy Advance hosted a large collection of accessories and peripherals spanning many diverse projects. The AGB-005, OXY-008, and their associated hardware pushed what the Game Boy could do and what players now expected out of portable multiplayer. While the future would be a world without wires, this period of the Game Boy's history demonstrated Nintendo's finest use of cable-based technology.

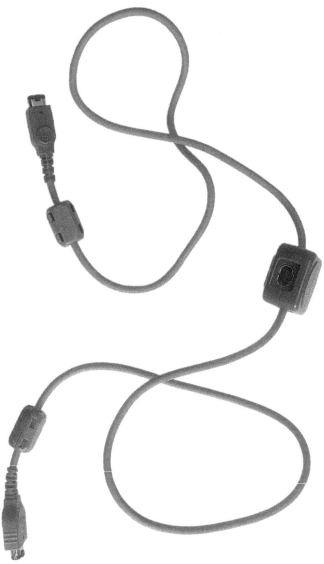

The AGB-005 Game Link Cable

The basic design of the AGB-005 accommodated 4-player games. Additional players connected their own cables into the middle hub. Unlike the earlier DMG-07, additional Game Boys were linked via "daisy-chaining". Player 3 connected to the first cable, and Player 4 connected to Player 3. Adding more players was relatively simple, and the AGB-005 handled standard 2-player games as well.

2-player modes worked much the same as before. On the Game Boy Advance, however, the speeds were greatly increased.

Thanks to the new MultiBoot mode, some games only required a single cartridge for multiplayer.

4-player mode effectively became a standard on the Game Boy Advance due to the AGB-005's improved design.

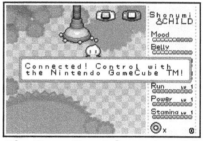

The Game Boy Advance's serial port was flexible enough to support many devices, including third-party peripherals and even GameCube communication.

The Link Cable supported enough data for first-person shooter duels.

**Release Dates:**

| | |
|---|---|
| AGB-010 | December 1, 2001 |
| AGB-014 | June 6, 2002 |

**Maker:**

Nintendo

**Legacy:**

Most pervasive and widespread card-reader for the Game Boy. Improved data capacity of cards with dot codes. Served as a basic model for some aspects of Amiibos.

Nintendo's video game consoles have a long history with card-scanning technologies. On the Famicom, two separate scanners were released: the Barcode Battler II and the Datach Joint ROM System. The Game Boy saw two more scanners when the Barcode Boy and *Barcode Taisen Bardigun* launched. While Nintendo actually licensed material for the Barcode Battler, the hardware for all of these products were third-party endeavors. For years, Nintendo abstained from directly entering this market themselves, leaving the task up to other developers. When the Game Boy Advance arrived, however, their plans had changed.

In late 2001, Nintendo brought the e-Reader to Japanese consumers, just in time for the holiday season. The very first models, known as the AGB-010, allowed players to swipe cards through a giant, bulky, specialized cartridge. Once the card passed through the built-in scanner, data would be transferred to the Game Boy Advance. It was a breakthrough from previous handheld card-reading attempts, requiring no cables or batteries. 64KB of flash memory was reserved for saving any data extracted from the cards. Another major change was the new "dot code" format, wherein data was stored as a 2D array of tiny printed dots, and each strip consisted of black and white points instead of barcodes. This allowed a single card to store vast amounts of information. For example, where Barcode Boy cards could only store a pair of 13-digit numbers on one side, e-Reader cards could squeeze entire minigames – graphics, sounds, and code – in just a few strips.

With this relatively massive increase in data storage, it was now possible to have full games spread across multiple cards. Nintendo initially supported their e-Reader with the Pokémon-e Expedition Base Set, an expansion of Pokémon trading cards that featured dot codes. Here, players could scan the cards to view Pokédex entries, download minigames based on Pokémon, and unlock different kinds of music. The e-Reader was even incorporated into trading card game battles. Some of the Pokémon cards had hidden abilities that caused random effects when used. By scanning them through the peripheral, the Game Boy Advance would determine what the outcome was, effectively using the handheld to roll digital dice.

In mid-September of 2002, the e-Reader came to North America. This accessory marked one of the first times a dedicated card scanner for a game console made its way to the West. The hardware itself had seen several alterations. Now called the AGB-014, its flash memory had doubled to 128KB. It also added a passthrough port for the Link Cable, opening up multiplayer possibilities and future communication options with the GameCube. The e-Reader would use the Link Cable to connect with other Game Boys as well, enabling various perks and rewards in select titles. Most telling of all, the e-Reader was now a gray and black add-on, ditching the older purple color scheme. For the American launch of the AGB-014, a number of NES games such as *Donkey Kong Jr., Balloon Fight,* and *Excitebike* were converted into dot code and sold as packs of cards.

Players had to scan a handful of dot code strips – typically around 10 – to fully construct NES software. Thanks to the improved memory capabilities of the latest version, however, these NES titles could be saved entirely to the e-Reader. In doing so, players could scan the cards just once but return to the game as often as they liked. Japan received upgraded hardware as well, known as the e-Reader+ to distinguish it from earlier models. Despite having access to these improvements, the Japanese market never received NES titles, making the software a rare American exclusive. Unfortunately, Nintendo refrained from giving Europe their own e-Reader. The only other region to launch the e-Reader was Australia.

Even though the e-Reader was perhaps the most advanced card scanner used for video games at the time, it garnered a lackluster response outside of Japan. By 2004, support for the device was all but canceled in North America. As new releases came along that year, games such as *Mega Man Zero 3* disabled e-Reader material in their western versions while promoting them in their eastern counterparts. The poor reception of the e-Reader and its unfulfilled potential may have had several causes.

The barcode scanning fad in Japan in the early '90s never properly materialized in the United States. Despite the rising popularity of trading card games in both countries, the e-Reader may have had trouble registering due to cultural differences in gaming. There was also a notable lack of content. After the initial set of NES games and Pokémon e-cards, only a handful of games actually used the e-Reader. When a sort of "second wave" of e-Reader compatible software began releasing in 2004, however, international audiences were left behind. If Nintendo and others felt that the e-Reader was unpopular, purposefully withholding later e-Reader support certainly ensured that would remain the case. Another explanation lies with the imminent launch of the DS. Perhaps to better focus marketing and internal resources on their upcoming console, Nintendo decided to cut off an item that had low sales volume.

Whatever the real reason, the e-Reader was nonetheless quite a technical achievement over previous card scanners. It came equipped with a small camera module capable of capturing a 402x302 pixel image, recorded in 7-bit monochrome. Functionally speaking, the e-Reader cropped this input to 320x246 pixels with a 1-bit color depth (pure black and white). Also inside the hardware, two LEDs acted as light sources, illuminating areas of the card as it was scanned. The camera had a scanning resolution of 1000dpi, sharp enough to read the incredibly small dots on each strip. Data was read per-scanline, with the hardware signaling to the e-Reader's software when processing was complete. From there, the software transferred scanline data to RAM, where it began analyzing the dot code. Each 320x246 portion of the strip was further broken down into 8x6 segments as necessary.

Nintendo licensed the dot code technology from Olympus Corporation and as a result were able to fit a great deal of information on each card. The dot codes themselves were stored in "long" or "short" strips, depending on which side of the card they were printed. Long strips could typically hold 2,912 bytes of data, while short strips could hold about 1,872 bytes. In contrast with regular barcodes, the information per-card was exponentially denser. The data itself could represent native code to run on the Game Boy Advance as well as emulated Z80 or 6502 code, along with a number of graphics or sounds.

Each strip consisted of several blocks of dot code. Long strips used 28 blocks, and short strips used 18. These blocks had a series of guide dots above and below the data sections to help the e-Reader detect when to start and stop parsing. On the left and right sides of the block were address columns which made sure the e-Reader read the block in the correct order. Each block also had a header, a brief section of data that described the dot code type (long or short), the total data size, the size of error correction data, and the error correction data for the block header itself. The format permitted Reed-Solomon data correction, meaning some data could be lost when scanned but later rebuilt. Since e-Reader cards were more complicated than traditional barcodes, they were potentially more prone to errors while scanning. Being able to fix most corrupted data allowed the e-Reader to operate in a user-friendly manner, reducing the need to swipe cards multiple times. Data was read block-by-block, and left to right and top-to-bottom within each block.

While the number of e-Reader compatible games was rather low, it managed to span both the Game Boy Advance and GameCube libraries. On the home console side, *Animal Crossing* was the first game to take advantage of the Link Cable passthrough port in conjunction with the GBA-to-GCN cable. The Game Boy Advance would scan the card then transfer data via the JoyBus protocol. Depending on the card, players would receive letters and presents from specific villagers, download new town tunes, unlock minigames on the Game Boy, unlock NES games on the GameCube, or download patterns and designs for shirts, umbrellas, or signposts.

While hundreds of *Animal Crossing* cards flooded the scene early in the e-Reader's lifetime, several *Pokémon* games added support for the unique cartridge. *Pokémon Ruby* and *Sapphire* had dozens of cards that unlocked special opponents players could battle in Mossdeep City. Also on hand were several exclusive berries that could be obtained by scanning the appropriate card. Most notable of all was the Eon Ticket, a card that granted players passage to the Southern Island for a chance to catch the legendary Pokémon Latios or Latias. It was given away as part of *Nintendo Power*'s 173rd issue in North America.

Other spin-off *Pokémon* games featured e-Reader support as well. In *Pokémon Colosseum*, the peripheral gave access to the "Card e Room" in Phenac Stadium. Players could then battle against VR Trainers in the Virtual Capsule. Using various "Battle e" cards, different trainers would appear, the stage itself might change, and certain Shadow Pokémon could be caught. *Pokémon Pinball Ruby and Sapphire* used e-Reader cards to give players distinct advantages, such as allowing them to choose a bonus stage, getting nine lives, receiving 99 coins or a Master Ball, or turning on the Pichu ball-saver. Other cards helped players encounter rare Pokémon. Unfortunately for both games, these e-Reader extras were only implemented in their Japanese versions.

*Super Mario Advance 4*'s cards gave players power-ups, presented a brief speedrunning demo of a particular level, or unlocked "World-e" bonus stages. There were a total of 38 e-Reader worlds available, each with their own unique theme and title. Hidden in these worlds were "Advance Coins", which players collected in order to get three new minigames. While the Japanese and North American versions of the game both worked with the e-Reader, only a limited number of cards were released in the West. In other words, some of these levels and minigames were unobtainable without hacking. *Super*

*Mario Advance 4* was a victim of Nintendo's eventual decision to scale down the e-Reader overseas. Nevertheless, the Wii U Virtual Console version rightfully restored these lost elements for gamers of all regions.

Not to be left out, Capcom's *Mega Man* franchises utilized the e-Reader later on in the device's lifespan. *Rockman EXE 4, 5,* and *6* used cards to customize Mega Man's stats, such as improving stamina and speed, changing the default body type for different attacks and defenses, and granting useful items such as Battle Chips, Sub Chips, Bug Frags, and money. *Rockman Zero 3*, on the other hand, used its cards for mostly cosmetic effects. When scanned, the dot codes would change the appearance of the resistance base, adding new items or animations to various corners of the facility. They also added new characters for Zero to interact with, along with accompanying dialog. The sprites of certain common items could be changed, and the effectiveness of Zero's weapons could be enhanced. Once again, these additional e-Reader features were present only in the Japanese versions. While most of these extras were translated and present in *Mega Man Zero 3*, their functionality was disabled as the relevant cards were never produced in other countries. Years later, however, all players could access them through either *Mega Man Zero Collection* on the DS or the multiplatform *Mega Man Zero/ZX Legacy Collection*.

Rounding out the list were a pair of Nintendo mainstays. *F-Zero: GP Legend*'s cards provided players with new machines, courses, and ghost data for challenging races. Yet again, only Japanese copies were supported in this regard. Although not explicitly advertised as an e-Reader game, *Mario vs. Donkey Kong* came with 12 secret levels. The popular Coro Coro Comic manga magazine gave away sets of cards unlocking five of these stages as part of a competition, with only 1,000 contestants receiving them. A sixth card was handed out during the 2004 Next-Generation World Hobby Fair. Cards for the remaining levels, however, were never distributed. The data still exists in every version of the game and can be accessed via cheat codes.

The e-Reader was not without its flaws. Its hardware was essentially an oversized game cartridge, with a bulky mass that made it top-heavy on the first models of the Game Boy Advance. For SP models, the exposed Link Cable passthrough port was unusable and sat uncomfortably close to the bottom edge of the handheld. Additionally, the large unit potentially interfered with players trying to work the controls. In either case, the weight of the e-Reader may have felt unbalanced at times. The cards themselves were less durable than cartridges, being susceptible to bending, ripping, or misplacement. If one strip of dot code was heavily damaged, some cards became completely useless. Although the e-Reader could save scanned games internally, there was only room enough for one at a time. Furthermore, while the cards themselves were not locked to specific e-Reader models, some games would only accept cards from their given region, a rare attempt at restricting content on the Game Boy based on the player's country. Lastly, actually using some of the cards in-game was a hassle at times, requiring two Game Boy Advances to link up.

Even though the e-Reader did not captivate worldwide markets, it was nevertheless a considerable success in comparison to every other card reader for the Game Boy, or for that matter any Nintendo system past or present. Altogether, over 3,000 individual cards were produced globally for the device, a number that greatly exceeded both the Barcode Boy and *Barcode Taisen Bardigun*. It allowed Nintendo to experiment with bonus material that mimicked DLC. In many respects, the e-Reader's cards were somewhat proto-Amiibo, acting as physical collectible tokens that gave players new content. While most of these unlockables had to be pre-programmed in advance – with the card serving as a key – the dot code was a big step towards more dynamically generated content in a few titles. The e-Reader may have stumbled with certain gamers, however, it ultimately gave Nintendo guidance and direction for future products and interactive toys.

The Nintendo e-Reader aka AGB-014

The e-Reader was the largest Game Boy Advance cartridge ever manufactured. It incorporated the card scanning hardware directly. The first versions sold in Japan (AGB-010) lacked a Link Cable passthrough, preventing them from being used with many of the later compatible titles.

Close up of the top side of the e-Reader

Several e-Reader cards

The e-Reader cards were surprisingly easy to pirate. It only required a decent scanner and printer.

Most cards had text and screenshots printed on them as well. For the NES titles, they functioned like a manual and featured tips and tricks for playing.

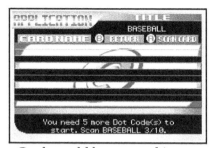

Cards could be scanned in any order. The e-Reader kept track of which dot codes were missing and which had been scanned.

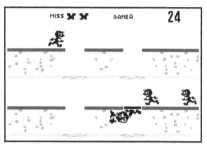

Thanks to dot codes, cards could hold enough data for game code, graphics, and sound.

Certain cards only worked in the e-Reader when linked to another Game Boy or the GameCube.

Some cards had more than just minigames, such as offering detailed information about the Pokémon and its Trading Card Game stats.

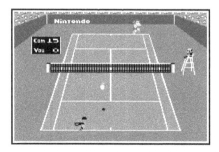

Entire NES games could fit on just a handful of cards.

**Release Date:**
March 8, 2002

**Maker:**
Nintendo

**Legacy:**
Continued Nintendo's experimentation with motion controls.

Nearly a year after the MBC7 debuted with *Koro Koro Kirby* in Japan, Nintendo presented a direct sequel at Space World 2001. In the demo, the Game Boy Advance and GameCube were linked together, with the handheld acting as the motion-based controller while the home console managed everything else. This upcoming game used the same technology that powered the original hardware. Now, however, it had been adapted for Game Boy Advance cartridges. The project was ultimately canceled, but this newly created cartridge would gain a fresh life in the following months.

On March 8, 2002, Nintendo published *Koro Koro Puzzle Happy Panechu!* The game tasked players with rearranging groups of block-like creatures called "panechu" around the screen. The goal was to pack them together by their colors, forcing them to disappear and clear the board. They could move up, down, left, and right. However, instead of mapping these actions to the standard directional pad on the Game Boy Advance, players had to physically tilt the handheld in those directions. *Koro Koro Puzzle* continued where the MBC7 left off, using the same ADXL202JQC accelerometer to judge how far the Game Boy moved.

Despite making a return, tilt cartridges didn't gain much traction. Only one other game, *Yoshi's Universal Gravitation* (also known as *Yoshi Topsy Turvy*) would go on to support it. Released on December 9, 2004, the game focused on Yoshi's adventure to free his island from the pages of a storybook. Here, the green dinosaur completed each level with a specific objective in mind, such as collecting a certain number of fruit or coins. The twist was that players could tilt the Game Boy Advance left or right to help Yoshi travel across various stages. When the handheld was turned, Yoshi could run up walls, roll along balls, swing from trolleys, and dash around half-pipes. Tilting was only one portion of the control scheme, however, as players could still move Yoshi normally with the directional pad, jump around with the A button, and lash out at enemies with the B button.

Like its predecessor, the Game Boy Advance tilt cartridges measured movement on X and Y axes. It's important to note that this hardware operated in a completely different manner from the gyroscope found in *WarioWare Twisted!* As tempting as it may be to lump them together given their roles in promoting motion controls, they used separate components and had programming specific to each. The most obvious way *Twisted!* contrasted with these tilt cartridges was the fact that it only detected changes in the Z axis. In comparison to games using the accelerometer, *Twisted!*'s gyroscope often required players to rotate the console like a steering wheel, which also changed the viewing angle more noticeably.

The Game Boy Advance tilt cartridges worked very similarly to the MBC7 as well. Specific memory addresses typically assigned to the cartridge's SRAM were repurposed to provide access to the sensor. Instead of reading back save game data, these addresses responded with 16-bit values representing the current amount of tilting. Once again, this data first had to be "latched", essentially updating then locking the current value so it could be read accurately. Software wrote only two bytes to the SRAM region to do so. After processing these X and Y values, it could calculate what actions needed to be performed. Both *Koro Koro Puzzle* and *Yoshi's Universal Gravitation* offered options to invert the Y axis, extremely useful for models such as the Game Boy Advance SP, Game Boy Micro, and DS. This wasn't a hardware feature but rather something done completely in software. Nonetheless it solved a key issue present in MBC7 games, which were unable to handle different orientations of the cartridge.

Even after staging a comeback on the Game Boy Advance, tilt cartridges struggled to define unique gameplay elements that would attract gamers. Although *Koro Koro Puzzle* made relatively good use of motion, the action simply wasn't as compelling as *Kirby Tilt 'n' Tumble*. While the former did take advantage of movement in all four directions, there was no real analog control nor any required skill for hand-eye coordination. Once the tilt reached a certain threshold, all of the blocks moved over to one side. The latter, however, incorporated even the slightest movements for fine-tuned rolling, allowing players to make precise choices about where Kirby would go. *Koro Koro Puzzle* was by design a game for the intellect rather than a test of reaction, a genre perhaps ill-suited for motion controls.

Related criticisms applied to *Yoshi's Universal Gravitation*. The game did make clever use of tilting to execute pinpoint actions, however, they were limited to simply turning left and right. When players shifted the cartridge forwards or backwards, however, nothing happened. No actions were mapped to the X axis, vastly constraining what the title could have achieved. In both *Koro Koro Puzzle* and *Yoshi's Universal Gravitation*, arguably only half of the cartridge's true potential was realized.

As the famed video game designer Shigeru Miyamoto once envisioned, the Game Boy Advance tilt cartridge would have allowed the GameCube to access the accelerometer. Software running on the Game Boy would record sensor data and pass it along via the GBA-to-GCN cable. From there the GameCube could translate those values into movement of on-screen characters and objects. Action could have even shifted back and forth between the player's TV and handheld. The hardware certainly had a chance to make unprecedented progress, conceivably giving Nintendo's home console motion controls a full generation before they began Project Revolution and produced the Wii. That possibility was never reached, however.

Additionally, *Diddy Kong Pilot*, was initially intended to have tilt controls, according to some of the earliest development builds. However, the idea was later scrapped before canceling the game altogether. Had Rare stuck to their original design, their title could have conceivably elevated motion-based input to new levels. In the end, that was not the case, and it left the handheld without any software that maximized the control scheme. Instead, the Game Boy Advance tilt cartridge earned mixed reception.

*Koro Koro Puzzle* was a decent, fun, and competent puzzle game; unfortunately Yoshi's outing was seen as mediocre. Neither title received the critical response seen in *WarioWare Twisted!*, which embraced its hardware and was carefully programmed around it. Like the MBC7, Game Boy Advance tilt cartridges only accounted for two games out of the entire library, with one being a Japanese exclusive. Although they didn't exactly set the world on fire, they did once again prove that motion controls had to be thoughtfully and deliberately designed for video games. It wouldn't be the end of Nintendo's fascination with the technology, however. These tilt cartridges were mere stepping stones to the Wii. When the next console generation arrived, the company would literally come out swinging.

*Yoshi's Universal Gravitation* GBA Cartridge

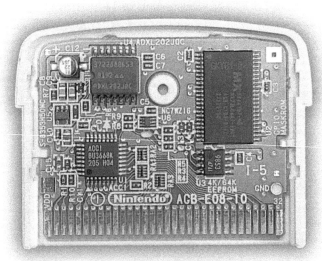

GBA Tilt Cartridge PCB

The Game Boy Advance tilt cartridges were very similar in shape to normal ones. They had larger, rounded tops however. *Yoshi's Universal Gravitation* used a green and white plastic shell, making it one of the few games on the system to appear in a non-standard color.

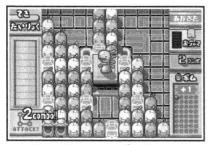

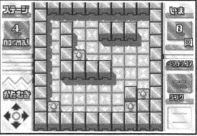

*Koro Koro Puzzle Happy Panechu!* had various modes of play. Here the enemy's stamina had to be depleted by triggering bombs.

The game had dozens of "IQ" puzzles that required planning to solve. Players carefully matched all the blocks on a given screen.

By tilting the cartridge, Yoshi could manipulate the environment and how he moved around the game's world.

There were various items in each level that interacted with the tilt mechanism such as rolling balls.

The software could handle tilting on several different systems.

**Release Date:**
November 15, 2002

**Maker:**
Kemco

**Legacy:**
Became the first officially licensed Game Boy hardware
dedicated to media playback. Brought new functionality to the
platform that inspired later products from other companies for
years.

After a year and a half on the market, the Game Boy Advance eventually became a multimedia device. Following the growing trend of portable, digital music, one company decided to give the Game Boy the ability to play MP3s. To achieve this goal, Kemco created the Game Boy Advance Music Recorder, a large cartridge that housed special hardware dedicated to playing and creating music files. This marked the first time any such device was officially sold for the Game Boy line of handheld systems, as it was licensed and approved by Nintendo. As consumers were gradually starting to pull away from CDs in favor of smaller devices with more storage, Kemco positioned its product as an option for gamers.

Released to the public in mid-November 2002, the Music Recorder featured a somewhat bulky, white or black cartridge shell. Inside, the PCB was folded into two parts, connected by a ribbon cable. On one end, a standard Game Boy Advance ROM provided the peripheral with its software. The other side contained components that handled MP3 decoding. While the Game Boy Advance could certainly decode MP3s manually with its CPU alone, it lacked the memory to hold large amounts of audio samples. Instead, dedicated circuits had to convert MP3s into a data stream that the Game Boy could read and playback. This route was later chosen by Nintendo's own Play-Yan, which also used extra hardware inside its cartridge to the same effect.

The Music Recorder came with a built-in slot that accepted CompactFlash memory cards. Users could transfer their favorite songs to the card, and from there the Music Recorder would scan and play any files it found. As a helpful gesture, the Music Recorder also came pre-packaged with a blank 8MB CompactFlash card of its own. While the overall capacity was quite small, it allowed people to use the Music Recorder right away without any additional purchases. However, as its name implied, the Music Recorder could also save audio to this storage as well.

Users had two methods of recording. First, they could use the Line-In port to connect the Music Recorder to any number of other sources. CD players, cassette players, PC audio output, stereos, other Game Boys: anything that output sound over a 3.5mm jack was fair game. The Music Recorder would take this audio and turn it into a custom GB3 file, writing it to the memory card for later playback. Additionally, the Music Recorder came with a built-in microphone at the top of the cartridge. Its purpose was to capture the user's voice. To that end, people could make notes and memos for themselves, or perhaps even record an episode of a podcast. Arguably the main draw of the microphone, however, was its use for karaoke, which the Music Recorder specifically targeted and supported.

Among all of the other types of cartridges released for the Game Boy Advance, the Music Recorder was the only one which required a AA battery to run. Part of the cartridge's shell had a cover that pulled away, allowing users to easily swap in fresh batteries. While the software could boot without a battery, that extra power was needed to handle MP3s. The Music Recorder showed an error message if it detected no battery or the battery was drained; it refused to continue unless the issue was addressed. The original packaging came with its own AA battery, once again letting buyers immediately put the Music Recorder to use. Its software constantly monitored the battery level and displayed an icon of the power levels.

The hardware functioned perfectly as a standalone device, requiring neither a PC nor a Game Boy Advance to listen to music. Once the MP3 files were loaded onto the CompactFlash card or recorded directly via Line-In, the Music Recorder was capable of playing songs by itself, pumping out tunes through its headphone jack. To accomplish this, the cartridge came equipped with five physical buttons on its backside. One controlled starting and stopping a track. Two more controlled moving forwards and backwards through track lists. The last two changed the volume up or down. Although the setup was very basic, it made the Music Recorder completely independent from other electronics. When playing music, it used a large, red LED at the bottom of the unit to indicate activity.

The Music Recorder did not stay exclusive to Japan. While Kemco was responsible for designing the hardware and software, the North American distribution rights were given to Radica Games and sold under the Gamester brand. It was renamed the Game Boy Advance Jukebox when it launched nearly a full year after the Japanese version. In all respects, both the Music Recorder and Jukebox were identical save for a change in translated software. The American variant naturally supported English menus and text. It continued offering customers out-of-the-box usability by throwing in a CompactFlash card, this time with a 32MB capacity.

Kemco provided an array of useful tools with the Music Recorder's software. Three main modes were available: Music, Memo, and Karaoke. Respectively, these would open the music player, record the user's voice, or let users sing along to their favorite songs. The music player itself was relatively standard, showing the name of the current song along with the playback time. It came with three different visualizations that animated in the background as well as an optional spectrum analyzer. More importantly, the player had an equalizer to adjust the tone of the music according to five different presets: Normal, Pop, Rock, Jazz, and Classic. As a bonus, vocals could be stripped from a track with the push of a button. Lastly, users could start and stop the music, increase or decrease the volume, or switch songs with the Game Boy's controls.

Inside the Music menu, the Music Recorder also grabbed live audio from its Line-In jack. Perhaps the most impressive feat here was the Music Recorder's "blank MP3 file" ability. When connecting to something like a CD player, for example, the Music Recorder would automatically detect the beginning or end of a song. With that, it would create a separate file for each new track. To do this, the Music Recorder waited until the volume dropped below a user-specified threshold for a certain amount of time, which usually indicated the start of the next song. This proved a simple approach that worked well with a range of audio devices. It was not foolproof, however, and could be disabled if necessary.

Memo, on the other hand, permitted users to record themselves. In the Options menu, the input volume could be dynamically adjusted for the best audio quality. The Music Recorder would sample the user's speech for a few moments and determine how best to adapt the microphone for future recordings. Related to this, the Karaoke mode played a song of the user's choice while recording them as they sang the lyrics. While not nearly as elaborate as more full-fledged karaoke solutions, the Music Recorder nevertheless offered a decent portable version. Karaoke mode featured voice cancellation as well, so users were free to add their own flair to the music. Once a song was finished, users could listen to the results of their work.

In all recording modes, the Music Recorder calculated how much time was left given the remaining memory of the CompactFlash card. Depending on the configurable bitrate – 128kbps, 96kbps, or 64kbps – the amount of storage needed per recording went up or down for GB3 music files. Lower bitrates saved space, however, it affected the overall sound quality. The GB3 format was actually just a regular MP3 file missing a proper header. Without that, many common or popular media players would not recognize them, restricting playback to Kemco's device. This limitation may have been an attempt at curbing potential piracy. Memo and Karaoke used PCM files recorded at 11KHz, which produced acceptable audio while still generating relatively small files. No matter how large the CompactFlash card, a maximum of 256 recordings each (768 in total) could be stored for Music, Memo, and Karaoke.

The Music Recorder dynamically interacted with its CompactFlash card in many ways as well. If the card was not correctly formatted, the software automatically performed the task for the user. Similarly, the Music Recorder could delete all of its music and recording files if necessary, returning the CompactFlash card to a relatively new state. Finally, users had the freedom to edit limited amounts of information about the songs themselves, such as changing the name and the artist fields. Without a working CompactFlash card, the Music Recorder failed to completely startup, as the storage was pivotal to its operation.

Due to the way the Game Boy Advance processed digital audio, it could not reproduce CD quality sound. Although the audio hardware was a great improvement over the previous generation, it still had certain drawbacks that were unfavorable for most music players. On top of all that, the handheld's built-in speaker only supported mono sound. To get around this problem, the Music Recorder optionally output audio through its own headphone jack, totally bypassing the Game Boy Advance and providing higher fidelity. Some years later Nintendo's own Play-Yan would do the same.

Despite having a wealth of features and being officially recognized by Nintendo, the Music Recorder remained somewhat an obscurity in its time. In truth, it competed with a variety of other MP3 players across numerous markets. It even had to deal with third-party unlicensed players on the same platform, such as the SongPro. Although its profile among consumers never rivaled the likes of the Apple's iconic iPod, Kemco's Music Recorder was an important step forward for Nintendo's portable game console. It helped establish the Game Boy Advance as a device that could extend itself to other forms of entertainment. Holding a license granted a sense of legitimacy to Kemco's endeavor, and from their early efforts other products would later appear. The Advance Movie Adapter, Game Boy Advance Video Cartridges, and the Play-Yan all shared conceptual roots with the Music Recorder. In effect, the hardware here was the start of a movement that ran throughout the Game Boy Advance's lifetime.

A brand-new GBA Music Recorder

Unlike many products for the Game Boy Advance, the Music Recorder came in a simple plastic package rather than a box. It sold with cables, a battery, and a specially-labeled CompactFlash memory card. The Japanese version included a mere 8MB card, a decidedly meager amount even by 2002 standards.

Music Recorder Front

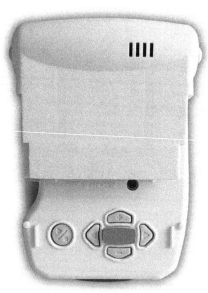

Music Recorder Back

The Music Recorder could work all on its own, thanks to a battery, a headphone jack, and several physical buttons.

The Japanese and English versions were largely the same besides some menu text and the loading logo.

Music, Voice Memos, and Karaoke mode were all available from the main screen.

Playing music brought up several different visualizers that changed to the beat and tempo of the sounds.

When recording via Line-In or the microphone, users could edit data such as the title and artist.

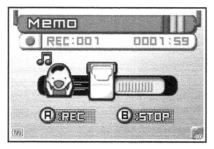

When recording files, a timer indicated remaining disk space.

**Release Date:**
   November 21, 2002

**Maker:**
   Nintendo

**Legacy:**
   Offered enhanced features compared to the last generation. Prepared the way towards built-in clocks as part of the base hardware for Nintendo's handhelds.

199

After the MBC3 mapper introduced real-time clocks to portable gaming in 1997, there was a steady expansion of Game Boy titles that utilized time as a mechanic. As the industry eventually pivoted from the Game Boy Color to the Game Boy Advance, this emerging technology would carry over into the new millennium. While rival consoles from Bandai and SNK followed Nintendo's lead to some extent, the Game Boy would ultimately be the most popular handheld platform for real-time clock functionality through the first half of the 2000s. Like its predecessor, the Game Boy Advance had certain cartridges equipped with built-in clocks that tracked the flow of time, even when the system itself had shut down.

Although Game Boy Advance cartridges were now physically smaller than the last generation, they still managed to squeeze in the necessary components for a real-time clock. Nintendo turned to the S3511 from Seiko Instruments. This bit of hardware proved much more detailed and complex compared to its counterpart from the MBC3 mapper. While both counted days, hours, minutes, and seconds, the S3511 supported years, months, day of the week, a distinction between AM and PM, and a 12-hour or 24-hour mode. It also allowed games to grab data in long formats (for the date and current time) or short formats (current time only).

The S3511 used a 32,768Hz crystal oscillator as well. Like the MBC3 mapper, the Game Boy Advance real-time clock was constantly powered by a coin cell battery, in this case a CR1616. Thanks to Nintendo's engineering, the battery was no longer responsible for maintaining both the clock and the cartridge's backup memory. On the Game Boy Advance, when the battery ran dry, game saves still worked. The clock would remain broken until a fresh battery was installed, however. Previously a dry battery would freeze the clock and wipe out any data in SRAM. This improvement was largely the result of shifting towards flash memory, FRAM, and EEPROM for backup data on the Game Boy Advance, none of which required batteries.

Reading and writing data to the real-time clock was more complicated than before. Game software took advantage of the Game Boy Advance's General Purpose Input/Output interface to manipulate individual pins connected to the S3511. The handheld reserved specific memory addresses for this interface, allowing software to access hardware embedded in different kinds of cartridges. All data to and from the S3511 was transferred serially, one bit at a time. Software issued specific commands along with any necessary parameters. Once the command was sent, the game could read back a response if expecting one. In this way, games could program the clock as well as check its status.

While the Game Boy Color saw a number of titles supporting the real-time clock, that count dropped quite a bit on the Game Boy Advance. A total of 16 games used the MBC3 variant, and across other mappers such as the TAMA5 and HuC-3, altogether 23 games used a clock of some sort. The next generation saw a mere 10 games use the S3511 for time-keeping. This was part of a broader trend, where game cartridges generally came with less and less unique hardware inside. Nevertheless, the few Game Boy Advance titles that did have real-time clocks put them to good use.

*Pokémon Ruby* and *Sapphire* were the first games to demonstrate this new type of cartridge. The clock managed the growth of berries, ensuring that the plants grew in stages after set intervals. An area within Hoenn called Shoal Cave had high or low tides depending on which hours the player visited. Certain portions of the cave were only accessible on a given tide. The Pokémon Eevee would evolve into Espeon during the day and Umbreon during the night. A few daily events occurred, such as Loto Tickets and the possibility of sailing to Mirage Island. Unfortunately, explicit morning, day, and night phases were scrapped from all mainline *Pokémon* games on the Game Boy Advance.

All three *Boktai* games had not only a solar sensor, but a real-time clock too. Players could set the date and timezone. The games then changed the environments according to the time of day. For example, after nightfall the settings darkened, and certain nocturnal enemies that were dormant earlier became active. The *Boktai* titles also estimated how much sunlight was normally available depending on the time of year and whatever location the player selected at the beginning. By the Winter Solstice, a place like Chicago would see sunset as early as 4:20 PM. Meanwhile, in Honolulu the sun wouldn't set until 5:55 PM. Rather than a one-size-fits all approach, the *Boktai* games took those differences into account.

The *Legendz* franchise incorporated the real-time clock into an "Auto Adventure" mode. When this option was selected, the games made a record of the current time and exited the main story. Based on the passage of time between this point and when the player tried to resume the story, one of the creatures on the player's team leveled up. The longer the wait, the more experience their partner obtained. By simply walking away from the game for periods of time, it was possible to create a strong group of characters primed for battle.

Only one *Mega Man* game sported a real-time clock. In *Rockman EXE 4.5*, players assumed the role of a NetNavi operator and joined forces with a wide range of Navis. The focus of this spin-off title was tournaments. Weekdays offered a regular series of tournaments for Net Battles. However, players could only participate if they signed up during the correct time slot. At 9:00 AM, 1:00 PM, 4:00 PM, and 8:00 PM, players had one hour to enter the tournament. Special tournaments advanced the plot but were only available on Saturdays and Sundays. Additionally the player's NetNavi managed a real-life monthly schedule. Certain events and characters only appeared on given days as well.

A late entry from Nintendo, *Sennen Kazoku*, had the player taking on the role of Cupid. The aim of the game was to guide a family via matchmaking and ensure it eventually grew into a thousand-year old lineage. Shooting various arrows at family members would inspire them or affect their moods as they went through their stages of life: growing up, getting a job, getting married, having children, and eventually dying. The simulation itself happened at an accelerated pace, where a few minutes translated into a few days. However, even when turned off, the game still progressed. Thanks to the clock, *Sennen Kazoku* could calculate the amount of time that had passed since the last save. Any events that took place while the Game Boy Advance was turned off were kept in a log that players could review upon starting.

In some regards, the Game Boy Advance's real-time clock was never fully exploited. Compared to the previous generation of *Pokémon* games, *Ruby*, *Sapphire*, and *Emerald* made far less use of time-based events than *Gold*, *Silver*, or *Crystal* did. Removing morning and night cycles was another blow, particularly as they were restored in every other mainline version thereafter. While *Rockman EXE 4.5* and the *Boktai* titles changed their games based on when they were played, the *Legendz* franchise was only notable for the time the player spent away from the game. This wasn't much of an issue with *Sennen Kazoku*, which followed a vision very similar to the earlier *Pocket Family* series. Regrettably, however, it was perhaps too heavily dependent on the real-time clock. If the battery ever ran dry, the game simply refused to fully boot up, unlike the other titles. This was not a problem with the hardware, rather it was just the way *Sennen Kazoku* was programmed. Overall, the use of real-time clocks was curtailed during the Game Boy Advance era, with a smaller number of supported games and a more limited amount of available content. Certain games would have benefited from a real-time clock, such as the *Harvest Moon* series, yet they passed on the opportunity.

Although the greatest potential of time-based games was never explored during this period, these special Game Boy Advance cartridges marked a slow but deliberate evolution. Their ability to track time far outstripped the earlier batch of MBC3 cartridges, provided a more consistent interface compared to the TAMA5 or HuC-3, and they offered better control than other options such as the Pokémon Mini's clock. Eventually, the real-time clock would permanently become fully integrated within Nintendo's handhelds. Their next portable console, the DS, used a cousin of the S3511 known as the S3518, which worked quite similarly. Despite lacking many games that showcased the clock, the Game Boy Advance continued to promote the concept, opening the way for better and more extensive hardware. In due time, nearly all software would have ready access to a functioning calendar, finally realizing a goal years in the making.

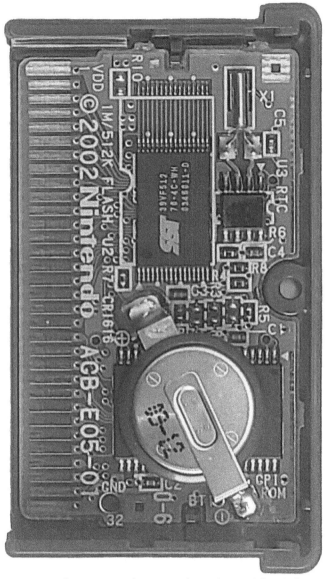

A complete view of a typical RTC cartridge PCB

Game Boy Advance Real-Time Clock cartridges often had the crystal oscillator soldered to the board. The previous MBC3 ones used simple tape. Either method kept an oscillator stable while it operated, ensuring accurate time-keeping. These cartridges used a slightly smaller CR1616 battery instead of a CR2025.

Boktai changed its settings to match the player's current time, even taking into account the timezone and current date.

Color palettes changed from bright or pastel in the day, to warm and vibrant at sunset, to gloomy at night.

In *Pokémon Ruby, Sapphire,* and *Emerald,* berries would grow based on the real-time clock.

Shoal Cave changed with the tides, and different areas could be explored depending on the hour.

*Sennen Kazoku,* had many events while the game was turned off.

*Rockman EXE 4.5* turned NetNavis into real digital assistants, with a working, programmable schedule and planner.

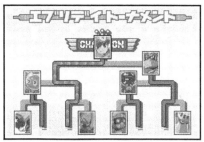

Tournaments required players to arrive at set times.

*Legendz*'s Auto-Adventure mode allowed characters to gain experience or learn new abilities while the game was turned off.

Once sufficient time had passed, the player's Legendz would return and share the story of their journey.

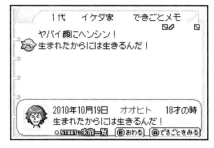

*Sennen Kazoku* kept a log of all that happened while the player was gone.

**Release Date:**
    March 20, 2003

**Makers:**
    Nintendo, Konami

**Legacy:**
    First and only officially rewritable Game Boy Advance
    cartridge released to consumers. Made Joy Carry content
    persistent and created a portable, miniaturized version of
    GameCube software.

With the Game Boy Advance's improved Link Cable capabilities, Nintendo's handheld and home consoles grew closer than ever. Players could connect the two systems in a variety of ways, the most prominent of which was downloading small programs to the Game Boy. In Japan, this feature was known as "Joy Carry" with the emphasis on that software's portability. For example, GameCube kiosks installed in various stores allowed customers to download minigames to their Game Boy Advances. They could carry the games home to continue playing. However, once the Game Boy was powered off, the minigames would disappear.

As the spring of 2003 rolled around, Konami sought a more permanent solution. With the release of their GameCube title *Hikaru no Go 3* in Japan, the company introduced a special piece of hardware called the Joy Carry Cartridge. It was in essence a rewritable game cartridge, similar in concept to the flashcarts popular with the homebrew scene. Different code, graphics, and sound could be transferred, completely changing what game was actually being played. Unique to the Joy Carry Cartridge was its official status as a fully licensed product for the Game Boy Advance. Despite its purple colorization, the cartridge itself used the same mold as other commercial games. It came with a label imprinted with a 2-digit factory code and was even designated its own 10-character ID: AGB-GHTJ-JPN. As far as Nintendo was concerned, this cartridge was a legitimate part of the Game Boy Advance's library.

The purpose of the Joy Carry Cartridge was to give players a mobile version of the ancient board game called Go ( 碁 ). Players strategically placed black and white stones on a grid to encircle their opponents. While the GameCube offered a story mode to progress through, two pieces of software could be downloaded to the Game Boy Advance. The first was *Igo Mondaishuu*, loosely translated as *Go Problem Collection*. This provided a host of specific Go puzzles and challenges that had to be solved, such as surrounding portions of the enemy's stones within a set number of moves. There were 200 of these in all, divided into four separate segments of 50, the maximum the Joy Carry Cartridge could hold at any given time. The second downloadable software was *Keitai Magnet Goban*, or *Mobile Magnet Go Board*. Focused primarily on multiplayer, it let participants battle in one-on-one or two-on-two Go matches via Link Cables. It also came with an option to view details of previous matches and a brief player profile complete with their name, their *Hikaru no Go 3* ID, and their win/loss stats.

Although the Joy Carry Cartridge may appear to be an otherwise normal Game Pak on the surface, underneath it contained components not seen anywhere else on the Game Boy Advance. It stored all of its data on 1MB of flash memory provided by a Sharp LH28F800BLE. The Joy Carry Cartridge was only the third cartridge with this kind of memory ever sanctioned by Nintendo for any Game Boy. During the initial connection between the Game Boy Advance and GameCube, a small MultiBoot program was loaded onto the handheld to manage the flow of data and rewrite the Joy Carry Cartridge. As new bytes arrived from the GameCube, they were gradually processed and saved. Previously, Joy Carry games vanished when the Game Boy turned off, but now they were long-lasting and persistent.

The flash memory itself was divided into 8KB sectors. A special permanent boot sector acted as the cartridge header and held the startup code. This section could not be erased and was setup during the manufacturing process. When consumers got their hands on it, the data was already read-only. It ensured that the cartridge would always try to boot properly. The rest of the data, however, could be freely manipulated. Like other products such as the GB Memory Cartridge or MBC6, the Joy Carry Cartridge accepted standard flash commands to handle reading and writing information. Technically speaking, the Joy Carry Cartridge is classified as a Debugging and Communications System cartridge, or DACS for short. The term most often refers to reprogrammable cartridges used for professional game development. The Game Boy Advance version of *Hikaru no Go 3* was the only instance where such a device was ever sold to the public.

Despite being a flashcart at its core, the Joy Carry Cartridge had some quirks that prevented it from being used for piracy. When loading ROM data from the cartridge, the Game Boy Advance could only address up to 32MB. Typically, games filled in data from the beginning of this area of memory, taking up as much space as necessary or however much they could fit on their ROM chip (which in most cases was less than the 32MB maximum). The Joy Carry Cartridge worked in reverse, with all of its data appearing at the end of the 32MB section of memory. Only the boot sector was mirrored to the start so the Game Boy could initialize the rest of the game's code located at the rear. This unusual setup stopped most games from working at all if they were copied to the Joy Carry Cartridge as-is. Additionally, the 1MB of flash memory was generally too small for commercial Game Boy Advance games, presenting yet another barrier for piracy. Nothing kept the Joy Carry Cartridge from being used for homebrew or personal programming projects, however, as long as these limitations were handled.

The Joy Carry Cartridge was perhaps one of the most thorough and ambitious attempts of the 6th Generation to bridge home consoles and handhelds. While other developers simply added small minigames when connecting the Game Boy Advance and GameCube, Konami was in effect splitting a single game across these two platforms. It served as a potential model for other Joy Carry games, allowing players to save data directly to the cartridge rather than having it erased once the Game Boy shut down. In theory, Nintendo could have produced a generic version that multiple GameCube games would have taken advantage of if players had purchased one. When the player was on the go, a portable version of the game would still be available for their entertainment. Unfortunately, such an idea was never pursued. Instead, *Hikaru no Go 3* stood alone, making it the only software to ever support this kind of feature. The Joy Carry Cartridge was in many ways ahead of its time in relation to the Nintendo Switch, foreseeing the market's desire to choose between playing their games in front of a big screen or in their own hands.

The Joy Carry Cartridge

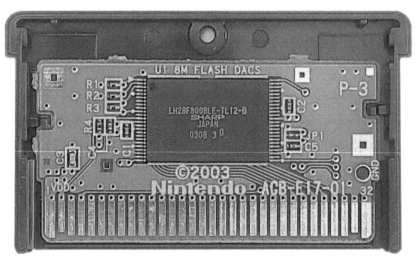

Joy Carry Cartridge PCB

The Joy Carry Cartridge is notable for being one of the few Game Boy Advance cartridges that featured a normal-sized plastic shell but had a different color than the standard dark gray. Many of the other colorful cartridges often had unique shapes and sizes, but not the Joy Carry Cartridge.

211

Two types of software could be downloaded to the Joy Carry Cartridge. *Igo Mondaishuu* is pictured above.

In *Igo Mondaishuu*, players could work through 200 different Go challenges and problems.

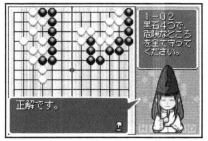

Each problem was unique and had specific requirements to fulfill in order to pass.

*Keitai Magnet Goban* acted as a mobile Go board for multiplayer. It recorded the results of matches and logged stats such as wins and losses.

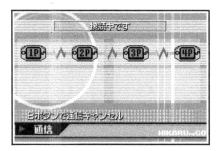

A 4-player version of Go was available in *Keitai Magnet Goban*.

**Release Date:**

April 24, 2003

**Maker:**

Takara

**Legacy:**

An early example of the "toys-to-life" gaming genre. The first franchise to do so on the Game Boy platform.

Many games often featured brightly colored and detailed creatures from other worlds. For the most part, these beings were never more than a collection of pixels and sounds, restricted to a purely digital existence. At best, a few toys or action figures for a franchise would come out, but these never played a direct role in the video games where the characters were most alive. There were, however, attempts to eliminate the gap as far back as R.O.B. on the NES or *ZXE-D* on the Sony PlayStation. These "proto-Amiibo" efforts predated the modern toys-to-life genre, and the Game Boy Advance had several contenders in that space.

The earliest instance came from the *Bouken Yuuki Pluster World* series. Set in a world of critters called "Plusters" and humans, the two could combine as one to become more powerful. Together, people and Plusters fought to restore peace in their respective lands. While Takara released two RPGs and one racing game based on *Pluster World*, they took player immersion to a new level by including the Multi Plust On System. This device plugged into the top of a Game Boy Advance, latching itself to the Link Cable port. It featured a circular pad where plastic figurines were set inside. Once the figurine was locked and secured by turning a dial, the player could use that to activate a specific Pluster within the game.

In the two RPGs, *Bouken Yuuki Pluster World: Densetsu no Plust Gate* and *Bouken Yuuki Pluster World: Densetsu no Plust Gate EX*, these allowed the main character to transform into a "Pluston", basically becoming a warrior with a costume that looked like the Pluster. They also gained abilities and attributes associated with that Pluster. In *Bouken Yuuki Pluster World: Pluston GP*, the figurines unlocked different racecars based on the Plusters. Each one performed differently in terms of top speed, acceleration, and handling. Plusters could be swapped mid-race as well, allowing strategies not seen in other games.

Each title sold as a special "starter set" edition packaged in a larger than normal box. Inside, players obtained the game itself, the Multi Plust On System accessory, and one Pluster figurine. The Plusters Wyburst, Beetma, and Beetma EX were found in the sets for *Pluston GP*, *Densetsu no Plust Gate*, and *Densetsu no Plust Gate EX* respectively. These starter sets were very important for new players, as each game was impossible to begin without the add-on. *Pluston GP* required the Multi Plust On System with an inserted figurine to start any race. Both *Densetsu no Plust Gate* games forced the player to transform into a Pluston early in the story and waited indefinitely until the hardware registered the figurines.

The figurines themselves were entirely plastic, containing no electronics whatsoever. Adorned at the top was a Pluster, while the bottom was largely hollow. Inside the base, a series of spokes were exposed. There were 22 unique Plusters recognized by the games, however, some Plusters had variants featuring different poses. The variants typically had enhanced or altered properties – such as Attack, Defense, and Speed – used for the LCD-based toys Takara released alongside the Game Boy Advance games.

These electronic devices had a small black-and-white display as well as an embedded Multi Plust On System of their own. Kids could plug in their Plusters and see them come to life without needing a Game Boy Advance. After transforming into a Pluston, they could play various minigames depending on the inserted Pluster. Additionally, up to four players could link up these devices to battle among themselves.

By expanding the use of the figurines outside of the video games, Takara tried to give people an incentive for collecting each individual Pluster. The games, unfortunately, didn't care about the variants. Although they were technically capable of recognizing these differences, they weren't programmed to take advantage of them. Whether the player inserted the regular Beetma or the Fighting Beetma version, they were ultimately treated the same. All of the games supported the initial set of Plusters Takara released first. A later set of EX Plusters were exclusively created for *Densetsu no Plust Gate EX*.

In reality, the Multi Plust On System used a very simple mechanism for detecting which figurine it currently held. Internally, the device had an array of pressure sensitive pads beneath its center. When a Pluster figurine was put in place, the spokes touched these pads. Depending on the configuration of the spokes, different pads were pushed down. Each pad reported its status to the rest of the Multi Plust On System hardware, which in turn forwarded that data to the Game Boy Advance. In the end, the Game Boy Advance received a 16-bit number that functioned as an ID for that specific figurine. By looking up this ID in a database stored in the cartridge's ROM, the games then determined if a valid Pluster was inside the attachment.

Due to the Multi Plust On System's reliance on physical, real-world objects, it was possible to make copies of the figurines and their spoke patterns. Today, some folks online even sell replicas of the

215

Pluster's base cut out from wood. Simply popping in the reproduction fools both the Game Boy Advance games and the LCD toys. Furthermore, a complete list of all available Pluster figurines and their exact spoke patterns has circulated on websites for many years. In contrast to later toys-to-life products, it is relatively easy to "pirate" the collectible characters for the Multi Plust On System.

Ultimately, both the peripheral and the figurines were perhaps only mildly popular. *Bouken Yuuki Pluster World* got its own anime and another line of toys from Takara (ones that changed a regular human into a Pluston, *Transformers*-style). However, after the third Game Boy Advance title, Takara abandoned the franchise. This emerging genre required a lot of momentum to maintain interest and engagement. Without new games and new figures, players could only do so much before moving on. Consider that the popular *Skylanders* series currently spans six games across multiple platforms worldwide, and there are hundreds of Amiibos for the 3DS, Wii U, and Switch supported by a huge amount of software.

The Multi Plust On System may not have changed the world, but today it represents what could have been. *Pluster World* tried to bridge the divide between items players could hold in their hands and the virtual worlds present in their video games, specifically at a time when the technology to do so on the Game Boy Advance was limited. In the absence of near-field communication, image recognition, or radio frequency identification, Takara developed something that proved straightforward and elegant in design. They achieved a new level of depth in gameplay that no one else had brought to the Game Boy as well. Although they were the first, they wouldn't be the last company to bring toys and handheld video games closer together.

*Bouken Yuuki Pluster World GP* Starter Set Box

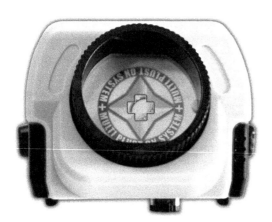

Multi Plust On Accessory

Pluster Figurine Wyburst

The Multi Plust On itself could feel a little clunky at times when attached to a Game Boy Advance, especially SP models. Nevertheless, it was the first toys-to-life product to hit the market for Nintendo's handheld. It aimed for simplicity by not including any digital components within the figurines.

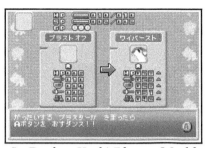

In *Bouken Yuuki Pluster World* RPGs, players could transform based on which Pluster they inserted.

The transformation granted them different powers and abilities in battle.

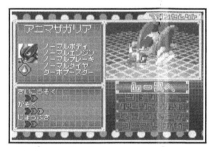

Before starting a race, players had to use a Pluster to transform their vehicle.

Like the RPGs, *Pluston GP*'s transformations granted different stats. Here they controlled how the vehicles moved on the race course.

In the turn-based RPG battles, players defeated random monsters.

**Release Date:**
> July 17, 2003

**Makers:**
> Konami, Nintendo

**Legacy:**
> First game hardware to incorporate direct sunlight, inspiring
> completely new and unprecedented game design.

In the middle of the summer of 2003, Konami launched a new franchise on the Game Boy Advance that featured gameplay mechanics previously unheard of in the industry. *Boktai*, as it was titled in the West, required direct sunlight in order to attack enemies. In a world taken over by the Undead, players assumed the role of Solar Boy Django, foiling the nefarious plots of several Immortal beings trying to destroy humanity. As expected, these villains were weak to the power of the sun. To make this concept a reality, a unique cartridge had to be created, one capable of capturing sunlight. The Solar Sensor was thus born.

Like a handful of other specialized Game Paks, the Solar Sensor had a slightly larger than normal outer casing. Inside, the cartridge's board contained a sensitive photodiode. Its purpose was to measure light, detecting both its presence and intensity. The Solar Sensor was tailored to pick up ultraviolet radiation, therefore, most artificial light sources would not activate it. Under ordinary circumstances, for example, the Solar Sensor ignored indoor lightbulbs. As a result, the *Boktai* games were hard to trick, although some exceptions did exist. The Solar Sensor worked with devices that emitted ultraviolet rays, such as blacklights or tanning beds, but those presented their own sorts of health risks under extended use. At any rate, the Solar Sensor largely achieved its goal, forcing players to operate outside or close to naturally lit environments.

A total of three *Boktai* games were produced for the Game Boy Advance, each using the same Solar Sensor. Rather than being something of a "one-hit wonder", Konami displayed a commitment to this unconventional technology. The series itself was created by none other than the famed Hideo Kojima, known for his work on the *Metal Gear* games. Given how innovative the Solar Sensor was, the hardware partly reflected the style and ambition of its mastermind. To this day, nothing comparable exists for other video games. The closest device would be the recent Joy-Con controllers for the Nintendo Switch, which come with powerful infrared cameras that can be used for nightvision or thermal mapping. Sadly, most games ignore these abilities, making the Solar Sensor truly one of a kind.

The actual sensor lay on the backside of the cartridge's board. This position allowed it to sit inside any model of Game Boy Advance and receive sunlight. As the sensor faced the player, it monitored UV radiation coming from behind them. Perhaps to avoid any undue interference, all three *Boktai* cartridges came in completely clear plastic shells. These conceivably allowed the Solar Sensor to grab sunlight at multiple angles, increasing its effectiveness over normal dark gray cartridges. The *Boktai* titles were another example of non-standard cartridge colors typically reserved for games with additional or exotic hardware inside.

When the player began their adventure, the games asked for the current time, date, and region. *Boktai*'s cartridges all sported real-time clocks in addition to Solar Sensors. Depending on the time of day, the time of year, and the specified location, the software calculated whether it was daytime, evening, or night, even accounting for seasonal changes. Each phase had its own settings and surroundings, with the game altering background palettes and replacing certain enemies. Although this feature wasn't strictly related to the Solar Sensor, it highlighted one of the very real consequences of using sunlight as a component of gameplay. Regardless of what time the game thought it was, *Boktai* was dependent on actual cycles of the sun. Once night fell, players potentially had to wait until morning if they needed to recharge their energy supply.

The Solar Sensor let Django unleash devastating light-based attacks that could stun or kill enemies. Using the Gun Del Sol at first and later the Sol de Vice to wield weapons like swords, players gathered sunlight to power up their offense. Each game had a gauge that tracked the amount of solar energy available to them. Attacking drained this meter, and when it reached zero, Django was unable to harm or stop undead foes. When the Solar Sensor detected sunlight, the meter refilled automatically. Players could also press the A button to quickly absorb energy themselves. The speed of this action depended on the strength of the sunlight hitting the sensor; the stronger the sun, the faster the charge. While roaming outside areas, Django could freely absorb the light, but inside dungeons or underground portions of the game, players needed to find shafts of light poking from above. These were essential for navigating enemy territory, however, they only appeared if and when the Solar Sensor registered any sunlight.

There were some passive effects of the Solar Sensor as well. So long as the device drew in light, it could collect and store energy for later use. Throughout all three *Boktai* games, numerous Solar Stations were scattered. They charged Django's energy with any surplus accumulated by the sensor, a useful tactic should players have to fight their way through the night. In *Boktai 2* and *3*, the Solar Stations' energy could also be used as currency. Naturally, this form of cash built up on its own when the Solar Sensor was exposed to sunlight. Additionally, both *Boktai 1* and *2* provided a feature called the Solar Tree, a plant that continually grew with sunlight. In the first game, players could plant different kinds of Solar Fruit, which could later be mixed together to grow new items. Successfully harvesting them also required sunlight. The second iteration of the Solar Tree was less extensive, but once it began to mature, it granted players useful defensive gear.

As was typical of Game Boy Advance cartridges with unusual hardware, the Solar Sensor's functions could only be accessed through the General Purpose Input/Output interface. The photodiode converted incoming light into a small electrical current. The sensor then recorded the resulting voltage, which represented the sunlight's strength. Afterwards, other components in the cartridge generated their own voltage, gradually increasing it in a linear fashion whenever the software dictated. Every time this internal voltage rose, a comparison was made against the previous one reported by the sensor. If these two were equal, the General Purpose Input/Output interface indicated to the game there was a match.

It was the software's responsibility to manually count each voltage increase, however. This number was essentially a digital value of how much sunlight was reaching the cartridge. Larger results meant brighter sources of light. The *Boktai* games constantly used this information to update the player's on-screen solar gauge. After polling the sensor, the software had to reset the internal voltage in order to repeat the process. The Solar Sensor could also be calibrated via software by reading the darkest level (i.e. covering the entire cartridge) as a baseline.

Using direct sunlight as an in-game energy source came with a host of potential dangers to the player, however. Ultraviolet radiation is harmful in prolonged and concentrated doses. Extended gaming sessions under harsh sunlight could possibly result in conditions as annoying as sunburn to ones as serious as heat stroke or skin cancer. Consequently, the *Boktai* games recognized these hazards and warned players accordingly. Going even further, however, the games had built-in mechanisms that aimed to prevent such situations entirely. If the Solar Sensor detected strong sunlight for a certain amount of time, it would trigger an "Overheated" status. In the first *Boktai* title, the Gun Del Sol would begin to malfunction, eventually becoming unusable until nightfall. This severely limited how well Django could fend for himself and made certain parts unplayable. In the *Boktai* sequels, Django would overheat instead. When his condition worsened, he would collapse and remain bedridden until players moved to find some shade.

The Solar Sensor once again pushed the boundaries of what kinds of things a Game Boy could achieve. Not only did it break new ground for Nintendo's handheld, it was a first in the world of gaming. The *Boktai* titles defied more traditional means of player interaction, and in the process created an experience that was unlike anything else. The Solar Sensor eventually saw some use on the DS when inserted into the system's Slot-2 for *Lunar Knights*. Unfortunately, outside of this example, the use of photodiodes or other similar hardware would remain exclusive to *Boktai*. Regardless, with a complete trilogy behind the franchise, Konami proved that even this niche mechanic was relatively well received and popular. It stands as one of the rare instances of video games actively encouraging and promoting people to play outside.

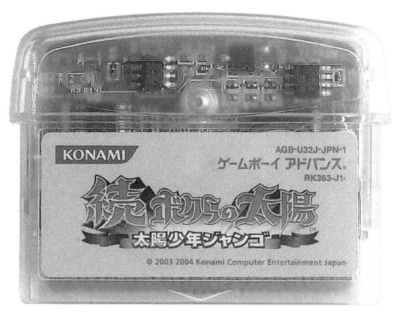

*Boktai 2* Cartridge Front

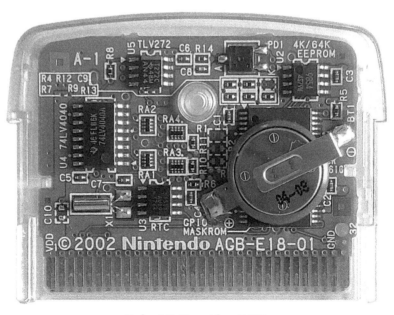

*Boktai 2* Cartridge PCB

The Solar Sensor itself, on the backside (black square, top left)

The Gun del Sol acted as the primary weapon in the first *Boktai* game, and it relied entirely on sunlight for firepower.

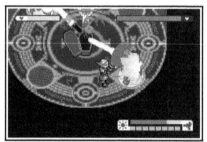

In order for the player to vanquish powerful foes, several boss battles made extensive use of the Solar Sensor.

As a safety measure, the games prevented players from exposing themselves too long under strong sunlight.

In open environments, players could freely absorb any available sunlight to supply their weapons with energy.

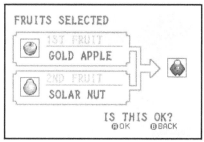

Sunlight was useful for more than just attacks. It could help grow various rare items.

Later games would expand Django's weaponry, even adding different elemental properties. They still required the Solar Sensor for power.

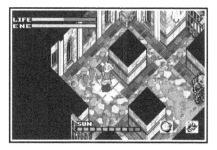

Some indoor environments only allowed small areas of sunlight.

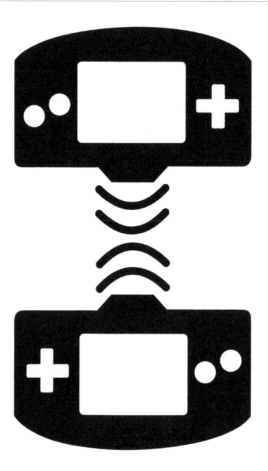

**Release Date:**
July 18, 2003

**Maker:**
Nintendo

**Legacy:**
Restored infrared communications on the Game Boy Advance.
First instance of a Game Boy controlling a robot.

Nintendo's handheld systems have a long history of using infrared signals for wireless communication. Even on its most modern console, the Nintendo Switch, infrared plays a role. Early efforts on the original Game Boy were created by third-party developers and restricted to a handful of specific game cartridges. Later, an infrared transceiver became standard for all Game Boy Colors. Unfortunately on the Game Boy Advance, built-in support for infrared was stripped from the prototype, leaving the final version barren in this regard. As a result, the Game Boy Advance supported the least amount of games with infrared connectivity of all the Game Boys. Nevertheless, it did manage to use infrared in at least one title for a very unique purpose.

The popular *Zoids* franchise features various characters piloting giant animal-like robots of the same name. Often in both the games and anime, a plucky protagonist stumbles upon a Zoid of their own, and circumstances force them into larger conflicts against different factions and even nations. *Cyber Drive Zoids: Kiju no Senshi Hyuu* followed a similar formula. While the main game focused on turn-based battles spread over a grid, it also had a mode where players could operate a real-life Zoid miniaturized as a toy model.

In 2003, Tomy Company released three battery-powered remote-controlled Zoid models as part of their "CDZ" series. These Zoids used infrared signals from a special remote to move around, shoot weapons, and participate in battles. Each one, for example, had a specific weak spot that could drop the unit's armor, and the toys kept track of hit points during matches. Tomy decided to expand the appeal of these CDZ models by making them compatible with the Game Boy Advance.

*Cyber Drive Zoids* achieved this by using the Game Boy Advance Infrared Adapter, also known as the AGB-006. While the Game Boy Advance lacked a native port for infrared communication, Nintendo created an add-on that restored this lost functionality. Once the AGB-006 latched onto the Game Boy Advance's Link Cable port, software could then send and receive infrared signals through the device. By sending the appropriate light pulses, *Cyber Drive Zoids* replicated the remote controllers that came bundled with the CDZ models. In many respects, Tomy's Zoids were similar to Bandai's WonderBorg on the WonderSwan, which also used infrared signals from a handheld console to control small robots.

Each copy of *Cyber Drive Zoids* came packaged with an AGB-006. The hardware was small enough to fit in a standard box for

Japanese games. This was the only title to utilize the AGB-006. Although Nintendo apparently went to some length to make the adapter – going so far as to give it a place among their other AGB-xxx products – it would remain exclusive to *Cyber Drive Zoids*. Buying that game, in fact, was the only way to obtain the accessory.

Once a save file of some sort from the main game was written, *Cyber Drive Zoids* enabled a menu for connecting the Game Boy Advance and CDZ model. By selecting a specific save, certain attributes of the player's Zoid from the game transferred over to the CDZ model's actions. For example, as the player upgraded their Zoid in the story mode, they could increase its speed. The CDZ model reflected this by moving faster than normal. A "Boost Mode" also existed, where the Zoid was temporarily invincible and moved at top speed. Depending on the level of the Zoid in the game, the CDZ model would be more agile or have better defenses when fighting.

*Cyber Drive Zoids* first performed a brief check to make sure the infrared adapter was connected. Afterwards, it loaded up a screen that mimicked the look and feel of a Zoid's cockpit. From here, players used the buttons on the Game Boy Advance to control their CDZ model, as long as they kept the infrared adapter within range of the model's receiver. The game helpfully displayed the commands being issued on-screen as well as the current speed and availability of the player's "Boost Mode". By using *Cyber Drive Zoids* and the AGB-006, players could gain access to a limited set of exclusive maneuvers, such as recovering lost hit points. This was thanks to the larger number of available buttons on the Game Boy Advance in comparison to the default remote bundled with the CDZ models. The standard controller only had a forward and back pad and two buttons, which paled before the Game Boy's wider range of inputs. As such, players could only take full advantage of their robots when using *Cyber Drive Zoids* and the adapter.

The AGB-006 used a rather simple protocol to communicate with the CDZ models. It sent a combination of 12 long and short pulses to the robotic toy, and the order determined the exact command being issued. Because these Zoids were meant to battle head-to-head, the protocol established two distinct "channels" for each combatant: ID1 and ID2. This ensured that one Zoid didn't accidentally receive commands intended for the other. The ID was embedded in every command, and a specific synchronization signal sent at the start of a battle told the CDZ model which ID it was to use. If it picked up a command with an ID that did not match, the command was entirely ignored.

While the AGB-006 was a fully functional transceiver, *Cyber Drive Zoids* only used half of its potential. Communication was strictly one-way, with the Game Boy Advance beaming infrared data outward but never accepting any incoming pulses. The default remote controllers packaged with the CDZ models operated in the same manner. There was no feedback whatsoever from the Zoids. It certainly would have been possible for the AGB-006 to receive data during fights given its broad area of reception. Nevertheless, no commercial software ever officially made use of the AGB-006's ability to read infrared light. Even so, the adapter provided its own interrupts that alerted the software when a new signal was detected.

In comparison to the built-in infrared hardware on the Game Boy Color, the AGB-006 offered many improvements. The effective distance for receiving signals was greatly increased, reaching as far as 1.8 meters. On the Game Boy Color, for example, it could do at best a dozen centimeters or so. The AGB-006 also detected infrared light at far wider angles, about 150 degrees horizontally and 165 degrees vertically. Previously, the Game Boy Color essentially required line-of-sight to work, and any deviation would result in lost or incomplete signals. In these technical respects, the AGB-006 was a massive step up from earlier infrared communication on Nintendo's handhelds. When it was sold, it was arguably the best infrared device ever designed for the Game Boy.

One bit of mystery remains buried in *Cyber Drive Zoids'* code. The game tried to access memory that controlled the infrared hardware on Game Boy Advance prototypes. However, as retail units ultimately removed the built-in infrared, the code basically did nothing. It may be a curious holdover from long ago. Perhaps the game was partially being developed while Nintendo perfected its prototypes. Perhaps a deprecated SDK was initially used. Although this oddity has no definitive explanation, it is interesting to see that the only Game Boy Advance title known to support infrared communication included some references to the outdated infrared port.

In their decision to get rid of native infrared support on the Game Boy Advance, Nintendo may have completely turned away developers from the technology. It's quite possible the company always intended to sell an adapter to resurrect this feature, but only if and when required by upcoming games. Only the people behind

*Cyber Drive Zoids* are known to have expressed such an interest, and to date the AGB-006 is completely tied to that software. It is also noteworthy that the numbering of the adapter itself (AGB-006) puts it between other accessories such as the Game Boy Advance Link Cable (AGB-005) and Battery Case (AGB-007). As both these two were released at the Game Boy Advance's launch, this suggests that the Infrared Adapter was originally intended for a much earlier debut. One can merely speculate whether or not the adapter would have seen higher adoption if it had been pushed sooner with more backing from Nintendo. In any case, a wireless adapter for the Game Boy Advance was released less than six months after the AGB-006. Any appeal the older device had was likely lost in favor of the newer one in short order.

In the end, the Game Boy Advance marked a rapid decrease in the popularity of infrared communication for handheld gaming. Despite eventually getting an adapter, the system never supported as many titles as its predecessor. After the AGB-006 became available through *Cyber Drive Zoids*, no other games utilized the hardware. Regardless, the infrared adapter demonstrated the potential to link video games and miniature machines. It provided a unique experience for *Zoids* fans and added value to the CDZ models themselves. The AGB-006 had a great deal of unrealized possibilities, however, it did provide one of the most advanced video-game-to-robot interfaces of its time.

*Cyber Drive Zoids* Box Front

*Cyber Drive Zoids* Box Back

The Game Boy Advance Infrared Adapter (AGB-006)

*Cyber Drive Zoids* 02—Cyclops

There were only a total of three CDZ models ever made. Though it was an impressive toy, it took some skill to master its movements, especially in the heat of battle.

233

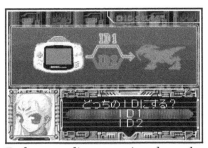

Before sending any signals to the CDZ model, players chose between two channels to avoid infrared interference.

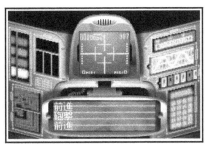

Once the adapter was detected, players viewed this screen while sending commands to their miniature Zoid.

The actual game itself involved turn-based combat on a grid. Players upgraded their Zoid as the story progressed.

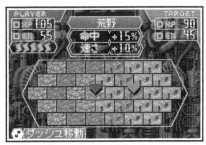

The player's Zoid had various attacks for different situations, including short-range and long-range assaults.

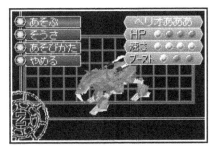

The player's stats from the game transferred over to the CDZ model.

**Release Date:**
2003

**Maker:**
Carrera

**Legacy:**
An early attempt at bringing modern interactivity to digital slot-car racing.

In the world of slot-car racing, enthusiasts can craft all sorts of challenging and exciting courses. Gravity-defying loops, crisscrossing lanes, dangerously sharp banks, and tricky turns are all fair game. Previously however, no one had ever thought to throw the Game Boy Advance into this equation. In 2003 one of the most prominent leaders of slot-car racing, Carrera, decided to add a more digital dimension to their product line. The result of their work was the Virtureal Racing System, or VRS, a specialized kit that allowed Nintendo's latest handheld to directly control slot-cars along a customized track.

Characterized as a "motor driver", the VRS served as the base of a given 1:43 *Carrera GO!!!* racetrack. Users could build the course as they saw fit, so long as the start and end of the track were properly connected to the VRS. The unit itself came with two permanently attached Link Cables for the Game Boy Advance, and by using the *Carrera Power Slide* software, racers could send their cars flying with the push of a button.

The goal behind the VRS was to create a more interactive experience than what was normally found in most slot-car setups. *Carrera Power Slide* could, for example, simulate fuel consumption or account for crashing off-road. Running out of gas or taking too much damage then required a pit stop. Although such effects were optional, they offered a much deeper level of play compared to regular slot-car tracks. Carrera additionally championed the Game Boy Advance as an "intelligent" controller, presumably one with finer handling of the car's speed.

As a game, *Carrera Power Slide* focused much attention on virtual isometric track racing, however, it had a dedicated mode called "Real Racing" that handled all functions related to the VRS. Once selected, players connected their Game Boy Advance to the hardware so *Carrera Power Slide* could identify the motor driver. A second Game Boy Advance could download a so-called "MultiBoot" program from the first handheld, even if the second player did not own a copy of the game. This small program contained everything the other player needed to participate in Real Racing.

Unlike newer *Carrera GO!!!* motor drivers, the VRS was not battery-operated. Instead, it plugged into a power source. Its singular button activated the device, and a bright red LED indicated its status. The VRS had to be turned on to use in any capacity, otherwise *Carrera Power Slide* wouldn't detect anything connected, and the Real Racing mode became completely inaccessible. When transferring the MultiBoot program to a second Game Boy Advance, the LED automatically turned off until the other handheld finished the download. Once the transfer was complete, the LED came back on and both players could begin their race.

A number of different modes were available through the VRS. Free Run was an unrestricted practice session. Timed Run pitted two racers against one another to see who completed the most laps in a given amount of time. Lap Race was another head-to-head match where racers competed for the total lowest time for a set number of laps. In Catch-Up, the first racer to finish an entire lap before their opponent did was the winner. Ghost Race recorded a slot-car's movements for one lap and let players race against a "playback" version. Stop Watch simply provided detailed logs on various lap times.

During races, input from the Game Boy Advance determined how the cars moved along the track. The A button accelerated, and Up on the directional pad entered a brief turbo boost. The L button performed a pit stop, as long as it was pressed within two seconds of starting a new lap. The Game Boy Advance screen displayed a wide variety of information such as current speed, crash damage, remaining fuel, whether the player was in first or second place, fastest lap time, current lap time, total race time, and current lap count. Although there were two separate lanes on the VRS, the software allowed racers to choose which one they wanted to control. Player 1 was not restricted to Lane 1, and neither was Player 2 restricted to Lane 2. The VRS also supported using the older hand controls for Player 2, so technically only one Game Boy Advance was necessary to start playing with a friend.

Installed in the VRS itself were two mechanical switches near the starting line. These tiny bits of plastic were triggered every time a slot-car ran over them. They allowed the VRS to keep track of the number of laps for each lane. Internally, the hardware used two digital counters and incremented them when the corresponding switches pressed down. These numbers were then reported back to the Game Boy Advance via the Link Cable. *Carrera Power Slide* monitored the lap time on its own, so the VRS was only responsible for updating the lap counter. When it was released, this was a very compact and well designed lap counting solution. Other mechanical counters were typically limited to a set maximum number of laps. Later electronic lap monitoring used infrared sensors but were often relatively expensive. In comparison, the VRS was quite cheap and could theoretically register an unlimited number of laps.

Depending on the curvature of a track and the speed at which a slot-car was moving, racers might accidentally careen off-course, at which point *Carrera Power Slide* acknowledged a crash. The VRS, however, had no real method of detecting when cars left their lanes. Rather than relying on the hardware itself, the software cleverly accounted for crashes by measuring how long the player stopped driving. The idea was that after a crash, the racer had to pause what they were doing to pick up and reset their car on the track. In all likelihood, the Game Boy Advance had to be set aside temporarily. These brief periods of inactivity while a race was in progress, therefore, were often signs of vehicular mishap.

Similarly, fuel usage was something calculated in software. *Carrera Power Slide* simply watched how long a racer hit the gas and periodically subtracted a given amount of fuel. Once a racer sustained too much damage or ran out of fuel, the software no longer transmitted the appropriate signals to the VRS that instructed the car to move forward. By entering a pit stop, *Carrera Power Slide* reset its damage and fuel levels and then communicated normally with the VRS.

To accelerate a slot-car, the Game Boy Advance sent a specific 16-bit command to the VRS. This told the hardware how fast to move the car and which lane to control. There were a total of 16 different possible speeds; the lowest one prevented any movement at all while the highest level was reserved for turbo boosting. In response to this command, the VRS would output the current lap counts for each individual lane. In order to accurately react to fast-paced racing action, the Game Boy Advance issued these commands rapidly many times per-second. As such, the speed of the slot-car and the number of completed laps were constantly updated.

Despite having so many advanced racing options, the VRS was not particularly well received. It struggled on the market and proved somewhat unpopular for traditional Carrera fans. Among the complaints against it was the cumbersome setup in contrast to normal *Carrera GO!!!* racetracks. Not only did players need the VRS, but they had to supplement the device with a minimum of one Game Boy Advance and the relevant game cartridge. Furthermore, the digital controls via the Game Boy Advance were seen as less flexible and less practical than the regular hand controllers. The standard mechanical controls used by many Carrera kits permitted cars to run at multiple precise speeds depending on how hard the button was pushed. Meanwhile, the Game Boy Advance was strictly binary, either ramping up to full throttle or quickly coming to a complete stop. The data displayed on the Game Boy Advance screen was not always quite useful due to the lack of lighting on early models and the need for racers to constantly focus on the track itself rather than the handheld.

Even though it was not a massive success, the VRS was well ahead of its time. By using a unique combination of software and hardware, it became one of the most sophisticated ways to race slot-cars. For years after the VRS launched, features like counting laps, timing laps, pit stops, and racer positions couldn't be found as a single all-in-one package from Carrera. These concepts wouldn't return in a cohesive manner until 2010 when the company unveiled the Carrera 30352 – 30360 digital racetrack components. The VRS was in many ways the predecessor of today's *Carrera Go!!! Plus* racetracks which use bluetooth, smart devices, and apps in place of the Game Boy Advance. Ultimately, the VRS acted as a guide for enhancing slot-car racing, and traces of its influence are present even in Carrera's most recent products.

VRS Motor Driver Box

There were a total of three different box sets for the VRS. The basic one (pictured here) came with just the motor driver itself. A more comprehensive Formula 1 edition came with a massive racetrack, two cars, and the *Carrera Power Slide* game.

Thanks to Carrera having a vast catalog of slot-car products available, players had a wealth of options when it came to expanding racetracks of their own. Almost any kind of course could be designed. The VRS could work with anything racers dreamed up, which potentially made the peripheral attractive for enthusiasts.

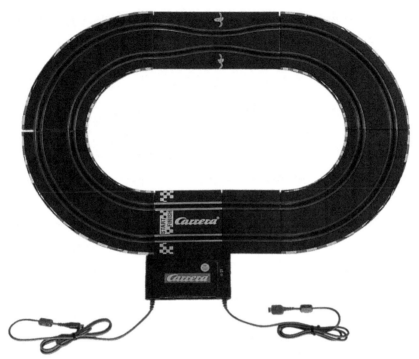

The VRS fully assembled with a small racetrack

Several Mario-themed cars were later made by Carrera

Real Racing sported plenty of different modes, taking advantage of the VRS in multiple ways.

Extra conditions, such as fuel consumption and the amount of damage from crashes, could be set before a race.

The screen shown during most races presented a great deal of information.

After a racer was declared the victor, the software displayed the lap times.

The software also gave awards for performance like best lap time.

242

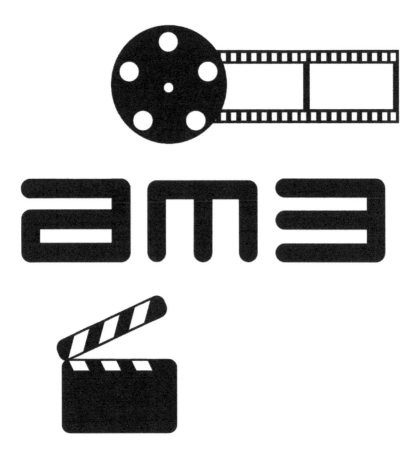

**Release Date:**
November 20, 2003

**Maker:**
AM3

**Legacy:**
First commercialized multimedia experience on the Game
Boy. Established Nintendo's handheld as a viable platform for
audio and video formats.

After the dawn of the new millennium, many consumers began turning their attention to mobile digital media. The likes of cassette and CD players gradually gave way to MP3 players such as the vastly popular Apple iPod. While music was a relatively easy target for many products, video somewhat lagged. Early dedicated video players were often quite expensive and had limited capacity. One particular corporation, however, saw a way to reasonably lower costs and reach a wide-ranging audience at the same time. Rather than completely manufacture specialty hardware of their own, they planned to use Nintendo's prolific handheld gaming console as a base.

On October 24, 2003, a Japanese company known as AM3 announced their latest endeavor, an adapter for the Game Boy Advance that allowed the device to read SmartMedia cards. Each of these cards would contain playable multimedia assets such as anime shows and films. The Advance Movie Adapter, as it was called, had a slot for SmartMedia cards on the side and plugged directly into the Game Boy Advance as a cartridge. Less than a month later, the adapter hit the market. It sold as a bundle and launched with several cards featuring episodes of *Detective Conan*. This marked the first time the Game Boy Advance was used not only for gaming but also as a video platform.

Thanks to the codec developed jointly by IMAGICA and Actimagine, AM3 could provide fullscreen video at 30 frames-per-second on the Game Boy Advance. Perhaps most impressive of all, the codec required no custom video hardware for decoding. Rather, the Game Boy Advance's CPU handled everything. The codec was in fact specifically designed to run on the portable system, taking advantage of its processor and audiovisual output capabilities. As such, AM3 was able to maximize compression while maintaining reasonable levels of quality. They claimed videos could be anywhere from 40 to 200 times smaller in size compared to the originals. A common 32MB SmartMedia card from AM3 could hold about 24 minutes of recorded content, long enough for a typical anime episode. Larger 64MB cards were capable of storing full-length movies, such as the first four theatrical *Pokémon* releases.

SmartMedia cards were a type of flash memory ranging from sizes as small as 2MB to as big as 128MB. The standard was initiated by Toshiba in the mid 1990s, competing with other formats such as MiniCard and CompactFlash. It became a notable storage medium for digital cameras. However, due to other formats like SecureDigital physically shrinking while increasing memory capacities, support for

SmartMedia began leveling off by the time the Advance Movie Adapter came about. Nevertheless, it offered AM3 cheap and widely available data. One additional consideration for the company may have been the format's ability to guard against unauthorized copying.

Every SmartMedia card had an unused block of bytes that could only be written to once, generally by the manufacturers themselves. In effect, each card held a permanent, unique 128-bit ID, which AM3 used as part of a copy-protection scheme. In order for their videos to play, a small file on the cards was decrypted with the DES algorithm. The unscrambled file contained its own 128-bit number, which had to match the currently inserted SmartMedia card's ID. As no two SmartMedia cards ever shared the same ID, users couldn't simply copy the contents of one card and transfer them to another. Although this method was far from perfect and could be overcome with enough time and resources, the goal for AM3 was to prevent casual piracy. Such a measure was likely needed to ensure that media companies would license their material. Without copy prevention techniques, these groups may have viewed the Advance Movie Adapter as a risk and avoided the product altogether.

The Advance Movie Adapter had built-in firmware to handle a range of tasks. Although it only measured in at a mere 11KB, the firmware provided all the necessary code for the Game Boy Advance's multimedia duties. Aside from setting up a boot environment, it pushed audio and video through the Game Boy's LCD and speakers. It constantly pulled data from the SmartMedia card, converting that binary information into pixels and sound samples. Additionally, the firmware handled basic playback features such as pausing and seeking forward/backward at speeds of 1x to 4x. Certain titles released by AM3 also supported chapter selection and simple interactive menus. Lastly, the firmware managed which files to read from the SmartMedia card, as well as anything that needed decryption.

AM3 had plans to promote other forms of entertainment through the adapter, such as game trailers and previews, pictures, music, education, e-books, karaoke, manga, and maps. Nintendo prohibited game distribution, however. Unfortunately, despite all of that potential, there were very few instances of the adapter being used for anything outside of videos sold to consumers. Nevertheless, AM3 carved out a relatively successful niche as it began operating a kiosk system that allowed people to write or re-write different videos to SmartMedia cards. Rolling out nationally in Japan in October of 2004, the kiosks would accept AM3 branded SmartMedia cards. By default, some of AM3's cards were blank, but for a fee spanning 100 to 400 yen, the machines would put movies or TV shows chosen by the user onto the medium. This service proved quite affordable, making it attractive to many interested in on-the-go video. Furthermore, AM3 grew its market by partnering with popular animes such as *Detective Conan, Pokémon, Crayon Shin-chan, Time Bokan,* and *Lelere's Genius Bokan,* appealing to a broad, young audience.

The hardware architecture of the Advance Movie Adapter remains quite distinctive among Game Boy peripherals. Covered in a black and white plastic shell, it exposed an extremely thin gap on the side for SmartMedia cards. As far as official products are concerned, such a characteristic was also shared by Nintendo's Play-Yan, which worked with SD cards. The majority of the Advance Movie Adapter's components were designed for reading data from either firmware or SmartMedia. When the Game Boy Advance first turned on, a small portion of the firmware was available right away. It executed a 1KB block of code that then loaded the rest of firmware into RAM. Due to the way the adapter handled mapping new data, only 1KB at a time could be transferred to a fixed location. Once the CPU issued a new command to read the next block, the old bytes were replaced with the incoming section.

After loading all of the firmware, the next step for the Game Boy was to start reading various metadata about the file layout on the SmartMedia card, obtain the card's 128-bit ID, and decrypt the special "lock" file used for copy-protection. Should this process fail, the firmware halted, preventing the system from doing anything further. Not even the initial startup animation with AM3's logo appeared. When successful, however, the firmware presented the user with a main title screen. From here they selected different episodes or chapters if available or started from the beginning of a single video. AM3's software periodically requested new 1KB blocks of data and parsed those bytes according to Actimagine's FastVideo codec as it played the media. The adapter provided an interface to request specific files stored in the SmartMedia's File Allocation Table, and it even alerted the CPU when reading past the given file size.

The Advance Movie Adapter was exclusive to Japan during its entire lifetime. It performed well enough for AM3 to support it for over four years, extending past the Game Boy Advance era and into the DS. With over 50 individual cards for different anime franchises, it was notably more expansive than its western counterpart, the Game

Boy Advance Video cartridges. In this arena, the adapter had several advantages concerning price, range of content, security functions, and arguably video quality. Perhaps the largest factor favoring the Advance Movie Adapter was that some of its videos were compatible with the Game Boy Player, whereas the entire Game Boy Advance Video series was purposefully programmed to not play on that hardware. On the downside, however, the adapter was somewhat cumbersome due to its large size; it constantly protruded from one end. Moreover, it required users to slide thin cards in and out of a narrow slot, an extra step compared to simply swapping the whole cartridge. The cards were small and may have been prone to getting scratched or lost.

Despite surviving well into 2007, AM3's adapter was surpassed and supplanted by other multimedia hardware. The Play-Yan came along in early 2005, allowing the Game Boy Advance to play arbitrary music and video files from a user's library. It even provided minigames in its first version. AM3 eventually released the DSVision, which was essentially a continuation of the Advance Movie Adapter but on the Nintendo DS. Here, SmartMedia cards were replaced with MicroSD cards, and content could now be downloaded through a special online store via PCs instead of standalone kiosks. Cellphones gained more and more multimedia capabilities each year, gradually evolving into the smartphones most know today. While the Advance Movie Adapter served an early role when choices were limited, other technologies quickly caught up, making it obsolete.

Although systems like Nokia's N-Gage and the Tapwave Zodiac were among the first to carry modern multimedia functions, AM3's work on the Game Boy Advance had a measurable impact on Nintendo's next handheld game consoles. It demonstrated that consumers wanted portable digital media and that they were comfortable accessing it through devices like the Game Boy. From the Advance Movie Adapter, other efforts followed suit. The likes of the DSi and 3DS both featured their own SD card slots and could play music files that users uploaded. As rivals such as the PlayStation Portable and Vita began natively supporting music, videos, and photos, the industry experienced a shift. People owned more and more media; what once was a novelty add-on was now an indispensable feature. Nintendo's path towards this realization rapidly accelerated with AM3's adapter.

*Detective Conan* Episode 1 AM3 Card and Adapter

*Detective Conan* Episode 2 AM3 Card

SmartMedia cards that featured the "ID" logo had unique, permanent 128-bit numbers used for copy-protection. AM3 SmartMedia cards came in 32MB or 64MB sizes.

Advance Movie Adapter Front

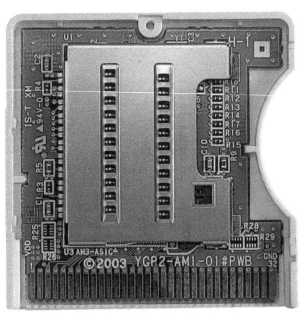

Advance Movie Adapter PCB

Not unlike DVDs, the videos on AM3 cards would offer a title screen before jumping into the episode or movie.

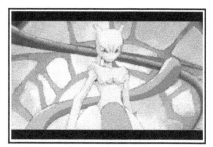

Normally, 32MB cards had enough space for a full 24-minute episode, while 64MB cards could fit entire animated films.

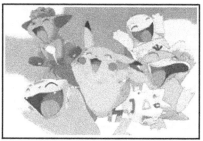

The adapter and its software took full advantage of the GBA's hardware to provide relatively decent audio and video playback.

Basic controls such as pausing and seeking forwards and backwards were available through the firmware.

The overall quality provided enjoyable, portable videos.

**Release Date:**
> December 11, 2003

**Maker:**
> Konami

**Legacy:**
> First ever interactive watch that communicated with a Game
> Boy. Further established the Game Boy's ability to function
> with a diverse set of accessories.

The range of devices the Game Boy could connect with was both vast and unbridled. Any idea, it seemed, was considered and implemented. Nothing was too outrageous or audacious, and technically speaking very little could stop the handheld video game console from interfacing with all kinds of hardware. Among this formidable array of peripherals was the Magical Watch, one of the few items that was as much an accessory for the player as it was for the Game Boy Advance. Produced by Konami, it represents the first and only time the Game Boy ever directly communicated with a wristwatch.

With the end of 2003 approaching, the game company released a title known as *Wagamama * Fairy: Mirumo de Pon! Hachinin no Toki no Yousei*. Based on the popular *Mirumo* anime and manga, players assumed the role of the fairy prince Mirumo, going on a journey to find out why the flow of time had stopped in his world and fix it. A basic adventure game sprinkled with a few minigames here and there, it would have been an otherwise ordinary piece of tie-in media were it not for the Magical Watch. The product itself came packaged with copies of the software, costing 6,800 yen for the whole bundle.

Unlike many other digital watches of this era, the Magical Watch came with a monochrome 32x32 pixel LCD screen capable of displaying small graphics and text. It was also outfitted with three buttons for user input and menu navigation and had a small, built-in speaker for various sound effects and alarms. Needless to say, it kept track of the current time and date as well through a crystal oscillator powered by a CR2032 battery. The most interesting specification of the Magical Watch was its serial port, modeled to work with a Game Boy Advance Link Cable. Through this, the Magical Watch transferred data to and from the Game Boy software, enabling the two to interact.

Aside from telling the time, the Magical Watch also featured three minigames. *Dash de Pon* had players controlling Mirumo during a short race. The goal was to move 100 paces within 30 seconds. To advance, the left and right buttons on the Magical Watch were pressed, alternating from one side to the other. If the player hit one side twice, Mirumo tripped and temporarily could not continue. Trip three times, and the player lost. *Dance de Pon* was a simplistic *Dance Dance Revolution*-esque minigame where Mirumo moved left or right in sync with several onscreen signs. Failing to do so three times resulted in a Game Over. *Catch de Pon* had Mirumo moving along the bottom of the screen collecting falling objects. As the minigame continued, the intensity increased. Missing anything three times ended the game.

Players gained points based on their performance in these minigames. When connecting the Magical Watch to the Game Boy Advance, these points were exchanged for special in-game items that aided Mirumo in his task to restore time. The video game version of the Magical Watch in the main story allowed Mirumo to stop and start time at will. Returning time back to normal was crucial to completing the game, however, doing so continually drained an energy meter. If that energy ran out, Mirumo was forced to complete a brief minigame in order to recharge his Magical Watch. Fortunately, the items players received from the real-life version of the Magical Watch allowed Mirumo to recharge on demand. In short, connecting with the Magical Watch granted players an advantage during Mirumo's quest.

The Game Boy Advance also sent data that unlocked extras on the Magical Watch itself. While playing the main game, Mirumo would meet other characters, adding their profiles to a "Fairy Picture Book". This list of characters, 60 in all, was simultaneously copied over to the Magical Watch while the device sent its items to the Game Boy. The Fairy Picture Book was present on the Magical Watch as well, allowing players to choose a character who would appear on the watch's home screen.

Common for such accessories on the Game Boy Advance, the Magical Watch utilized the serial port's General Purpose mode for communications. There were four stages involved in the Magical Watch's protocol. The first was simply a start signal initiated from the Game Boy Advance, causing the Magical Watch to prepare for the next phase. Afterwards, the Game Boy Advance uploaded a total of 80 bytes, one bit at a time. During this part, eight bytes of Fairy Picture Book data from the Game Boy Advance were transferred over to the watch and saved on that device. The other 72 bytes represented commands that instructed the Magical Watch to respond with its own data. For the following phase, the Magical Watch returned nine bytes that the Game Boy Advance interpreted as various special items, plus an 8-bit checksum to ensure everything was sent correctly. Finally, the Game Boy Advance sent a stop signal to end all transmissions.

To be clear, the Magical Watch was not a genuine smartwatch or anything close to one. Instead it was a sort of companion device akin to the Pokémon Pikachu 2 or Pocket Sakura. All three served a similar role, granting exclusive content via points when connecting to a Game Boy and offering various simplistic activities on a small LCD screen. In Konami's case, the Magical Watch was a marketing move to sell more merchandise for a well-known franchise. While it added some interesting functionality to the main game, it was not overwhelmingly useful. Mirumo could charge up his time starting/stopping abilities easily enough by collecting common items scattered literally everywhere. Even without help from the Magical Watch, players could readily power up Mirumo's energy bar when merely walking across the screen in many cases.

Although the Magical Watch was something along the lines of a gimmick aimed at children and fans of *Mirumo de Pon!,* it nevertheless contributed to the world of gaming peripherals. It further proved that there really were few, if any, major limitations on what the Game Boy could connect to. As long as developers and engineers could imagine it, there was always a way to link the handheld and another machine together. The Magical Watch may not have been as revolutionary as some of the other subjects in this book, yet it covered new ground all the same. It's especially worthwhile to note that the Game Boy itself evolved from the Game & Watch handhelds, which shared some lineage with calculators and wristwatches. In a strange and convoluted way, the Magical Watch allowed the Game Boy to come full circle.

The Magical Watch

Among all the items featured in this book, the Magical Watch is one of the few wearable ones. It was designed to act independently from the Game Boy Advance and made for a charming, standalone accessory for *Mirumo* fans.

The Magical Watch from another perspective

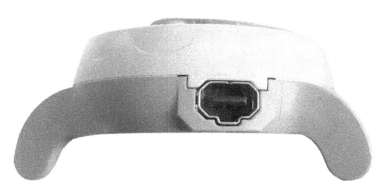

Side-on view of the watch's Link Cable port

Unfortunately, the Magical Watch did not come with its own Link Cable! Despite coming in a large plastic-encased set along with the game, this accessory required players to source their own cables. As the Game Boy Advance eliminated the infrared port from the Game Boy Color, the only means of communicating with the handheld was via the Link Cable.

Various character portraits could be unlocked on the Magical Watch as part of the Fairy Picture Book.

The watch featured three minigames where players controlled Mirumo. These rewarded points based on performance.

A total of 60 characters were available, including some villains!

The portraits were displayed on the main screen of the watch along with the current time.

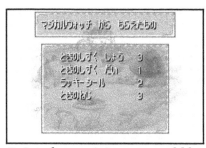

Points from minigames could be converted into useful items when connecting with the Game Boy Advance.

Most of these bonus items helped charge up the in-game Magical Watch.

If the in-game Magical Watch lost its energy, it had to be replenished by completing a short minigame.

The Fairy Picture Book data was taken from the Game Boy Advance and sent to the watch.

Using the in-game Magical Watch was the only way to make progress.

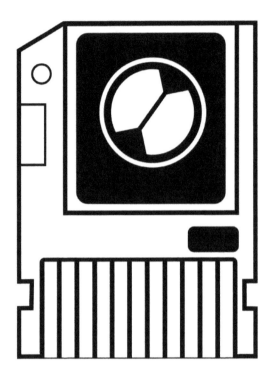

**Release Date:**
December 12, 2003

**Maker:**
Takara

**Legacy:**
Added a level of immersion so that real-life gameplay closely
resembled the fictional world of the *Battle Network* franchise.

In the early 2000s, the *Mega Man* franchise had something of a renaissance on the Game Boy Advance. Two new series appeared on the handheld: *Mega Man Zero* and *Mega Man Battle Network*. Both went on to launch numerous sequels and revitalize interest in the overall brand. Quite notably, *Battle Network* inspired an entire generation of fans and spawned anime, manga, toys, collectibles, and board games. With the release of *Mega Man Battle Network 4*, Capcom joined forces with Takara to bring players the Battle Chip Gate and a level of immersion that exceeded anything before it.

Throughout the fictional world of *Battle Network*, people used living electronic programs called NetNavis to fight various computer viruses. These "operators", as they were known, inserted combat data contained on Battle Chips, and the NetNavi could then execute devastating attacks. The gameplay of each *Battle Network* entry revolved around this concept, where players selected these chips and then guided their NetNavi against enemies. For the first three games in the series, this was nothing more than highlighting the chip via a cursor and pressing buttons during real-time battles. *Mega Man Battle Network 4*, however, introduced the concept of Chip Gates, large accessories which allowed players to insert physical Battle Chips to engage their foes.

There were three different iterations of the Chip Gates: the original Battle Chip Gate, the Progress Gate, and the Beast Link Gate. Each functioned in the same manner. They connected via the Link Cable port of the Game Boy Advance and came with an exposed slot for Battle Chips. During fights, the player stuck the chip inside, which then activated a given attack. This sequence reflected how operators in the *Battle Network* world fought viruses, aligning the player's actual experience as closely as possible to the game.

Each Chip Gate supported hundreds of real-life Battle Chips that directly corresponded with ones found in the games, further deepening the illusion that players had become NetNavi operators. Separate sets of Battle Chips were produced for each version of the Chip Gate and were only compatible with that particular device. The unique size and shape of the chips meant the hardware would only accept ones designed for that model. With each new *Battle Network* game, the types of virtual Battle Chips available were changed and rearranged to keep enemy encounters fresh and interesting. Some were outright removed in place of brand new ones, and almost every Battle Chip used different numbering from one game to the next.

Since the physical Battle Chips matched their digital counterparts in these regards as well, they could not be transferred across sequels.

The usage of each Battle Chip Gate varied considerably between supported games. In *Battle Network 4*, inserting the original Battle Chip Gate unlocked the Operation Battle mode. Here, the player had limited control over their NetNavi, unlike the main game. Instead of manually dictating every movement, the player instructed the NetNavi to follow several tactics and focus on certain rows of the battlefield. While the NetNavi had some autonomy, the player had to regularly insert Battle Chips so an attack could be launched. This mode was completely optional, but it demonstrated how Chip Gates would integrate into later *Battle Network* games. Operation Battles also featured a multiplayer mode to go up against a friend.

*Rockman EXE 4.5: Real Operation* took the concept behind Operation Battles and massively expanded them. While Operation Battles were previously an extra bonus in *Battle Network 4*, here they were the heart and soul of the entire game. Rather than simply defeating a series of enemies, *Rockman EXE 4.5* played much like a regular *Battle Network* adventure with an overworld of the internet, a unique storyline, random battles, and a few tournament modes. Each and every battle, however, had the player's NetNavi acting independently for the most part. Like the Operation Battles of *Battle Network 4*, the Battle Chip Gate was used to send attacks to the NetNavi in real-time. In this game, however, the NetNavi could move around the battlefield more efficiently and perform limited actions without relying on the Chip Gate.

*Mega Man Battle Network 5* brought back Operation Battles as an unlockable mode, although it used the system from *4.5* where NetNavis had greater freedom to move around. In the main game, the Progress Chip Gate allowed players to swap into different NetNavis during battle if the appropriate Battle Chip of that character was chosen. This permitted players to use multiple strategies for various situations, as normally they only controlled MegaMan.EXE.

*Rockman EXE 6* was far more ambitious than its predecessors. Inserting the Beast Link Gate caused players to transform into an overpowered "BeastOut" version of MegaMan.EXE, capable of rapid-fire buster blasts, auto-targeting enemies with Battle Chips, and unleashing special charged-up attacks. Normally this mode was limited in duration, but with a Beast Link Gate plugged in, BeastOut became permanent. The Beast Link Gate let players insert Battle Chips in any battle during the main story. Unlike the previous titles,

*Rockman EXE 6* gave players full control of their NetNavi while using a Chip Gate. Lastly, when certain NetNavi Battle Chips were inserted into the Beast Link Gate, players could temporarily use that character via the Link Navi System. Alternatively, players could also imbue MegaMan.EXE with the powers of other NetNavis via the Cross System. These chips carried a small amount of EEPROM that held data representing that NetNavi's level. They could be leveled up and enhanced using the Link PET_EX, a *Battle Network* inspired electronic toy also manufactured by Takara.

Unfortunately, only the Japanese version of the sixth *Battle Network* game supported the Beast Link Gate, as the accessory was exclusively sold in that country. At this time, the popularity of the Chip Gates was waning in the West, so other versions disabled or removed portions of the game related to the Beast Link Gate. It is still possible to enjoy some of the extras activated by the hardware, such as the infinite BeastOut mode, but only when using a hacked version of *Battle Network 6* or an emulator.

One other *Mega Man* game managed to support the original Battle Chip Gate, even though it was from a completely different sub-series. *Mega Man Zero 3* unlocked four different minigames when select Battle Chips were inserted at the main start screen. Using Battle Chips with an odd number ID unlocked Phantom's minigame, while even number IDs unlocked Harpuia's minigame. Fenrir and Leviathan's minigames required the RedSun and BlueMoon Battle Chips respectively. Although there were other ways to unlock these minigames, using the Battle Chips was typically a faster, easier shortcut.

Despite having three distinct models, each Chip Gate operated in very much the same fashion on a technical level. Every Chip Gate began in a "standby" mode where it waited for a start signal from the Game Boy Advance. In this standby mode, the Chip Gate responded to any transfer with its 16-bit ID. These IDs allowed the games to determine which model was currently in use. The ID therefore prevented an incorrect model from communicating with an incompatible *Battle Network* game. After the software determined what kind of Chip Gate was connected, it sent the start signal, a series of transfers that commanded the Chip Gate to begin processing Battle Chips.

From this point, the Chip Gate would continually send a packet of data that contained the Battle Chip ID of anything inserted in its slot. If this value returned zero, nothing was currently inside the

Chip Gate, however, a non-zero value indicated that a Battle Chip was present. By monitoring these changes, the video games could detect when players were using physical Battle Chips and which ones they had specifically chosen.

Each Battle Chip had a set of exposed metal contacts similar to those seen on SD cards or game cartridges. Although the individual pins were visible from the outside, underneath the plastic covering some were connected to each other. Depending on which pins were linked, a different circuit was created once inserted into a Chip Gate. That information then determined the ID of the Battle Chip and was passed along to the Game Boy Advance. It proved a simple and effective solution that quickly converted the physical attributes of a Battle Chip into a digit.

The Battle Chip Gates all had Link Cable ports of their own. Many Game Boy Advance accessories that attached to the Link Cable port did not permit multiplayer gameplay while using the device, however, the Chip Gates were an exception. With the inclusion of an additional port in the Chip Gate itself, players could battle friends in one-on-one matches using real Battle Chips.

Capcom and Takara saw a lot of success with the Chip Gates and their related products. Not only did the Game Boy Advance hardware see support across five *Mega Man* titles, the Battle Chips were used in various electronic toys and even found their way into an arcade game: *Rockman EXE Battle Chip Stadium*. For the Game Boy, it was rare to have third-party companies back such peripherals over several years and revisions. The Chip Gates, therefore, stand against a common trend in the industry where such efforts quickly and quietly disappeared from the market.

Today the Chip Gates have seen a resurgence in popularity along with the *Battle Network* franchise as a whole. With the vast array of Battle Chips available, they've become something for fans to collect. They leave a legacy that shows just how close video games can bring players into another world. The Chip Gates were eventually succeeded by the Wave Scanner on the Nintendo DS, which used cards instead of chips, although the key ideas behind both remained the same. The Chip Gates paved a path of heightened interactivity that few games to this day have replicated.

A selection of Battle Chips for the original Battle Chip Gate

Battle Chips for the Beast Link Gate

The original Battle Chip Gate

The Progress Chip Gate

The Beast Link Gate

Battle Chip Gate with a Battle Chip inserted

In *Mega Man Battle Network 4*, the Battle Chip Gate unlocked Operation Battles. Players used different Navis from the game.

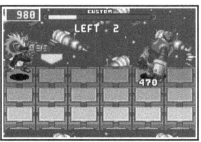

Fights were semi-auto. As the Custom Gauge filled up, players could slot in real-life Battle Chips for attacks.

*Rockman EXE 4.5* took Operation Battles further in its own spin-off, complete with an overworld.

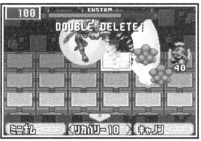

Battling in *4.5* was improved. The Navi was still semi-auto, but some attacks were available even without using the Chip Gate.

The built-in Link Cable port allowed multiplayer matches too.

Not to be left out, *Mega Man Zero 3* let the Battle Chip Gate unlock special minigames.

The minigames could be unlocked by other, more difficult means, so the Battle Chip Gate acted as a welcome shortcut.

Operation Battles returned in *Mega Man Battle Network 5*. It now used the same system from *4.5*.

*Rockman EXE 6* gave players complete control of the Navi when using the Beast Link Gate. It also made them vastly overpowered!

The Beast Link Gate also let players swap characters out or fuse with them.

**Release Dates:**

| | |
|---|---|
| AGB-015 | January 29, 2004 |
| OXY-004 | September 13, 2005 |

**Maker:**

Nintendo

**Legacy:**

Nintendo's first attempt at local radio-based multiplayer. Laid the foundations for future wireless communications. Established precursors to both the DS Download Station and Nintendo Zone.

The Game Boy Advance brought many changes to its multiplayer setup. Simultaneous 4-player games became common, with more supported titles than the DMG-07 on the original Game Boy ever mustered. Transmission was faster, supplying more data per-second than any other previous Nintendo handheld. It also offered a variety of different modes, letting the Game Boy Advance communicate as it saw fit with other Game Boys, GameCubes, and even non-gaming devices. Despite all of these newfound advantages, the Game Boy Advance was still restricted in one important regard: it relied on cables in a world that was increasingly cutting the cord.

The future was wireless. As forward-looking as the Game Boy Advance had been in 2001, it found itself behind the times as the years progressed. Thanks to its Link Cable port however, the system could expand its capabilities near endlessly by simply inserting an accessory. To untether the Game Boy Advance, Nintendo presented the AGB-015 as its solution. Officially known as the Game Boy Advance Wireless Adapter, this add-on granted the console over-the-air communications. When attached, players could send and receive data from nearby friends, all at a distance and without cables. Initially, Wireless Adapters were bundled with copies of *Pokémon Fire Red* and *Leaf Green*, the first games to feature the latest peripheral. Eventually, over 40 games would support it, a decent amount considering how late into the handheld's lifespan it was introduced. A separate version under the code OXY-004 was produced specifically for the Game Boy Micro due to the different shape and style of its Link Cable port.

The Wireless Adapter used radiowaves for transmission and came with a 2.4GHz ISM band transceiver. It allowed up to five players to participate in a single multiplayer session. Its optimal range was somewhere around three meters, however, some intrepid gamers have reported it working to some extent at 70 meters. Games could use Single-Pak and Multi-Pak modes through the adapter as well. All participants needed the Wireless Adapter, but players without cartridges could still download the necessary data from the host. When a Game Boy Advance with no cartridge started up with the Wireless Adapter plugged in, the peripheral provided a MultiBoot app that would then launch. This program showed players a menu, listing the names of any games hosted nearby that the adapter could detect. Once a game was selected, those players could join in as clients, and the rest of the multiplayer data was downloaded.

While games were only designed with five players at most (one host and four clients) for ordinary multiplayer scenarios, some games found other ways to increase the player count. *Pokémon Fire Red* and *Leaf Green* had a dedicated "Union Room" made especially for the Wireless Adapter. It acted as a sort of virtual lobby where up to 39 Pokémon Trainers could meet, engage in limited chat, trade monsters, and battle them head-to-head. This marked the largest local multiplayer mode of a Nintendo system at the time. It easily beat the Pokémon Mini's maximum six players via infrared or *Chousoku Spinner*'s 10 players via the HuC-1. Across other handhelds, it was only challenged by the Neo Geo Pocket Color's Wireless Communication Unit's 64 players.

Less than two months after its launch, the Game Boy Advance Wireless Adapter brought along a new service from Nintendo. On March 25, 2004, the company debuted JoySpot, a special digital data distribution system available in select Japanese stores. Somewhere on the premises, a Game Boy Advance fitted with a specially programmed game cartridge and a Wireless Adapter would constantly operate from within a box. The entire terminal, known as the JSP-001, would offer players unique opportunities if they entered the store with their own Game Boy Advance and adapter.

For the *Pokémon* games, players could test their skills in "Pokémon Challenge Battles". Here, Trainers entered any Pokémon at Level 30 or lower. The JoySpot service would then match them with a virtual opponent of a comparable level. The system ranked the top 20 players, even displaying their names on a public monitor for others to see. The JoySpot also served Mystery Gifts to visitors. As additional games began to support the Wireless Adapter, content through the JoySpot was updated. For *Mario Golf: Advance Tour*, players could obtain 16 different types of SP clubs. *Hamtaro: Ham Ham Games* gave exclusive friend cards. The second and third *Boktai* games used JoySpot to level up Blind Boxes, thus giving players better items. Perhaps most curious of all, however, was *Sennen Kazoku*, which used JoySpot for a "God Recommended Marriage Partner Introduction Service", i.e. matchmaking based on what other players had been there before.

Nintendo's JoySpot only lasted a little over a year. It was shutdown on July 8, 2005. By the time the Game Boy Micro and its version of the Wireless Adapter retailed, the JoySpot experience was finished. This fascinating service was effectively the precursor to DS Download Stations and the Nintendo Zone, which echoed many of the same ideas but on a larger scale and execution. While its short duration may suggest it was either unpopular or experimental, the truth may be that Nintendo simply switched focus to their next generation handheld, the DS. Despite the company's claims of treating the dual-screen console and its predecessor as equals, it quickly became evident in the mid-2000s which one would dominate the future.

The Wireless Adapter was unfortunately not backwards compatible with other Game Boy Advance titles. Communication required software to follow a special protocol, so older games were essentially prohibited from using the adapter. To access the Wireless Adapter, a game had to first reset the device, using the Link Cable's General Purpose mode and manually controlling a few brief signals on the serial port's pins. Afterwards, the Game Boy Advance and adapter would transfer data back and forth in 32-bit chunks. Software had to follow a "login process" with the adapter, sending the word "NINTENDO" and waiting for an inverted response.

Once the login was complete, the software could issue commands to the adapter along with a number of parameters for them. Ordinarily, games began by creating a session with the Wireless Adapter, then they would broadcast basic information such as the room name for multiplayer. During the in-game setup, the software often asked players to either act as the host or client. When choosing to be the host, players typed in an 8-character name for their group. This allowed multiple Wireless Adapters to run at the same time in close proximity, but the unique names helped friends choose the right host. Wireless Adapter compatible software was also expected to send a few configuration settings to the device, but afterwards they could finally open a multiplayer session.

The host constantly pinged for clients once a room was created. Likewise, clients continually searched for available rooms and tried to connect to the host. Once all sides had established contact and the host agreed to begin, the games exchanged data related to their own multiplayer programming. During this time, the host and client Wireless Adapters would transmit 32-bit values accordingly, almost as if they were physically linked together. Once the multiplayer game was finished, all sides could quit the current session and join other rooms if they wanted to.

Although the Wireless Adapter was quite advanced when it came out, several factors were stacked against its success on the market. The primary issue was that games had to be built to specifically utilize the device rather than having the adapter serve as a drop-in wireless fix. It did not work with previous games. For new titles choosing to include multiplayer, they would need different code to handle not only this adapter, but also existing Link Cables widely used by most players. Care had to be taken when programming multiplayer modes around the Wireless Adapter to avoid latency problems with transmissions or extra timing concerns due to the protocol itself. In addition to putting more work on developers, the Wireless Adapter was also a late arrival. General interest from both gamers and those in the industry gradually shrank a year later as the DS came along with built-in wireless hardware.

Nintendo could have possibly made hardware that translated standard Link Cable transmissions into wireless signals. Third-party efforts such as Majesco's Wireless Link were sold for the Game Boy Advance. However, there may have been technical difficulties in that route. While Majesco's product did indeed work quite well in a number of cases, it wasn't 100% compatible. Nintendo might have felt such a device would not be acceptable without a higher degree of reliability. One way to guarantee that reliability was to make new hardware with its own communication methods. New software would have to be tested by the developer and ultimately approved by Nintendo themselves, thus enabling a consistent level of quality. This path ensured upcoming games ran smoothly but at the cost of backward compatibility and a comprehensive list of supported titles.

Nevertheless, the Wireless Adapter set Nintendo on the road to better things. When it came out, the Wireless Adapter represented Nintendo's most ambitious push for cord-free multiplayer since the Mobile Adapter GB. By the time consumers finally got their hands on the DS, wireless multiplayer was the default. In every subsequent handheld from the company, wireless communication would be ubiquitous. It even reached a point where Nintendo's handhelds and home consoles could talk to each other under certain conditions, such as games that promoted Wii-to-DS or Wii U-to-3DS connectivity. Their work on the JoySpot emphasized their vision for other local and globally networked features and services such as StreetPass and SpotPass much later. It may be easy to forget the Wireless Adapter due to the sparse amount of available software, but its role in ushering Nintendo's next wave of communication is something to remember.

The wireless adapter attached to a Game Boy Advance

The AGB-015 was designed for the original Game Boy Advance and Game Boy Advance SP models. Like other accessories such as the Infrared Adapter, Battle Chip Gates, and GameCube-to-GBA Cable, it came with hooks that allowed it to latch into two slots at the top of the handheld.

The OXY-004, on the other hand, was designed exclusively for the Game Boy Micro and had no such hooks. Instead, it fit in snugly and securely, almost like a small cartridge. As with many of the Micro's peripherals, the OXY-004 is somewhat rare and difficult to find.

AGB-015 Front

AGB-015 Back

In Japan, a special red and white Famicom edition of the AGB-015 was released. It was rather uncommon for Game Boy accessories to have such variants, although Nintendo had previously done so for the Game Boy Camera and Game Boy Printer.

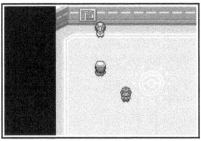

The Union Room in *Pokémon Fire Red* and *Leaf Green* allowed numerous players to mix and mingle wirelessly.

Available games were hosted as "rooms" that others nearby could join in.

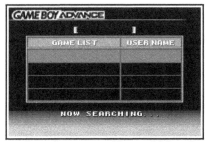

The adapter itself would load software onto the Game Boy that could search for players hosting sessions.

Despite being wireless, gamers often had to maintain a relatively close distance to avoid communication errors.

The wireless mode was separate and distinct from the Link Cable.

**Release Date:**
July 29, 2004

**Maker:**
Bandai

**Legacy:**
Most expansive and ambitious toys-to-life effort of the 6th Generation. Introduced electronic components into its figurines.

277

The Game Boy Advance hosted not one, but two separate toys-to-life franchises. Each had their own hardware dedicated to reading specially crafted figurines and translating them into usable game data. Although it was not the first company to target this particular market, Bandai improved and perfected the formula with its *Legendz* games. In this fictional world, Legendz were powerful creatures trapped inside hexagonal crystal-like structures known as "Soul Dollz". To awaken them, players had to use a wide range of tools such as a Talispod, a Talisdam, or the Soul Doll Adapter.

Each Soul Doll figurine could be plugged into one of these aforementioned devices. The Soul Doll Adapter was designed exclusively for the Game Boy Advance games and allowed various Legendz to participate directly in battle. Talispods and Talisdams were sold as individual electronic accessories. They had a small LCD screen along with several buttons. After inserting a Soul Doll, the character appeared as a small monochrome sprite, and different activities could raise their level and strength. Talispods had a slot for only one Soul Doll, while the Talisdams had a total of three slots and allowed a sort of fusion of Legendz when putting together certain combinations.

Two compatible titles were released for the Soul Doll Adapter – *Legendz: Yomigaeru Shiren no Shima* and *Legendz: Sign of Necrom*. Each was a typical turn-based RPG, however, all of the fighting was handled by the player's team of Legendz. To add one to the current party, the Soul Doll had to first be "reborn". For this initialization process, the Soul Doll Adapter attached to the Game Boy Advance via the Link Cable. Afterwards, the software communicated with the Soul Doll Adapter and read any information stored inside the figurine, such as the nickname of the Legendz, its current level, its stats, and its current owner. On the Game Boy Advance, only one person could register their name to the Soul Doll at a time. The games offered the option to erase any user data for a fresh start, however.

There was no method of obtaining new Legendz in either game without using the Soul Doll Adapter. In fact, the hardware was required to play at all, as both story modes mandated the "Doll Initialization" of a specific Soul Doll near the beginning. The games waited indefinitely until the Soul Doll Adapter read the data for "Hexadragon". Fortunately, the *Legendz* games were sold as starter sets, featuring larger than normal boxes that included the adapter and Hexadragon. To expand the team, the player had to buy more Soul

Dollz separately. These often came in sets of three, but a handful were sold by themselves as part of DVDs or through gachapons.

Bandai made a grand total of 103 Soul Dollz by the time they released *Sign of Necrom. Yomigaeru Shiren no Shima* sold before some of the later Soul Dollz were created, so a few incompatibilities existed, and the game would not recognize the newer set. *Sign of Necrom*, however supported them all. Some Soul Dollz were considered important to the larger plot in the *Legendz* games and could not be added to the team, although they still made a brief appearance when the player tried to initialize them. Bandai created a number of variant Soul Dollz as well, and the games sometimes changed or enhanced their base stats when initializing them.

Perhaps one of the more interesting aspects of the Soul Doll Adapter was how it interacted with real-time clocks present in game cartridges. Each *Legendz* game came equipped with a battery-powered crystal oscillator used by the Game Boy Advance to keep track of time even when the system itself was turned off. Players could send their Legendz on an "Auto Adventure" where the creature could train on its own when the game shut down. The Soul Doll for that Legend was placed in the adapter, and then the software recorded the start time of their adventure.

Once a certain amount of minutes had passed, the journey ended and the same Soul Doll had to be placed back in the adapter. After reading data within the Legendz, the game displayed a few cutscenes describing all that had happened while the player was away. The Legendz then received experience points and possibly learned new abilities. Although the Soul Doll simply acted as a physical key that unlocked this feature, it offered a creative way for gamers to get the most out of their figurines even when not actively playing.

The Soul Doll Adapter had a handful of other features as well. Legendz could temporarily hold objects from the inventory. Although only a single type of item could be selected, the Soul Dollz would save up to nine duplicates. The Legendz also recorded brief 16-character messages that players could change at any time. Additionally, the Soul Doll Adapter was responsible for frequently updating the combat abilities of a Legend, such as their stamina, physical strength, and defense. The player could remove a Legend from their roster in the games but completely restore them later using the Soul Doll and the details stowed within.

Each Soul Doll possessed a small amount of memory which the Game Boy Advance accessed through the Soul Doll Adapter.

Tucked inside the black portion of the figure's base was a 1KB EEPROM controller, a chip that contained data for the Legendz and allowed software to read from or write to its contents. The Game Boy Advance communicated directly with the Soul Doll Adapter and sent serial commands that set the memory address to look up and the data to transfer to or from EEPROM.

Only the last 256 bytes of the Soul Doll's EEPROM data was used by the video games. The remaining sections may have been reserved for the Talispod and Talisdam toys. These areas presumably would have had information such as the preferred humidity and temperature of the Legendz as well as other types of attributes. The Game Boy Advance titles, however, used the final section to hold the nickname of the Legendz, their owner's name, various flags related to the "Auto Adventure", and an ID number.

This ID number determined what creature the Legend would become during initialization. Although every byte of EEPROM was writable, the games weren't supposed to change the ID at all. As such, the ID set at the time of manufacturing was never touched, and players did not have to worry about suddenly getting different Legendz than the ones they purchased. However, it was still possible for homebrew software to arbitrarily alter the value. With some hacking, a single Soul Doll could be transformed into any of the others.

Despite spanning several video games and running a manga and anime series, the *Legendz* franchise was short-lived. By 2005, it had run its course, having released all of its software and hardware and finished its multimedia presence. Bandai would not revisit the world of *Legendz*, unfortunately. Nevertheless, it helped further establish one of the key elements behind the toys-to-life genre in gaming: the ability to store and transport user data.

The Soul Doll Adapter and its various Legendz were well ahead of their time, appearing nearly a decade before Nintendo's Amiibos for instance. In many regards, the adapter itself mirrored the Portal of Power from *Skylanders*, albeit on a much smaller scale. *Legendz* was not the first attempt to merge toys and video games on the Game Boy, but it did create an experience that closest resembles what people today expect when bringing toys into the digital realm. Even in its obscurity, the Soul Doll Adapter paved the way for future endeavors, offering a prime example for others to replicate.

The Soul Doll Adapter

A collection of Soul Dollz

Soul Dollz contained information such as their current level, nickname, and owner.

During the "rebirth" process, the Legendz would introduce themselves, giving insight on their personalities.

Battles were one-versus-one turn-based affairs.

Using the Auto-Adventure mode, Legendz could level up when the game was turned off.

A player could have various Legendz on their current team.

**Release Date:**
July 30, 2004

**Maker:**
Digital Act

**Legacy:**
Brought video-based phone calls to the Game Boy. Only the second time the Game Boy was officially involved in telephony, and the only official instance of simultaneous audio and video capture on the Game Boy.

In modern times, the age of smartphones has made video-based communication an almost trivial phenomenon. Nearly everyone carries with them a technologically advanced device capable of connecting to others at great distances. People all across the globe can easily see and hear each other in real-time. While this fantastic development is common today, in the past it was a concept that seemed quite far from being realized. The progress cellphones and computers made towards videoconferencing was slow yet gradual. Nevertheless, the Game Boy Advance managed to play a role during this challenging period.

Around the middle of September 2003, the Japanese company Digital Act announced a brand new product in the works. Known as the Campho Advance – short for Camera Phone Advance – it was envisioned as hardware that would allow the Game Boy Advance to act as a standard phone enhanced with video transmission. The peripheral, an oversized game cartridge, featured a front-facing camera to capture the user. On the side, it had a slot to accept a phone jack as well as a port to accept a microphone headset. Using the Campho Advance, the Game Boy could execute video-calls over an ordinary landline connection.

Initial advertising showed the Campho Advance in a silver color scheme with an estimated cost of 13,000 yen. Some 10 months later, Digital Act would finally begin selling the unit. Now the Campho Advance came in a red cartridge, and the price had risen to 19,000 yen. Upon launch, the company declared that only 10,000 Campho Advances had been made. This small opening, perhaps meant to test the waters, was further limited by another factor. To purchase the hardware, users had to buy it directly from Digital Act. Orders were only accepted via mail from a form printed off of their website. Anecdotal evidence suggests a small number of Campho Advances may have found their way onto wider markets. In any case, the product itself was rather expensive and elusive.

At 110,000 pixels, the camera's resolution provided decent and serviceable image quality. During calls, the user's face was pictured on-screen alongside the other party. It operated at a rate of five frames per second, however, it may have updated at a slower rate depending on the conditions of the telephone line. The Campho Advance aimed to simplify the process of setting up a video-call. Thanks to using the Game Boy Advance as the base, all the user had to do was plug everything in and turn it on. The software on the Campho Advance had clear, easy to follow menus and proved relatively straightforward. Although it used telephone lines to deliver audio and video, the Campho Advance did not work with faster, more advanced means of communication. The likes of ASDL, ISDN, and broadband internet were incompatible with its design. In 2003, Digital Act spoke of supporting broadband at first, but the final product had no such function.

The Campho Advance's package came filled with a variety of essentials. First and foremost, the box held a phoneline cable as well as a line-splitter. With the latter item, users could keep their existing phone plugged in and ready to use while the Game Boy and Campho Advance could be hooked up whenever necessary. As mentioned before, the Campho Advance used a headset with a microphone for voice input, and one was included by default.

Perhaps most interesting, however, was the power supply. Because of the energy demands of the Campho Advance, the Game Boy did not provide enough electricity for it to run. Instead, the Campho Advance needed external power. It had a slot to accept a regular AC adapter for the Game Boy Advance SP, known as the AGS-002. Thankfully, Digital Act bundled their own adapter, a rather unique one colored red just like the Campho Advance. Curiously enough, the Campho Advance was incompatible with both the original Nintendo DS and the DS Lite; each system failed to boot even with the power supply attached. To be fair, Digital Act produced the Campho Advance long before Nintendo's newer handhelds reached retail.

Although rather basic, the Campho Advance's software offered a number of adjustable options. Users could input contact data for other people with entries for their name and phone number. A dialer was present as well; here, a 10-digit number was entered, and the Campho Advance then initiated a call. The peripheral could receive and answer incoming calls as well. The software had several settings for the camera, such as the brightness of the picture or flipping the image. Both the speaker and microphone volumes were configurable. Additionally, users could specify whether to use pulse or tone dialing for their phoneline.

To be clear, the Campho Advance was a marvelous triumph for Game Boy hardware, demonstrating once again that Nintendo's handheld could extend itself anywhere given the right engineering. However, the Campho Advance was not exactly a runaway success. It gained little popularity and to date its known sales numbers are exceedingly small. Several reasons conceivably explain its lackluster adoption among consumers. First, it was not a small investment to make for the unit alone, along with a Game Boy Advance if necessary. On top of that, the Campho Advance was not widely distributed, being rather cumbersome to order compared to other products. Having only a few thousand units on hand meant stock was very limited from the start as well. Another mark against the Campho Advance was its immobility. While the Game Boy is famous for being a portable device, in this case it remained uncharacteristically stationary hooked up to power supply and landline cables.

The biggest challenges to the Campho Advance came from the evolving cellphone market of Japan. New phones were constantly pushed out with better specifications and access to faster wireless networks. By the time the Campho Advance arrived, it was only barely superior to the Kyocera VP-210, the first notable videophone publicly available and five years old at the time. Both had the same resolution in regards to the camera, but the Campho Advance generally had a faster framerate. Even so, it wouldn't take much for others to quickly surpass this performance. More pointedly, the Campho Advance lacked the ability to roam with its users, making cellphones a more attractive proposition. Needless to say, the Campho Advance was shortly outdated.

Despite not having made a significant dent in the market, the Campho Advance was at the time a wonderfully futuristic device, representing the technology of tomorrow. This vision wasn't necessarily wrong, as nearly every pocket today carries the tools to make video chats on demand. Digital Act erred only in using the Game Boy Advance as their platform of choice. While the handheld was great at gaming and providing an intuitive interface, it just couldn't overcome the dominance of new cellphones. That does not, however, diminish the Campho Advance's achievements. Although a handful of third-party unlicensed cartridges used built-in phone jacks for internet connectivity on the original Game Boy, none used them for phone calls or even two-way video transmission. The Campho Advance was also the only officially licensed camera for the Game Boy Advance and the second ever licensed camera for the entire Game Boy family. Besides the Pocket Sonar, no other cartridge competed against the Campho Advance's power consumption. In comparison to its peers, the Campho Advance certainly deserves recognition.

Campho Box Front

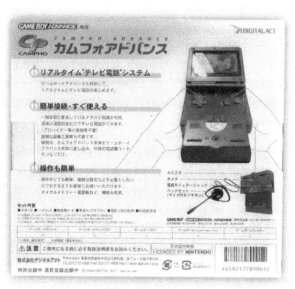

Campho Box Back

Like many Game Boy and Game Boy Advance accessories, the Campho Advance came in a larger than normal box. It was one of the few peripherals that had nothing to do with media playback or gaming.

Inside the Campho Advance box

To get users up and running immediately after purchase, the Campho Advance came packaged with a wide range of materials. These included: a headset, a splitter for a phone cable, an actual phone cable, a power adapter, and the Campho Advance itself.

Having such an extensive amount of items come as part of the package made the Campho Advance accessible and relatively easy to handle. Installation involved simply hooking up the power and phone cables, putting the cartridge in the Game Boy, and turning it on.

The Campho Advance

Campho Advance seated in an AGB-001

The original Game Boy Advance lacked any sort of screen lighting; as a result it was not ideal for the Campho Advance. An AGS-001 or AGS-101 were better choices. Neither the DS or DS Lite were compatible with the Campho Advance however.

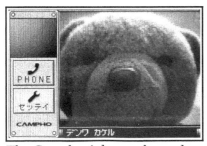

The Campho Advance booted up to this default screen.

Its software offered several configurable options such as volume controls.

Some of the options even manipulated how the camera worked, such as brightness options depending on the user's environment.

The Campho Advance could directly call other phones. The software allowed users to enter names and numbers.

It supported sending and receiving calls just like any regular phone.

**Release Date:**
> October 14, 2004

**Maker:**
> Nintendo

**Legacy:**
> Improved motion control technology compared to previous iterations and provided Nintendo with their first major "hit" game associated with this emerging control scheme.

291

Towards the middle of the 2000s, Nintendo continued dabbling with motion controls. The technology had yet to reach their home consoles, remaining absent on the GameCube despite earlier plans to do so via linking the Game Boy Advance. Instead, their experiments were limited to handheld platforms. While games such as *Kirby Tilt 'n' Tumble* generally received favorable reviews worldwide, subsequent motion control games like *Command Master* and *Koro Koro Puzzle Happy Panechu!* were released exclusively in Japan with far less fanfare. Nintendo's first efforts at motion controls were genuinely innovative, yet they lacked a "killer app" that would sell the overall idea to consumers.

The situation changed, however, when the company launched *WarioWare: Twisted!* in late 2004. As part of Wario's new franchise, the game revolved around simplistic "microgames" that lasted only a few seconds. The player had to complete the goal shown on-screen or lose the microgame. A series of these microgames were played back-to-back rapidly, increasing in tempo on later stages. Losing a total of four microgames resulted in a Game Over, forcing players to restart. After a set amount of microgames had been completed, a Boss microgame began. While these concepts were largely the same from the previous *WarioWare* title, Nintendo added a completely new dimension to its gameplay. Rather than use the control pad at all, directional input was replaced with specialized motion control hardware.

*Twisted!* packed a piezoelectric ceramic gyroscope developed by NEC TOKIN, embedding it inside the cartridge. This component, known as the CG-L43F, measured rotational angular velocity. It is not to be confused with the MBC7 mapper or Game Boy Advance Tilt Cartridges, which used completely different electronics. A key distinction between those accelerometers and the gyroscope in *Twisted!* was the direction their sensors detected. The CG-L43F worked along the Z-axis, reporting changes when the Game Boy Advance rotated like a steering wheel. The accelerometers, on the other hand, reported changes in the X and Y-axes when the Game Boy Advance tilted left, right, forward, and back.

The new hardware proved much more accurate than the older accelerometers, giving *Twisted!* a wide range of fine analog input. Various microgames took explicit advantage of this capability, with some requiring quick and wild spins, and others requiring slow, deliberate movements. *Twisted!* also reintroduced force-feedback on the Game Boy Advance. Similar to the MBC5 Rumble Cartridges, a small vibrating motor was attached to the PCB. At various times, the motor would activate during microgames. It marked the return of rumble after years of absence following its debut on the Game Boy Color. *Twisted!* was one of only two titles on the Game Boy Advance that ever featured such haptic cartridges, making it a truly unique game among the system's library.

Like a few other cartridges with additional hardware on the Game Boy Advance, *Twisted!* used the General Purpose Input/Output interface. By writing to select memory addresses normally dedicated to the cartridge's ROM, the game's software could send and receive information related to the gyroscope and operate the rumble functionality. The rotation data came in the form of a 12-bit value, the result of a process called analog-to-digital conversion, or ADC. Once the software signaled to the hardware to begin this conversion, the gyroscope eventually returned its data serially, one bit at a time.

After collecting all 12-bits, the software then knew how fast the Game Boy Advance was moving and the direction of any motion. The hardware specified a median value representing zero movement at all. Values higher than the median denoted clockwise rotation, while values lower than the median denoted counter-clockwise rotation. By calculating how far these values were from the median, the game also determined the player's speed. As such, it was possible to distinguish between minor turns and intense spinning. *Twisted!*'s rumble was handled by a single bit on the General Purpose Input/Output interface. Setting that bit to "1" turned the motor on, while flipping it to "0" turned the motor off.

As far as cartridges go on the Game Boy Advance, *Twisted!* was very much something of an oddity, physically speaking. It was the fifth largest cartridge of its era, only coming up short when compared to the Campho Advance, Music Recorder, GlucoBoy, and Nintendo's e-Reader. This is particularly noteworthy given that cartridges shrank once the Game Boy Advance was released, and making oversized ones was generally avoided during this time. Regardless, Nintendo broke this convention in order to improve their motion controls. Most of the space inside of *Twisted!*'s cartridge – the giant hump – held up the gyroscope, with some area left over to tuck in the rumble's motor. Additionally, it was one of the rare titles that came in non-standard colors as well: white in Japan and clear overseas. In all respects, no other cartridge quite looked like it.

In contrast with their previous attempts at motion controls, Nintendo gained critical acclaim from *Twisted!* The method of input was rather basic in concept, but the clever design and short length of each microgame made the overall experience fresh and inviting. Until *Twisted!* arrived on the scene, Nintendo had yet to really land a hit with these types of games. It did suffer some criticism, namely that the screen could be hard to see at times when moving the Game Boy Advance, a common issue with handheld motion titles. Nevertheless, *Twisted!* demonstrated that there was indeed a willing market for these types of games, so long as the control scheme was fun and the gameplay itself was carefully thought out and implemented.

Even as *Twisted!* garnered much praise for Nintendo, the future of motion-based gaming would temporarily leave the company's handhelds for their next home console, the Wii. After the last Game Boy Advance Tilt Cartridge arrived in December 2004, Nintendo abandoned this type of control for the duration of the DS and DSi's lifetime. Rather than motion, the focus shifted to touchscreen technology and how games could best exploit a secondary screen. While third-party solutions such as Activision's Motion Pack would partially fill the gap, motion controls wouldn't seriously return in handheld form until the 3DS launched with a built-in gyroscope of its own. Ultimately, gyroscopes would find their way onto the Switch, baked right into each Joy-Con.

Although Nintendo only released a small handful of motion control games on the Game Boy, this work prepared the gaming giant for one of their most ambitious and revolutionary products yet. In many ways, the MBC7 mapper and Game Boy Advance Tilt Cartridges were all small, preliminary steps taken to realize a larger goal. Arguably, game developers had not quite tapped into the full potential of motion mechanics, but with *Twisted!* Nintendo had finally found a winning formula and a path that could carry them on into the future. Thanks to the precision of the gyroscope and its brilliant if quirky gameplay, *Twisted!* served as a guide for the Wii, highlighting the value motion could add when done properly.

*WarioWare: Twisted!* Cartridge

*WarioWare: Twisted!* PCB

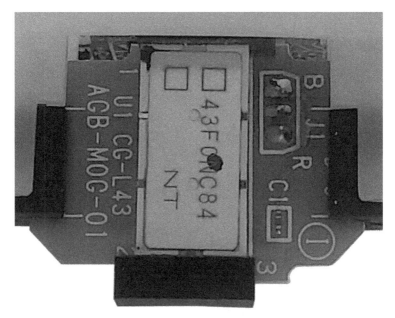

Close-up of the gyroscope

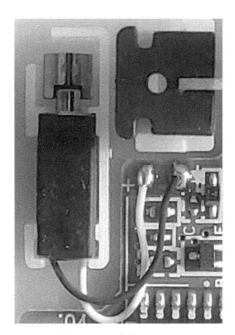

Close-up of the motor

The game avoided using the directional pad. Even menu navigation required spinning the Game Boy.

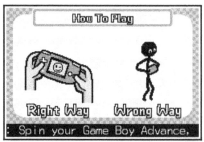

The gyroscope worked on the Z-axis, shifting the left and right ends of the system up or down.

The microgames were short and wacky, but they made good use of the motion hardware.

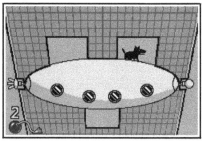

Some microgames utilized the gyroscope's precision, forcing players to move the Game Boy slowly.

The rumble feature could be turned on or off.

As the player progressed, the overall speed of the microgames intensified, making the action all the more frantic.

A few microgames actually didn't use motion controls. Some had players pressing the A Button at the correct time.

Boss stages were longer and slightly more complex than normal microgames.

Players had to complete a set number of microgames to advance. Failing four of them resulted in a Game Over.

Not everything was a microgame. Some fun extras had no goal or end.

**Release Dates:**

| | |
|---|---|
| Play-Yan | February 21, 2005 |
| Play-Yan Micro | September 13, 2005 |
| iQue MP4 | End of 2005 |
| Nintendo MP3 Player | December 8, 2006 |

**Maker:**

Nintendo

**Legacy:**

First and only time Nintendo produced a dedicated multimedia device for one of its consoles.

By the mid-2000s, the Game Boy Advance had already demonstrated it could serve as a platform for portable videos and mobile music. Kemco's Music Recorder allowed users to enjoy their MP3 collections on the go. With AM3's Advance Movie Adapter and Majesco's Game Boy Advance Video cartridges, there were several options that practically turned the console into a handheld TV. Unfortunately, consumers lacked a cohesive all-in-one package that covered both audio and video. Furthermore, AM3 and Majesco limited their products to commercial entertainment such as anime, cartoon shows, and feature films. Those with their own movies had no legitimate way to view them on the Game Boy Advance. While each company pushed the system into new territory, the console's multimedia revolution was still incomplete. Nintendo themselves, however, ultimately changed that with the release of the Play-Yan.

Otherwise known as the AGS-006, it was a specially designed cartridge capable of playing a range of different content. Like most Game Boy Advance cartridges with additional hardware, the Play-Yan came in an oversized plastic shell, one with several unique features. Foremost, it exposed a small slot on its side. Here users inserted a standard SD card containing the files they wanted to play. Additionally, the top of the Play-Yan had a small headphone jack. While the Play-Yan could use the Game Boy Advance or Nintendo DS' speakers, it could also output audio directly through the jack. This allowed the Play-Yan to bypass the hardware limitations of either system. For example, the headphones could play music in stereo as opposed to the mono audio of the Game Boy Advance. The overall fidelity of the sound would also vastly improve.

Perhaps most unexpectedly, the Play-Yan was not "compatible" with the original Game Boy Advance model that launched in 2001. Anything from the Game Boy Advance SP and onward, however, would do just fine. In truth, the Play-Yan worked on all Game Boy Advances, however, due to its power consumption, only newer ones were recommended. The Play-Yan supported several formats when it first arrived. For video, both the ASF and MP4 containers could be used, with MPEG-4 as the video codec, and G.726 and AAC as the audio codecs respectively. Videos could run at a maximum of 30 frames-per-second, more than enough for most standard definition material. For music, the Play-Yan supported MP3 files. The software could extract ID3 tags as well, presenting information such as the title and artist when playing. However, aside from displaying preview thumbnails for videos, the Play-Yan did not support static images such as JPEGs, GIFs, PNGs, or even BMPs. Depending on which system was used, the Play-Yan had a fairly impressive battery life, ranging from 4-5 hours with video and 16-20 hours with music.

The Play-Yan's ability to play audio and video of reasonable quality was not the result of software alone. Hardware inside the cartridge – an Alpha Mosaic VC01 – handled all of the decoding and acted as a multimedia coprocessor. Its job was to take pressure away from the CPU and free up computing resources. This approach differed greatly from the Advance Movie Adapter or the Game Boy Advance Videos, both of which used custom file formats that the Game Boy could natively parse without any additional components. The VC01 was the first in a long line of VideoCore products. Today, under the BroadCom company, newer versions of the VideoCore power devices such as the Raspberry Pi. As the VC01 did not deal with picture files, this perhaps explains the Play-Yan's inability to process them.

The VC01 relied on firmware supplied by the Play-Yan. When booting the cartridge, the software would manually upload default firmware from ROM. Later, if a firmware update file was found on the SD card, the newer version would be uploaded as well. The original Play-Yan, for example, was not able to play certain types of video until Nintendo issued an update. While it may seem odd that firmware needed to be uploaded each and every time the Play-Yan was turned on, this method ensured that the device was never permanently bricked by a bad update. Other Nintendo products, such as the Wii Speak, followed a similar philosophy of constantly loading firmware.

Audio and video were not the only things the Play-Yan initially offered. In its first iteration, the AGS-006 had a selection of 13 mini "Garage Games" that users could download as special ASF video files from Nintendo's website. By placing them on the SD card, the software would run these simple games. They all took place inside the small window normally dedicated to a video's thumbnail. In *Wave*, players were part of a human/stadium wave and timed their motions correctly. *Avoid* had players assume the role of a bat dodging projectiles from all directions. *Nekoroid* starred a cat rolling on the floor shooting lasers at incoming targets.

While all of the Garage Games may technically classify as downloadable content, in reality they were actually pre-programmed into the Play-Yan's ROM. The software specifically looked for certain

ASF files as a means of unlocking the games, but all the code, graphics, and sound were already stored on the cartridge. As the ASF files contained no executable code, this prevented the Play-Yan from becoming a potential hacking target. Historically, Nintendo had been very careful in this regard on the Game Boy, especially with downloadable content. It reflects how most of their handheld "DLC" up to this point, particularly on the Mobile Adapter GB, merely acted as keys to enable data locally available from ROM.

The first model of the Play-Yan was not sold in stores, rather customers had to order it directly through Nintendo. However, on September 11, 2005, the original Play-Yan was discontinued. In its place, the company introduced the Play-Yan Micro, an updated version that could play MP4 files out of the box. It was virtually identical to the previous Play-Yan with cosmetic changes to the software's interface. The Micro version removed the Garage Games, unfortunately. It launched on the same day as the Game Boy Micro did in Japan, becoming available online through various outlets. Curiously though, it never made its way into physical retail stores.

Towards the end of 2005, the Play-Yan Micro began selling in Chinese markets under the name iQue MP4. The only major known difference in the iQue branded version was the language translation. Nearly a year later on December 8, 2006, the Play-Yan would come to Europe with a name change of its own. Simply called Nintendo MP3 Player, it used different hardware than either previous Play-Yan. Here its features were strictly reduced to audio playback, eliminating ASF and MP4 support altogether. Aside from that, the interface remained the same as the Play-Yan Micro. Regrettably, no version of the Play-Yan ever came to North America.

A number of controls within the Play-Yan's software enabled it to function as a highly competent media player. For both audio and video, it could dynamically adjust the volume with the directional pad. In addition to pausing, users could skip forwards and backwards a few seconds at a time. The Play-Yan conveniently offered a bass boost effect to deepen certain tones within a song. It was also capable of artificially increasing surround sound. For video, it allowed several levels of brightness to get the best picture. The overall quality, however, ultimately depended on the encoding used in the files. Like most MP3 players, the Play-Yan could shuffle through songs randomly and loop through them. Included with each copy of the Play-Yan was a CD-ROM disk with the software "MediaStage 4.2 for

Nintendo". Its purpose was to convert videos into ASF files compatible with the Play-Yan.

Quite interestingly enough, the original Play-Yan's interface implemented a selectable light and dark mode, changing the color palette entirely to suit the user. This was a rather rare feature in 2005 for mobile devices, one that would only really take off a decade later. The Play-Yan split its interface into audio and video, simplifying the process of sorting out the user's media. It also took advantage of folders to organize music and sorted those files alphabetically. Unlike the Game Boy Advance Video cartridges, the Play-Yan was compatible with the Game Boy Player, letting users play media on their TVs. Although it was possible to do so, the Play-Yan remained constrained in terms of picture quality. Working with 240x160 compressed video had its limits after all.

The Play-Yan would only function properly when a formatted SD card was present in its slot. If no card had been inserted, the Play-Yan failed to boot completely. Instead, it would show the user a brief message explaining the problem. The software checked for any filesystem errors as well, as those prevented it from processing any files and folders. Furthermore, only certain SD cards were compatible with the Play-Yan. Typically, the Play-Yan could not recognize cards greater than 2GB in size, with some exceptions. In general, the maximum allowed size was 1GB. Even then, some cards from various manufacturers simply did not work. Thankfully at the time, Nintendo provided a thorough list of common cards that the hardware would or wouldn't accept. As SD cards continually grew in storage capacity, compatible cards became harder to come by.

Among Nintendo's many efforts to spread into new territory, the Play-Yan in particular stands out. It marked the first time the company sold a multimedia experience of this kind on any of their platforms. Nothing like it ever existed in Nintendo's product lineup before, and to this day they haven't made anything similar. With the Play-Yan, Nintendo not only directly acknowledged the Game Boy Advance's potential as a portable, personal media device, they moved to make that a reality. More significantly, it was the first time users could officially bring both their own songs and videos to the Game Boy rather than relying on just a handful of licensed offerings or homebrew solutions. In a period where dedicated players were often costly, the Play-Yan distinguished itself as a familiar and inexpensive way to get audio and video on the go.

The original Play-Yan

PCB of the original Play-Yan

Original Play-Yan Box Front

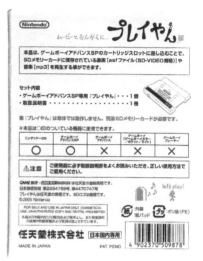

Original Play-Yan Box Back

MediaStage 4.2 PC software used to convert video files

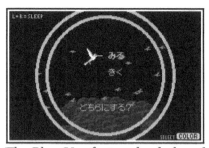

The Play-Yan featured a dark and light color scheme, long before "dark mode" became common in software interfaces.

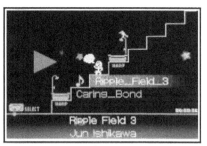

The music player presented tracks as different steps. It offered a number of quirky, playful animations.

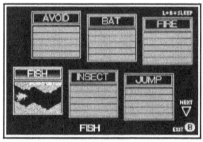

13 so-called "Garage Games" were available for download on the original Play-Yan. They were brief, simplistic minigames.

For the first time ever, Nintendo allowed users to upload their very own videos onto the Game Boy Advance.

The Play-Yan could also generate thumbnail previews for videos.

**Release Date:**
> September 9, 2005

**Maker:**
> Nintendo

**Legacy:**
> Nintendo's last Game Boy Advance cartridge with special hardware aimed at enhancing gameplay. Marked the end of force-feedback hardware built directly into cartridges.

In contrast with the Game Boy Color, the Game Boy Advance saw a huge decline in the overall number of specialized cartridges. Regarding rumble support, only two such games featured motorized force-feedback. The second entry came late in the handheld's lifetime, in the fall of 2005. *Drill Dozer* followed the adventures of Jill and her eponymous drilling machine. By spinning the drill forwards or backwards, players could defeat enemies and break through barriers. Taking full advantage of the hardware's rumble, *Drill Dozer* let players upgrade the drill with secondary and tertiary gears, ramping up vibrations the longer they were running.

The cartridge used in *Drill Dozer* was only slightly bigger than other ordinary ones on the Game Boy Advance. Inside it housed a small motor that shook periodically. It operated similarly to the older MBC5 Rumble Cartridges on the Game Boy Color. Like many Game Boy Advance cartridges with unique hardware built-in, *Drill Dozer* used the console's General Purpose Input/Output interface to control vibration. By simply writing a "1" or a "0" to a certain area of memory, the motor started or stopped. Once triggered, it would shake until disengaged. To create different levels of intensity, these ON/OFF transitions varied in length.

*Drill Dozer* represents the last time Nintendo's dedicated haptic hardware was included in the cartridge itself. A little more than a month later, *Metroid Pinball* introduced the world to the DS Rumble Pak, effectively beginning a new era of handheld rumble. With the advent of the Nintendo DS, game cartridges continued to grow smaller, making it less appealing for developers to cram extra hardware inside. After *Drill Dozer*, users needed to plug additional accessories into the console itself for rumble support, following the model established by the Nintendo 64. After rumble evolved into a Slot-2 add-on for the DS, it vanished altogether on the 3DS before ultimately becoming part of the Joy-Cons on the Switch today.

*Drill Dozer* marks the end of Nintendo's specialized Game Boy Advance cartridges designed to enhance gameplay in some form. It's also Nintendo's last known use of larger-than-normal cartridges housing such hardware. Although several oversized cartridges for the DS did exist – such as a TV tuner and an azimuth – they focused on areas unrelated to video games. *Drill Dozer* was an acclaimed game, and today its cartridge illustrates how Nintendo slowly integrated rumble as a key built-in component of their portable consoles.

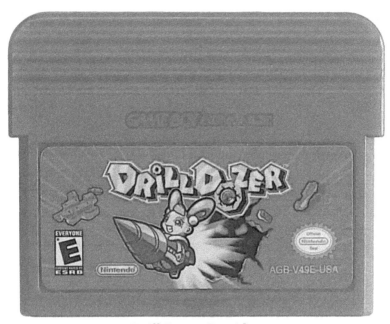

*Drill Dozer* Cartridge

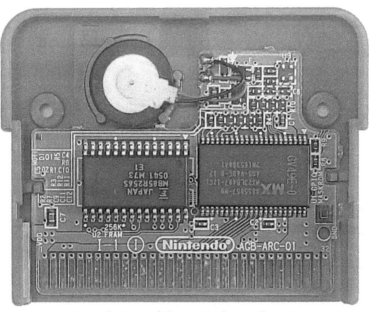

Internal view of the cartridge and motor

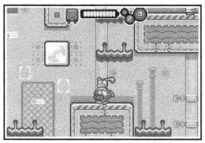

*Drill Dozer* had a number of interactive objects, such as this block that flung players when drilling in reverse.

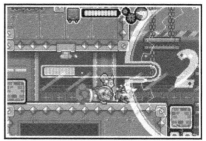

In addition to solving puzzles and overcoming obstacles, the drill could be used to defeat foes.

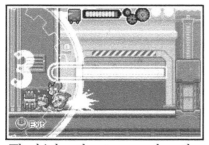

The higher the gear number, the faster the drill spun. All the while, the rumble increased in effect as well.

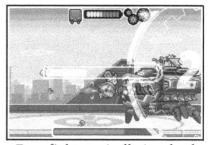

Boss fights typically involved lots of attacks, so the rumble cartridge made these matches even more intense.

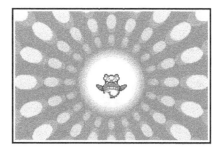

The game also rumbled to give animated sequences an extra punch.

**Release Date:**

November 14, 2007

**Maker:**

Guidance Interactive

**Legacy:**

First and only medical device officially allowed on any Game Boy handheld. Delivered a revolutionary new approach to tackling diabetes in children. Marked the end of all special Game Boy peripherals.

As this book has highlighted numerous times, throughout its history, the Game Boy became a vehicle for many things other than video games. Over the years, it was used as a general computing device with a simple interface and input system. The handheld would evolve into a platform capable of supporting various activities such as fishing, sewing, internet browsing, audiovisual playback, and even video telephony. One domain in particular, however, remained out of reach. Not until very late in the Game Boy Advance's lifetime did a peripheral emerge that finally took Nintendo into the medical field.

The GlucoBoy was first conceived of by Australian inventor Paul Wessel. Noting how his diabetic son would often carry his Game Boy around no matter where he went, Wessel became inspired to create a new product. He started designing a Game Boy cartridge that doubled as a blood testing tool. The goal was to help encourage those with juvenile diabetes to check themselves regularly. Not only would the GlucoBoy provide hardware to analyze blood glucose levels, it would offer games that rewarded children for performing the test. This brilliant combination of electronic entertainment and pediatric health was the first of its kind on the Game Boy.

Unfortunately it was initially a bit too unprecedented for Nintendo. The company refused to approve the GlucoBoy for some years. One problem was merely a lack of awareness regarding juvenile diabetes, a relatively rare disease in Japan. The other and perhaps larger issue was that of liability. Out of an abundance of concern, Nintendo likely balked at licensing any sort of medical device, fearing what might happen if it ever failed or malfunctioned. Improperly managing glucose levels can lead to severe medical complications, and Nintendo would have been keen to avoid any such trouble. Examples of Nintendo's extreme caution regarding health and safety are evident in the Virtual Boy's lack of head-mounting, the copious Wii Remote warnings found in many games, and the 3DS' reminders to take a 15 minute break during long play sessions, as well as age recommendations for the stereoscopic screen.

Nevertheless, Wessel kept pursuing the GlucoBoy, and eventually it was given Nintendo's blessings as an officially licensed product. After an abbreviated and somewhat rushed development period, it launched exclusively in Australia on World Diabetes Day, selling for approximately $300 AUD. Although it was an incredibly late entry to the Game Boy Advance library, it still managed to sell around 70,000 units. Thanks to the secondary cartridge slot on both the original DS and DS Lite, the GlucoBoy was compatible with the next generation of Nintendo handhelds while working with millions of Game Boys from the previous generation.

The GlucoBoy came as an oversized white cartridge. In the center sat an ovular LCD screen that displayed the current test results. The hardware was capable of detecting glucose levels as low as 1.1 mmol/L and as high as 29.2 mmol/L. In addition to this amount of precision, the GlucoBoy only required a small amount of blood for the test itself, a mere 0.6 uL. Also helpful was its ability to store the last 500 test results internally. Testing strips were inserted into a small opening at the very top of the GlucoBoy. Once stuck into the device, it began processing the blood sample relatively fast, taking about 10 seconds.

After a patient's blood had been tested, the results were read by the software and converted into "Glucose Reward Points", or GRPs. These points could then be spent in a variety of ways when playing the GlucoBoy's games. They could unlock minigames, for instance, or be treated as currency to buy certain items or power-ups. The amount of points given was dependent on several factors such as how consistently the patient tested, whether or not the test was performed timely, and whether the glucose level was within a satisfactory range. The reward's algorithm was carefully constructed to provide children with the incentive to test themselves regularly and maintain healthy levels of blood sugar.

Two main games were present on the GlucoBoy: *Lost Star Saga* and *Knock'em Downs*. The first was a traditional 2D turn-based RPG with a science fiction setting. Two selectable protagonists had to locate missing members of their starship crew, fighting hordes of enemies along the way. *Knock'em Downs*, on the other hand, was an action RPG with a somewhat light-hearted carnival theme. Players roamed the map completing various quests and fighting foes in real-time with weapons such as guns that fired teddy bears and jellybeans. Both games allowed players to spend their Glucose Reward Points on items that would help them progress through the story. Three minigames were unlockable via Glucose Reward Points as well. *Solar Wing* was a horizontal space shooter, *Plexus* was a *Breakout*-like game, and *Raccoon Rancher* was a puzzle game tasking players with separating raccoons with a controllable fence.

Although the GlucoBoy was eventually released after years of wrestling with Nintendo, its time on the market would be short-lived. As Guidance Interactive was preparing to launch the GlucoBoy internationally, the German pharmaceutical corporation Bayer purchased the smaller company. As they planned on making a newer version of the GlucoBoy for the DS, Bayer decided to destroy any unsold stock. Tragically, the GlucoBoy never saw a proper release outside of Australia, and the loss of their remaining wares limited its numbers to just the initial 70,000 sold during the product's brief year on shelves. Today, it stands as one of the rarest Game Boy peripherals, one in dire need of preservation.

The GlucoBoy was nevertheless a massive achievement for the Game Boy. It ingeniously combined the thrill of video games with daily blood monitoring to keep kids with Type 1 diabetes healthy. While health-based video games had existed for quite some time, their focus was almost entirely on exercise and fitness. The GlucoBoy, however, broke new ground by shifting its attention to a specific medical condition. Not only was this a first for Nintendo, it was something new for the whole industry. Most impressively was the fact that the GlucoBoy received a sequel device shortly after it was introduced. The Bayer Digit was marketed worldwide and thrived on the most successful handheld consoles of all time.

This revolutionary approach to tackling childhood diabetes sadly marked the genuine end of exotic peripherals for the Game Boy. For over 18 years, the Game Boy served as a proving ground for fresh and interesting hardware, an incubator for wild dreams and ideas. Thanks to Nintendo's constant delay of the GlucoBoy, the product would sell almost three years after the DS had been introduced. By this time, the Game Boy Advance was losing support among developers. Bayer acknowledged as much with the Bayer Digit. Many other companies were simply moving on. The same spirit of creativity would follow, however, leading to many more unique add-ons for the DS. With the mantle handed down to the next generation, the GlucoBoy was the last device representing the Game Boy's ability to innovate.

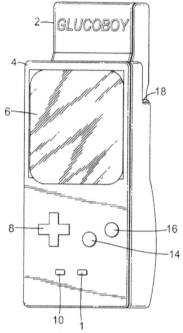

The GlucoBoy as envisioned in the original U.S. patent application

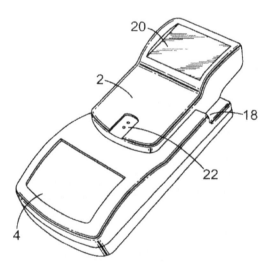

Another angle of the GlucoBoy in the patent application

315

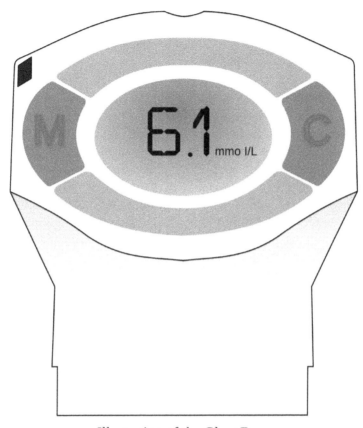

Illustration of the GlucoBoy

The GlucoBoy is an incredibly rare and seldom seen piece of hardware. It's so obscure and hard to find that none could be procured for this book! Nevertheless, enjoy a helpful illustration based on what few photos of the unit actually exist. This amazing device would signal the end of a long era of exotic Game Boy peripherals. To the very close, the Game Boy's add-ons were ever impressive.

Despite being so diverse and varied, all of the items featured up to this point have one thing in common: they were sold to customers in some shape or form. This is actually a distinction worthy of note. Not every product eventually appeared on the market. In fact, there are plenty of examples where hardware never left the prototype phase. Today, a few of these exist only as rough drafts, plans that were ultimately abandoned. Somewhere along the path of development, the hardware was shelved. There are many reasons why an accessory or peripheral might have been dropped. At times, funding ran out, spelling the end of the project's life. In other instances, the underlying concept behind the hardware proved infeasible or unworkable.

This category of Game Boy hardware is often difficult to properly document. Generally, these products are created privately by companies, removed from the public eye. At most, a few pictures or bits of text from an old magazine are all the evidence that these devices were ever imagined at all. More commonly, unreleased hardware is discovered purely by accident. A couple are only known today thanks to online data leaks, for example, or from former employees talking about their past experiences in the industry. In many cases, however, hackers and enthusiasts happen across traces of these would-be peripherals buried deep in a game's code. Without the right circumstances, these items would likely remain lost in obscurity, forgotten by all but a few handful of aging game developers.

While it is impossible to say for certain what role unreleased peripherals may have played if they had ever been sold, they are nevertheless an integral part of video game history. Each one represents potential that, while unrealized, still had its merits in the context of gaming. A product may have failed to materialize for many causes, but that does not change the fact that it once had a chance to make an impact. Even if the results would have been unimpressive or lackluster, it makes for an interesting story about what ideas simply did not work. On that basis, they can help us better understand the overall progression of the industry.

The following section covers some of the products we know might have existed on the Game Boy. It would be misguided, however, to say it is a definitive list or even anywhere near complete. In recent years, new hardware has been uncovered rather frequently. Who's to say what else lies hidden away, entombed in some far off storage unit or left to rot in a secluded pile of boxes? What other confidential documents might make their way onto the web, revealing something that a company decided to drop? No one knows for sure.

Not everything discussed in these pages relies on the hypothetical, however. Because research in this area is always ongoing, efforts to reconstruct a few of these would-be devices has grown recently. For a handful of the items covered, they can be brought back to life either physically through reproduction hardware or virtually through emulation. Others are not quite at that point yet and are still waiting for someone bold enough to take the initiative. In any case, the mystery surrounding these seemingly lost artifacts of the past may yet be broken when given enough attention.

Perhaps one day we will reclaim all of it for ourselves. To reach that point, gamers and historians alike will have to keep prowling archives for any loose data that escapes from the secretive vaults of corporations, scouring for the smallest clues left behind, and analyzing every bit of evidence out there. Until then, however, we can marvel at what the gaming world might have looked like in a different timeline based on what facts and details have currently been uncovered so far.

**Expected Release Date:**
April 1989

**Maker:**
Nintendo

**Potential Legacy:**
Could have been the earliest Game Boy accessory ever to add new functionality outside of multiplayer. Could have established Link Cable add-ons as the de facto method of expanding the Game Boy's capabilities.

Unknown to most, the Game Boy was supposed to launch with more than just the Link Cable as an accessory. In fact, if everything had gone according to plan, this would have been the earliest known peripheral on the handheld unrelated to multiplayer, beating the Barcode Boy by a solid three years. The release of *Alleyway* should have been followed with a special "Vaus" Controller. The device would have been similar to the one that came with the NES version of *Arkanoid*, featuring a small rotary dial and at least one button. By turning the dial left and right, players were to move the in-game paddle – also known as the "Vaus" – with which they could bounce balls back at blocks at the top of the screen.

For years, the Vaus Controller remained a complete mystery. While debugging his Game Boy emulator in early 2019, Frédéric Hamel came across some odd behavior when running *Alleyway*. Digging deeper, he found out that the game was trying to process input over the Link Cable despite being a single-player game. The code inside caused the paddle to move left or right depending on the values it received. This information established the theoretical existence of a Game Boy Vaus Controller.

Further probing by members of the NESdev forums revealed some of the inner workings of the controller. It would have communicated over the Link Cable in 16-bit bursts. The first byte contained an ADC value representing movement of the dial, allowing the game to determine if it was being spun to the left or the right. The second byte was dedicated to button input. Only a single bit here was actually used. It combined the role of two normal Game Boy buttons, allowing the user to exit the pause screen and load up a new ball on the paddle.

In the end, the Vaus Controller may have simply been too awkward and unwieldy for players. It would have required holding the Game Boy in one hand and the controller in the other, not an easy setup given the first Game Boy's size and weight. Another possible configuration, placing the Game Boy down or leaning it up against a surface was more practical but brought up issues of positioning the screen correctly. It also would have made the Game Boy drastically less portable, an image Nintendo may have well wanted to avoid, especially for a brand new product that heavily advertised on-the-go gaming.

Despite those design flaws, the Vaus Controller would have brought precise, analog movement to the Game Boy, something that really wouldn't happen until the first MBC7 cartridges were released

11 years later. Compared to the standard directional pad, it could have vastly aided the player's accuracy. The Vaus Controller was actually brought to other systems, such as the MSX and PlayStation 1. Even the DS had a Slot-2 version demonstrating that the concept could work on portable platforms given the right approach.

No prototypes of the hardware have ever been found. The Game Boy's Vaus Controller may have only ever been code, something the developers cooked up but never seriously pursued manufacturing. The only exact information available is that Nintendo left the programming inside the game cartridge's ROM. Rather than clean it up, they simply let it be. For almost 30 years, it went largely undetected, so for a time it was an effective way to hide it from prying eyes. Nonetheless, today it is possible to recreate the Vaus Controller on one's own. Grabbing a microcontroller and soldering a few wires, intrepid tinkers and makers could potentially revive it. Unlike many later accessories, its operation is incredibly straightforward and simple. Perhaps one day in the future it will be reborn.

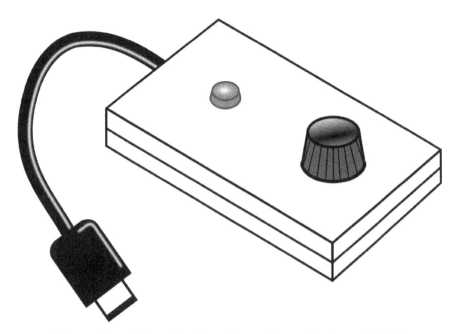

Illustration of how the Vaus Controller might have looked

It's impossible to say for certain exactly how the Vaus Controller would have appeared, had it been released. Nevertheless, it would have most likely taken its design cues from previous Vaus Controllers on other systems. The NES/Famicom version of the Vaus Controller, for example, would have been one of the most recent at the time of the Game Boy's launch.

It's highly probable that the Game Boy Vaus Controller would have had a dial-like knob that rotated in either direction, allowing players to control the paddle. It would have also featured at least a single button for additional input, such as setting up a new ball.

**Expected Release Date:**
December 1991

**Maker:**
Xanth Software

**Potential Legacy:**
Could have massively raised the maximum number of multiplayer participants in Game Boy titles. Would have put the Game Boy on par with rivals such as the Atari Lynx in this regard.

Not long after the Game Boy's release, Nintendo began working on a way to expand the number of systems that could link together. The eventual result was the DMG-07, also known as the 4-Player Adapter. Parallel to those efforts, however, another company began experimenting with a similar solution. Xanth Software's *Faceball 2000*, the Game Boy's earliest first-person shooter, paid special attention to its multiplayer mode. The original version of the game, *MIDI Maze* on the Atari ST, featured a 16-player mode. By daisy-chaining MIDI ports on the computer, a small local network could be created. This ambitious concept was carried over to the Game Boy port.

Robert Champagne, the lead programmer and artist for *Faceball 2000* examined the specifications of the Game Boy Link Cable and came up with a solution. Using a custom in-house connector he'd built, daisy-chaining multiple Game Boys became possible. This adapter turned out not only to be low cost, it also worked very well in testing, readily handling up to 10 players. It would have attached to a standard Link Cable on one end, plugged into the serial port of another Game Boy, and exposed a new Link Cable port for the next Game Boy to connect with.

The team at Xanth Software were unaware of Nintendo's plans for the DMG-07 when their own connector was being made. As originally proposed, every copy of *Faceball 2000* would have been bundled with this adapter. Unfortunately, right near the end of the game's development, Nintendo denied them permission to use the adapter. Instead, Xanth Software was forced to use the "official" method with the DMG-07. Rather than strip out the existing code, Champagne merely added DMG-07 support. *Faceball 2000* would simply detect which Link Cable setup was being used and execute the correct code. As a result, the game technically still supports 16-player deathmatches even though the necessary accessory was never released.

According to Champagne himself, there was no limitation regarding the number of players *Faceball 2000* could handle. 16 was chosen as the maximum, keeping it in line with *MIDI Maze*. The adapter worked by having all the Game Boys connected in a circular manner. Player 1 would begin a serial transfer, passing data along to the second Game Boy. Player 2 received Player 1's input and then responded. Instead of sending data back to Player 1, it communicated with the next Game Boy, Player 3. The process repeated. Every Game Boy received input from the previous one and passed their output to the next one in line. The process ended when the last Game Boy output data back to Player 1. At this point, the loop was complete and data had been transferred to each system in the network.

Nintendo may not have wanted to create confusion or competition for its DMG-07. Despite that, the 4-Player Adapter saw poor adoption among game developers, and support for the peripheral only extended to a small list of titles. This ultimately prevented *Faceball 2000* from showing consumers just how powerful the Game Boy could have been with 16-player action. It would have been a good selling point to match the Atari Lynx, which used daisy-chaining cables for large multiplayer games and even boasted of it through advertising.

Thankfully, all is not lost. Since Champagne left the code for the special connector in *Faceball 2000*, people can make their own versions. A number of hobbyists have been doing just that in recent years, splicing together cables and wires and unlocking multiplayer sessions with at least five or more participants. Others have found that the Game Boy Advance Link Cable can be purposefully misused to replicate a daisy-chain connection, with some bold testers successfully reaching 15 player matches. Additionally, this adapter could be added to existing emulators with network capabilities. The overall design of *Faceball 2000*'s daisy-chain connector is relatively basic. Perhaps soon the world will see dedicated physical and virtual recreations. It would finally bring to life something that for years was misunderstood by the community.

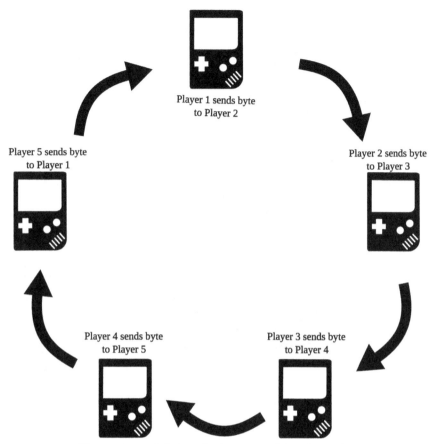

Illustration of daisy-chain networking in action

With the daisy-chain, every member of the network sends their own byte to the next node. Think of it like passing a dinner dish around the table. As the nodes keep passing around bytes, eventually each member will have received each other's bytes.

**Expected Release Date:**
December 1992

**Maker:**
Source R&D / Fabtek

**Potential Legacy:**
Could have started a new era of Game Boy hardware that focused on areas outside of gaming, expanding the handheld to new heights. Could have inspired others to make exotic devices. Would have been the most complex accessory of its time for the Game Boy.

While the Game Boy is famous for having a large collection of non-gaming related peripherals, some may assume it was a trend that started later in the system's lifetime, perhaps around the launch of the Camera and Printer. However, history shows that this idea began far earlier in the form of the WorkBoy. This device was supposed to transform the Game Boy into a miniature handheld personal computer, capable of performing dozens of small office tasks on the go. Had it been released, the WorkBoy would have been the first add-on of its kind on the Game Boy, having nothing to do with boss battles, high scores, or any sort of gameplay whatsoever.

The product itself was to be a small QWERTY keyboard that attached to the Game Boy via Link Cable. It had additional keys such as directional arrows, capitalization, secondary options, and shortcuts to nine different applications. Furthermore, it contained a real-time clock and speaker, utilized for the clock and alarm features. Last but not least, it came with a modest amount of DRAM to store data. The WorkBoy was rather small, measuring in at about 5.75x3.5x2 inches altogether, perfect for holding in one's hands. It required two coin cell batteries to operate, the first Game Boy accessory to need some sort of external power.

Eddie Gill, an inventor from the United Kingdom, came up with the WorkBoy's concept. He was among the first people to realize the Game Boy's potential as a general computing device that was cheap and easily accessible in terms of user interfaces. The WorkBoy's software was developed by Source R&D while the production of the hardware itself was handled by Fabtek in the United States. Its first appearance at the 1992 Consumer Electronics Show in January exposed the world to the Game Boy's endless possibilities. From there, the WorkBoy was spotted on TV networks and even made its way onto the pages of *Nintendo Power*. It was set for release in December of 1992, however, it mysteriously vanished.

For years, many assumed the WorkBoy had been completely erased. The demo units were either long gone or possibly destroyed, and there was no trace of mass production. The WorkBoy remained something of a ghost, existing only as images from a magazine or TV clip. In 2020, however, a series of data leaks found their way online. As part of Nintendo's "lot check" of Game Boy titles, a bunch of previously unreleased ROM files went public. Among them was a near final version of the WorkBoy's software. Within days, Lior Halphon (known as LIJI32), the author of a prominent Game Boy emulator, examined the ROM and reverse-engineered the WorkBoy's behavior. As a result, the SameBoy emulator could access most of the WorkBoy's functions, digitally recreating an experience that was once thought lost for good.

Parallel to the WorkBoy's virtual resurrection, video game historian Liam Robertson contacted Frank Ballouz, the former head of Fabtek. Not only did Robertson manage to track down an intact WorkBoy that Ballouz had in his possession, but he also uncovered the story behind the product's demise. Initially, the WorkBoy would have sold in the $80 to $90 USD range. However, Nintendo would soon cut the price of the Game Boy in 1993, making the WorkBoy rather costly in comparison. Adding to that problem, there was a sudden spike in DRAM prices thanks to manufacturing issues. These factors ultimately led Ballouz to cancel the project.

The WorkBoy would have communicated with the software on the cartridge to transform the Game Boy into a PDA. It had 12 apps in total including a clock, a calculator, a temperature and measurement converter for U.S. and metrics systems, currency exchange rates, bank account management, miscellaneous notes, a calendar, an appointment scheduler, and a phonebook that used the Game Boy's speaker to autodial numbers. To supplement the WorkBoy's internal memory, the cartridge had backup RAM as well. While most of these functions are trivial for modern smartphones, at the time it would have made the Game Boy a powerful business tool.

After spending decades hidden in the shadows, the WorkBoy has finally been recovered, both physically and digitally. The hardware represents a lot of unfulfilled plans that would have been groundbreaking. It would have beaten the Barcode Boy to the market, making it the most complex peripheral of its time. It would have solidified the use of real-time clocks on the Game Boy five full years before the MBC3 mapper was ever introduced. It might have inspired other companies to pursue similarly bold accessories, perhaps shortening the great gap of unique Game Boy hardware that ran from the end of 1992 to midway 1997. Had the WorkBoy sold in stores, it would have established uses for the Game Boy outside of video games much sooner than most know it today. Sadly none of that happened. Thankfully, however, the story behind the WorkBoy endures and its history has now been faithfully recorded.

The WorkBoy as featured in *Nintendo Power* Issue #36

**Expected Release Date:**
December 1999

**Maker:**
Nintendo

**Potential Legacy:**
Could have been one of the smallest, portable color printers available to consumers. Would have made Nintendo the only company at the time to pursue color prints through a game console.

When the Game Boy Printer launched in early 1998, it broadened the capabilities of handheld video game consoles. Now players could create a variety of materials, ranging from photographs to high score sheets. Shortly after that, however, Nintendo had plans for a newer model. The upgrade would have done away with the monochromatic color scheme in favor of a wider, richer palette. If everything had gone accordingly, the next printer would have technically supported thousands of different hues. Unfortunately, the so called Game Boy Printer Color never existed. For almost 20 years, in fact, only a select few people even knew Nintendo had considered making it. Until recently, it was very much a relic hidden in obscurity.

In 2019, a video game preservationist known online as LuigiBlood discovered the presence of some strange menus while digging through *Mario Artist Paint Studio* on the 64DD. Through further reverse-engineering, references to two previously unheard of peripherals were revealed. The first was a Nintendo 64 add-on called the 64GB Cable. Evidently, it would have been a Transfer Pak-like device that either exposed a Link Cable port for the Game Boy or else came with a built-in Link Cable. With this, the Nintendo 64 could communicate through that cable in the same manner as a normal Game Boy. The chief difference here was that the Nintendo 64 would have to first use its JoyBus protocol to send and receive any data over the cable.

LuigiBlood found the purpose of the 64GB Cable was to transfer data to either the standard Game Boy Printer or an entirely unknown version called the "Pocket Printer Color", which they later dubbed Game Boy Printer Color. This mysterious variant evidently functioned quite similarly to the original printer, except it came with several extended features. Perhaps most importantly, the Game Boy Printer Color would have processed 5-bit color data, designating 32 shades for each Red, Green, and Blue channel, for a total coverage of 32,768 colors. It would have been an exponential leap over the previous four shades of gray. Secondly, the Game Boy Printer Color was supposed to have doubled the horizontal resolution compared to the last generation. Based on the code found in *Mario Artist Paint Studio*, the device would have had a memory buffer big enough to store a 320x240 image, and it could optionally switch between 160 or 320 pixels for the print width.

*Mario Artist Paint Studio* is the only title known to support the Game Boy Printer Color. It would have sent detailed photos and pictures from the Nintendo 64 to the device, allowing players to have miniature, physical copies of their own. Although neither the 64GB Cable nor the Game Boy Printer Color were ever sold to the public, the game still has code that fully supports these accessories. Rather than stripping them away from the final product, it was simply disabled and made inaccessible by normal means. For years, evidence of the Game Boy Printer Color remained undisturbed, as few people had both the skills and interest in the 64DD to poke around its programming.

There's no clear reason why gamers wouldn't get to see the Game Boy Printer Color, although there are several plausible theories. The hardware itself may not have been simple or cost effective to produce. For such a wide range of colors, the Game Boy Printer Color would have to change its printing process, a move that may have been expensive or impractical. Even when achievable, the end result could have proved unfriendly to operate, particularly for Nintendo's younger audience. A simpler explanation lies with the 64DD itself. The system was not as popular as the company had hoped; they could have scrapped both the 64GB Cable and Game Boy Printer Color to focus resources elsewhere.

Perhaps the Game Boy Printer Color was never anything more than a fanciful idea at Nintendo, a "what if" concept they previewed in software but later rejected. To date, no hardware prototypes have been unearthed, and no Game Boy Color software has been shown to hold code similar to *Mario Artist Paint Studio*. The situation may change in the future, depending where people spend their time looking. For now, however, the Game Boy Printer Color can be experienced through emulation and a bit a hacking. With its inner workings out in the open, it's possible for anyone to make their own hardware recreation.

A menu from *Mario Artist Paint Studio* representing the Printer Color

A preview of a colorized image before printing

**Expected Release Date:**
Between 1999 and 2002

**Maker:**
Nintendo

**Potential Legacy:**
Would have rapidly advanced Nintendo in areas of wireless communication. Would have also brought internet connectivity to the Game Boy years before Nintendo became fully committed during the 7th Generation.

335

Although a handful of unforeseen circumstances prevented the WorkBoy from launching in late 1992, this failure did not deter the device's creator. Eddie Gill moved on to make several products for Nokia, however, he never lost the desire to tinker with new ideas and experiences for Nintendo's handheld. Years later, he would devise the PageBoy, an accessory that would have enabled long-distance wireless communication on the Game Boy. Despite the WorkBoy's mishaps, Gill wanted to make an improved peripheral along the same principles, something to demonstrate the console's capabilities beyond gaming.

The PageBoy would have handled a great deal of activities such as e-mail, web connectivity, and photo messaging, all of which would have been powered by the same radio frequency commonly used by two-way pagers. Most of its planned features involved interacting with other users or remotely grabbing data. For example, its mail functionality permitted animations and sound effects. Messages were to be sent directly to individual PageBoys, as each would have its own number. While PageBoys could talk to one another, people without the add-on could call telephone operators and send messages if they provided a specific user's number. The PageBoy's software also supplied up-to-date information from news stories, weather reports, and sports events.

Perhaps the most notable ambition of the PageBoy was its idea for Game Boy TV, a "Live Mode" sort of webpage that would have been refreshed in near real-time. It would have pulled in new data every 30 seconds with as much as 400 characters of text per minute. Here, Nintendo would have dealt out exciting and exclusive previews of upcoming titles for their platforms. In addition to streaming the latest developments straight to users, Game Boy TV used a special data format that stylistically enhanced these messages. Each visual effect was pre-programmed into the PageBoy, so the overall transmission itself would use only a small amount of bytes.

Gill and others proposed several more concepts for the PageBoy that revolved around Nintendo. A Mario-themed search engine called "Ask Mario" let users enter in queries such as items for sale. A miniature mobile version of *Nintendo Power* was suggested as well, complete with scaled down text, images, and pages. The PageBoy was also pitched as a way to unlock special content in certain games. As it was originally imagined, the PageBoy would communicate with Nintendo if the user had a certain game, at which point they would give these players items or other bonuses. With this, the PageBoy potentially enabled DLC and could have brought about time-limited events. Last but not least, the PageBoy could transmit high scores for various games, letting Nintendo display the top players on Game Boy TV.

To accomplish these feats, however, the PageBoy needed a way to connect with existing Game Boy cartridges. The product was modeled to fit into the Game Boy Color's cartridge slot while simultaneously offering a second slot of its own. In this way, it somewhat mirrored the likes of the GameShark cheat device. Players would have been able to choose between booting the PageBoy or the inserted game cartridge. During the Game Boy Color's startup sequence, pressing Down on the directional pad would activate the PageBoy, an ingenious workaround for its time. The PageBoy could then read all data on the cartridge to identify the game and any save files present. Those same saves could also be modified in the case of receiving DLC.

Additionally, the PageBoy was intended to work with the Game Boy Camera and Printer. Since the PageBoy could read cartridges, it had the ability to pull pictures taken on the Game Boy Camera. These images were to be used as profiles for known contacts or simply sent to others for fun. Photo extraction from the Game Boy Camera was a rare feature, having only ever been implemented briefly on the 64DD. While most of the messages received by the PageBoy were optionally saved to the device itself, everything could also be output on paper thanks to the Game Boy Printer.

As the scope and size of the PageBoy became apparent to Gill, he sought out Nintendo's cooperation. Both sides were interested in the product, and it would have been a first-party item developed under Nintendo. The company investigated its viability from 1999 until 2002 under the codename Cheetah. The hardware would have ran on two AA batteries, used some amount of built-in memory, sported an internal clock and alarm, vibrated when receiving new messages, and cost a mere $50 USD. The wireless service would have been entirely free for users as well. However, as history shows, the PageBoy was eventually canceled and shelved.

While the wireless networks in North America easily supported the PageBoy's specifications, no cheap alternatives existed in Europe or Japan. Nintendo felt the appeal of the PageBoy was that it gave users a chance to connect globally. It was meant to be universal rather than regional, and without that all efforts were eventually abandoned. These were the reasons given by Nintendo at least. Curiously, however, many of the opportunities present in the PageBoy were duplicated by the Mobile Adapter GB. Perhaps Nintendo never fully pursued the PageBoy due to it possibly conflicting with their plans for the adapter. It's worth considering that the Mobile Adapter GB was specific only to Japanese markets, yet they launched and promoted it anyway. The adapter's existence negates some of the company's logic for dropping the PageBoy project, especially given the host of other Japanese-only online services for the Famicom, Super Famicom, and 64DD.

In light of this evidence, the PageBoy may have never been realized simply because it was not feasible in Japan, something a Japanese company was not comfortable with. Whatever the cause, the PageBoy would remain nothing more than a mock-up model and a few PowerPoint files. No physical prototypes were produced. Had the situation been different, the PageBoy would have been massively ahead of its time, pushing the Game Boy into mobile territory that phones would take years to catch up. It could have jumpstarted wireless functionality on Nintendo's handhelds, potentially bringing aspects of both the Mobile Adapter GB and the Game Boy Advance Wireless Adapter to a wider audience much sooner. As few steps were taken towards producing a working PageBoy, it sadly remains a fanciful "what if" peripheral.

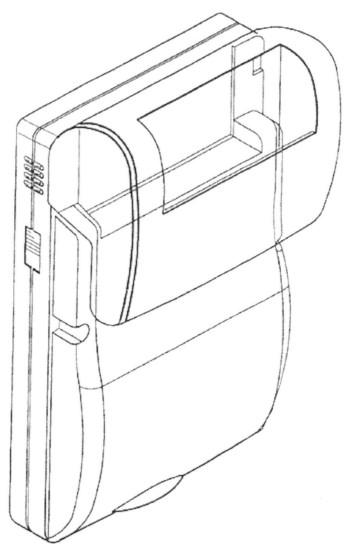

A U.S. patent illustration of one variant of the PageBoy

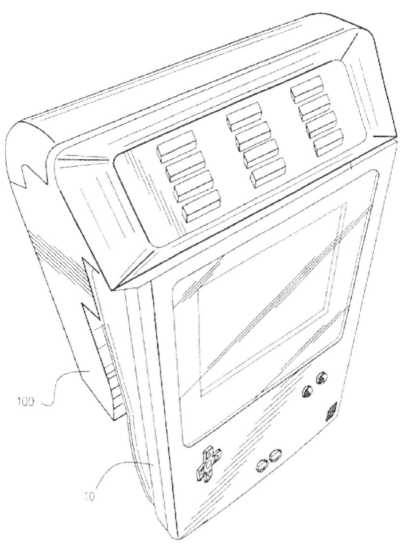

A U.S. patent illustration of another PageBoy variant

**Expected Release Date:**
July 2000

**Maker:**
Media Factory

**Potential Legacy:**
Would have brought about a new method of barcode scanning to video games. Would have been the only time a Game Boy Color title interacted with the Sega Dreamcast in some form.

341

During the Game Boy era, the platform saw multiple barcode scanners released. The trend proved steadfast and continued well into Nintendo's DS age. While these devices focused on scanning physical media such as cards, one peripheral for a certain game would have changed all of that. Launched for the Game Boy Color in July 2000, *Sakura Taisen GB* became notable for working with a special accessory called the Pocket Sakura, which in many regards mimicked the Pokémon Pikachu 2. The game and the Pocket Sakura communicated via infrared to unlock bonus material. This, however, was not the full extent of *Sakura Taisen GB*'s infrared capabilities.

If things had gone differently, the game would have communicated with a second device. Known only as the "TV Adapter", the add-on was to plug into the Game Boy's Link Cable port. Afterwards, players could have used the adapter to scan a barcode. The source of that barcode, however, would have been an actual TV set. The original plan was to work in conjunction with *Sakura Taisen* on the Sega Dreamcast, which would display a barcode in certain scenarios as a reward. Unfortunately, this feature was never implemented, although remnants still exist in the Dreamcast game. A specific icon for the TV Adapter's barcode is mentioned in the manual, and the icon itself can be seen in the "One Long Day" mode.

No physical prototypes have ever been found, and the only images of the TV Adapter come from unused graphics pulled from *Sakura Taisen GB*'s ROM. However, based on those 8-bit pictures and some of the leftover programming also found in the cartridge, it is possible to speculate how it would have functioned. The player would have likely had to manually move the TV Adapter across the barcode shown on their TV screen. The adapter probably used some type of basic camera to detect light and dark transitions.

Perhaps most interesting is how this data was transferred back to the Game Boy. Judging by the game's code, it would have used an obscure feature of the Link Cable's pins. Only one pin was typically unused during data transfers, Pin 4. Most Link Cables and peripherals didn't even have connections for Pin 4. Nintendo designated it as "reserved", generally making it off-limits for developers. On the Game Boy Color, Pin 4 did have some unique uses. It could toggle a certain bit in an area of memory normally dedicated to infrared communications, even though the actual input did not come from the infrared port. Nevertheless, the unused code in *Sakura Taisen GB* read this bit constantly, suggesting this was how it operated. Using Pin 4, it may have been capable of sending data faster than standard transmissions over the Link Cable.

The TV Adapter was discovered in 2021 by a group of translators patching the game from Japanese to English. They stumbled upon the adapter while examining and studying the infrared handling code. The menu for the TV Adapter works perfectly, and under some conditions it can be accidentally triggered without any special hardware using the original game cartridge. Evidently, the barcodes would have unlocked a variety of extras: a Hard Mode for minigames, items to increase character stats while training, shop discounts for select items, bonus points for the shop, and photos and portraits of different characters. Amazingly, the code for receiving these rewards remains intact rather than buried or disabled.

Currently, no one knows the exact reason why the TV Adapter never became a reality. Perhaps the product drew too much power over the Link Cable. Use of the Link Cable's Pin 4 may have caused its cancellation as well. The practice would have been frowned upon by Nintendo, especially since it might have been incompatible with the upcoming Game Boy Advance. The device may have simply been too costly. At any rate, if the TV Adapter had come about, it would have been a dramatic departure from other barcode readers, acting in a manner similar to modern smartphones reading QR codes. It potentially could have been the one and only piece of Game Boy Color hardware to take advantage of Pin 4. What's more, it would have been the first example of some kind of Game Boy-to-Dreamcast connectivity. Thankfully, given the state of the game's code and that fact that all of the valid barcodes are known, someone could conceivably make a reproduction TV Adapter some day.

The TV Adapter being detected in *Sakura Taisen GB*

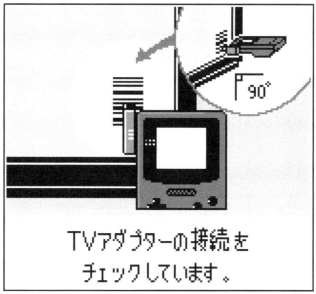

An unused screen from the game demonstrating the TV Adapter

**Expected Release Date:**
    Between 2002 and 2004

**Maker:**
    Nintendo

**Potential Legacy:**
    Would have resurrected features once found in the Game Boy
    Camera. Could have brought colorized photography to
    consumers and further established the use of cameras for
    video games.

In February 1998, the Game Boy Camera and Game Boy Printer were launched simultaneously. It was Nintendo's intent from the start to pair them together. The two peripherals went hand-in-hand at first, although the Game Boy Printer saw greater use across multiple games during its lifespan. At one point Nintendo had planned a colorized upgrade to the Game Boy Printer, however, they ultimately decided not to bring that product to consumers. Despite this setback, the company went ahead and developed a successor to the Game Boy Camera instead.

At the 2002 Electronic Entertainment Expo, a new device was unveiled and demonstrated on the floor. Called the Game Eye, it was a multicolor digital camera created for the Game Boy Advance. Like the Game Boy Camera, the Game Eye featured image capturing and processing hardware built directly into the cartridge. The unit itself was a gray Game Boy Advance cartridge with a large protruding bar at the top that stretched out horizontally to either side. On the left end sat a camera buried within the Game Eye's cylindrical case. The right end acted as a knob, allowing the camera to rotate towards or away from the player.

While the Game Eye was touted as a standalone project, its GameCube connectivity was the highlight at the time it was shown. The unreleased GameCube title *Stage Debut* was essentially a more modernized version of *Talent Maker* from *Mario Artist: Paint Studio* on the 64DD. Players could take pictures of their own faces on the Game Eye and upload them via the GBA-to-GCN cable. The face would then serve as a texture for a 3D model that could execute a variety of wacky tasks, such as dancing and performing on stage for a virtual audience. Some amount of editing was planned, such as altering facial features and hair. It was Nintendo's closest attempt yet to create what eventually would become Miis.

The Game Eye was capable of recording player profiles, complete with a picture of their face and information such as name, age, sex, personality type, hobby, birthday, personal comments, weight, and body shape. Naturally as an independent device, it also featured an option to save images directly to the cartridge. The camera had a higher resolution than the original Game Boy Camera and used the L and R triggers on the Game Boy Advance to zoom in (2x max) or out. The Game Eye would have been able to send multiple pictures to compatible software such as *Stage Debut*. Known as "sheets" according to technical documents, the Game Eye queued up batches rather than transmitting each one separately.

The following year at the 2003 Electronic Entertainment Expo, another version of the Game Eye appeared. It was reworked now with a new look. The prototype was still a cartridge housing a camera, but it no longer had a long bar. Instead it had a shorter tube-like appendage coming from one end of the plastic shell. Nintendo had removed the dedicated knob, apparently making the camera on the end directly adjustable through twisting. Interestingly, these models were not explicitly labeled as the Game Eye but rather simply called "AGB Camera No. 7".

Unfortunately, that was the last the world ever saw or heard of the Game Eye. The project was quietly shelved. *Stage Debut* never released for the GameCube, and so the Game Eye never even had a flagship title. As *Stage Debut* depended so heavily on the canceled handheld accessory, it is little wonder Nintendo eventually ceased work on that game as well. Not everything was thrown away, however. Important elements from both the Game Eye and *Stage Debut* were incorporated into later products. The concept of Miis would flourish widely during the Wii era. On the DS, Nintendo produced the Facening Scan accessory, a small Slot-2 cartridge with an embedded camera intended for makeup and "facial expression training". Eventually, built-in cameras on the DSi and 3DS would be used to capture the user's face for various in-game models or regular photo taking.

For gamers today, the Game Eye remains a lost piece of history. The only traces still present are images and footage of its brief time at gaming conferences. Despite all of the data leaks Nintendo has suffered in recent years, no solid leads have turned up regarding the camera or the GameCube software. Perhaps Nintendo has a copy or two hidden away in one of their archives, sitting abandoned through the decades. Only time will tell if more details about the Game Eye surface.

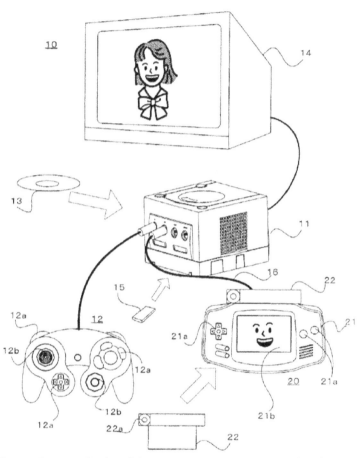

The Game Eye, as depicted in a patent, connecting to the GameCube

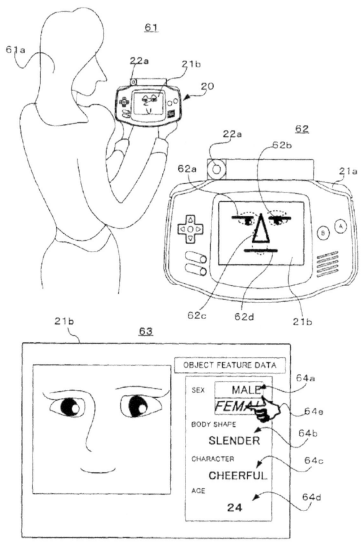

Another patent drawing of the Game Eye's face-capturing features

Illustration of the first Game Eye prototype model

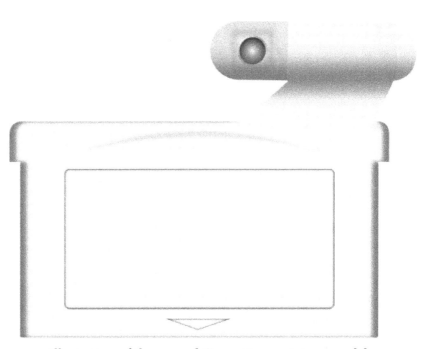

Illustration of the second Game Eye prototype model

**Expected Release Date:**
Between 2004 and 2006

**Makers:**
Nintendo, iQue, BroadOn

**Potential Legacy:**
Would have brought the Game Boy Advance back online. Had the potential to set the standard for downloadable games on Nintendo's platforms. Was the most advanced cartridge ever designed for the Game Boy.

At the start of the 6th Generation of video game consoles, Nintendo finally seemed poised to launch themselves into the online sphere. On the handheld front, the Mobile Adapter GB brought internet connectivity to a number of Game Boy titles, and the possibilities of the GameCube's broadband and dial-up adapters had yet to be fully explored. Unfortunately, the Mobile Adapter GB's service ended relatively quickly, and the GameCube featured online gameplay in just a handful of situations. The 7th Generation marked Nintendo's true awakening regarding the internet after years of false starts. Before the DS arrived, however, another attempt was made to put the Game Boy Advance back in cyberspace.

In 2004, a company known as iQue began designing and building a project called the NetCard. The device was to have been a highly specialized Game Boy Advance cartridge that connected directly to a player's computer. To achieve this, the NetCard came equipped with its own USB 1.1 port capable of accepting USB Mini cables. As the NetCard and the PC were linked together, data could be transferred back and forth between each side with the computer doing all of the actual networking. Nevertheless, it would have enabled the Game Boy Advance to play online. Additionally its 128MB of built-in NAND flash memory opened the way for various downloads of all sorts, including entire games.

On that note, the NetCard was an attempt to bring more of Nintendo's Game Boy Advance library to China in a way resistant to piracy. iQue started localizing games in 2004, but due to rampant bootlegs on the handheld, they stopped in 2007, having only released eight works altogether. The NetCard would have added various layers of security to enforce copy-protection. Most notable of them were the dual ARM7TDMI CPUs embedded in the cartridge itself. The plan was to have one of these processors dedicated to tasks such as handling input/output, memory operations, and digital rights management.

This design was very similar architecturally to the Wii, which also had an ARM CPU called the "Starlet" with comparable functions. Another company called BroadOn was responsible for producing these components in both cases, making the NetCard something of a predecessor to the Wii. Furthermore, the NetCard implemented the same E-Ticket system later found in the Wii. This would have permitted the NetCard to manage and verify its digital downloads, almost as if it were installing software. The Game Boy Advance would have essentially had the equivalent of Wii Channels, at least on the Chinese market. During the NetCard's development, iQue actively discussed running critical code on one of these ARM CPUs, thus forming another obstacle against piracy.

Thanks to a native storage capacity that far exceeded any other cartridge of its time, the NetCard had potential as an officially licensed flashcart. It was capable of handling all manner of save data formats used by Game Boy Advance titles, from flash ROM, EEPROM, and SRAM/FRAM. Nearly any game could have been written to the NetCard via PC. However, the NetCard also did more than just video games. The peripheral supported a complete multimedia experience as it displayed movies and pictures and played music files too. Like the Play-Yan and Music Recorder, the NetCard had a 3.5mm headphone jack to bypass the Game Boy Advance's speakers and provide high quality audio.

Perhaps iQue's most extensive push towards real-time online gaming came in the form of their *Pokémon* project for the NetCard. The untitled game was to use *Fire Red* and *Leaf Green* as a base with both online and offline modes available. In the absence of an internet connection, players would have been restricted to a smaller pool of monsters to catch. Meanwhile, the online portion gave access to the full set of collectible creatures. Depending on the player's location (determined by their IP address) different Pokémon would be found. A weather system would have been implemented too based on where the player lived, adding an unprecedented level of variety to the franchise. The game was to be used with the NetCard along with another device with a "PC screen", presumably just the player's computer running and displaying graphics. The Game Boy Advance could have served as a controller as well. A tournament mode was also discussed with 3D models on the "PC screen".

Despite being proposed in 2004 and having large amounts of development behind it, the NetCard was never sold. As iQue continued to lay the groundwork for the NetCard, it likely became evident that the underlying product was growing outdated the longer it delayed coming to the market. Before iQue quietly dropped the NetCard, Nintendo was probably starting their own efforts to make the DSi. Not only would the next DS model remove the Game Boy Advance cartridge slot, it would assume nearly all of the roles the NetCard aimed to fill. The DSi would launch with 256MB of flash memory along with an SD card expansion. It offered fairly robust cryptographic functions, meaning the dual-CPU setup in the NetCard was unnecessary to prevent piracy. With its built-in Wi-Fi, the DSi could connect online with ease, needing no extra hardware or cables. The new handheld even worked with media such as photos and music. An online storefront provided digital distribution of games and apps. Everything envisioned by the NetCard became standard features of the DSi.

For the longest time, however, the NetCard's very existence remained shrouded in secrecy, possibly known to only a handful of iQue, BroadOn, and Nintendo employees. It wasn't until the summer of 2020 that news of the cartridge spread through online publications and social media. As part of a large set of data leaks from Nintendo, information about the NetCard began appearing. Evidently, the entire development repository for the device was posted for anyone to take a look at. Data miners and researchers found dozens of previously unknown material about the project, from demos, PowerPoint presentations, archives of code, and even a modified emulator used for testing NetCard programs. Despite the wealth of details in the leak, no prototype was known to exist at the time. No one knew for certain whether any sort of physical model had actually been produced. The story surrounding the NetCard took another surprising turn of events shortly after the leak. For the author of this book in particular, things became personal even.

*As news of the NetCard hit Reddit, someone asked me if it would be possible to emulate the cartridge. My main goal is to see that every piece of exotic Game Boy hardware is thoroughly examined and preserved, and that means making sure virtual versions can work on anyone's PC. I responded that, yes, in theory the NetCard could be emulated as long as we knew exactly how it worked. Obviously the data leak provided more than enough information to do so, but it would be illegal to use proprietary information without authorization. I said to this person that I needed to have a real, actual NetCard in my possession so I could reverse-engineer it. However, I replied that the chances of this happening were very low. It wasn't like a prototype would just appear out of nowhere, right?*

*Well, as I browsed other subreddits, I came across a new thread in /r/Gameboy where someone claimed they actually had a NetCard! Apparently this user had obtained the peripheral some time ago, however, they hadn't been able to identify it. In truth, they thought it was some kind of Play-Yan variant, which was very understandable, as it shared the same kind of cartridge mold and looked very similar. However, with all the news about the NetCard going around, the user connected the dots and concluded that they might have something special on their hands. Indeed, when they opened up the cartridge, it looked quite convincing. It certainly wasn't some random pirate cartridge; by all appearances it was legit. The whole thing was hard to believe at first. What were the odds that hardware no one knew about for over a decade would suddenly just show up out of nowhere? Its status changed from unheard of, to lost forever, to suddenly found all within a week.*

*At any rate, I contacted the user on Reddit through private messaging. It was a long shot, but I offered to buy the NetCard from them. After a while, after shopping around for other potential buyers, the user came back with an asking price of their own. If I said no, they planned to put it up on an auction. Their deal would have cost a pretty penny, to be sure, but what were my chances of getting even the slightest opportunity to obtain the NetCard ever again in my lifetime? The auction might have skyrocketed in value. If some random collector won, there was a distinct possibility the NetCard would just end up sitting on a shelf, a mere trophy rather than an artifact that needed to be studied and understood. I figured if I passed it up now, I wouldn't get to buy it a second time. You can always make more money, but it's hard to make up for regrets. This was a chance to get an up close inside look at Nintendo's hidden history and share it with the world.*

*After some negotiation and financial exchanges, the NetCard prototype arrived at my residence later that week. I was quite eager to start picking it apart and examine how it worked. Unfortunately that proved to be a fairly large task, so even at the time of this writing, I still haven't begun to unlock its secrets. That's a project that may take quite a while to unfold, especially since I'm technically prohibited from using any information from the 2020 data leaks. Eventually, however, I know we'll be able to reclaim all that Nintendo buried.*

The NetCard would have been a fascinating piece of hardware had it released. With its multiple CPUs and PC connectivity, it was by far the most complex and advanced Game Boy cartridge ever devised. The effort behind the NetCard demonstrated the handheld could still push boundaries. iQue was willing to bring a new dimension of online gaming to a population that was neither Japan nor the West. As their own internal documents showed, they would have taken popular Nintendo series such as *Pokémon*, *F-Zero*, and *Mario Kart* to new heights that wouldn't be seen until much later. In many ways, it was anywhere from one to five years ahead of its time regarding online features, storage, apps, and content management. While the NetCard today ultimately remains another fanciful "what if" peripheral, there's a good possibility we could yet recover the mysteries it left behind.

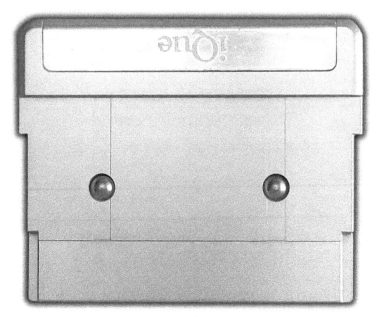

NetCard Front

NetCard Back

NetCard PCB Front

NetCard PCB Back

Close up of the top of the NetCard

The NetCard at an angle

The NetCard fitting into an AGB-001

The NetCard fitting into an AGS-001

**5th Generation of Video Game Consoles:** Also known simply as the 5th Generation, starting in late 1993. Covers home consoles such as the Sony PlayStation, Sega Saturn, and Nintendo 64. It also covers handheld consoles such as the Game Boy Color, Neo Geo Pocket, and WonderSwan.

**6th Generation of Video Game Consoles:** Also known simply as the 6th Generation, starting in late 1998. Covers home consoles such as the Sega Dreamcast, Sony PlayStation 2, Nintendo GameCube, and XBOX. It also covers handheld consoles such as the Game Boy Advance, Pokémon Mini, and Nokia N-Gage.

**7th Generation of Video Game Consoles:** Also known simply as the 7th Generation, starting in late 2005. Covers home consoles such as the Nintendo Wii, Sony PlayStation 3, and Xbox 360. It also covers handheld consoles such as the Nintendo DS and Sony PlayStation Portable.

**Accelerometer:** An integrated circuit capable of measuring changes in acceleration. Employed in a handful of Game Boy cartridges to measure tilting on certain axes and provide motion controls.

**ADC:** Stands for "Analog-to-Digital Converter". Changes analog input (continuous and infinitely variable values) into digital output (finite and discrete values). Examples include microphones capturing real sound waves and converting them into digital audio samples.

**AGB:** Stands for "Advance Game Boy", typically used as part of a model number for individual Game Boy Advance products in the form of AGB-xxx, where "xxx" is a 3-digit number.

**AGS:** Stands for "Advance Game Boy SP", typically used as part of a model number for individual Game Boy Advance SP products in the form of AGS-xxx, where "xxx" is a 3-digit number.

**Amiibo:** Nintendo's toys-to-life figurines, compatible with various games across the Wii U, 3DS, and Switch. Uses near-field communication and stores data internally.

361

**ARM:** A series of CPU architectures designed by Arm Ltd. Known for powering embedded devices. ARM CPUs are found in Nintendo consoles such as the Game Boy Advance, DS, 3DS, and Switch.

**BIOS:** Stands for "Basic Input/Output System". Code that typically handles booting. May provide other useful functions post-boot.

**CGB:** Stands for "Color Game Boy", typically used as part of a model number for individual Game Boy Color products in the form of CGB-xxx, where "xxx" is a 3-digit number.

**CMOS:** Stands for "Complementary Metal Oxide Semiconductor", used to make analog circuits such as image sensors.

**Codec:** A device or program that encodes and decodes data, such as audio or video signals.

**CompactFlash:** A type of flash memory for storing large amounts of data on a card-like medium. Created by SanDisk in 1994 and saw adoption in products such as media players and digital cameras.

**CPU:** Stands for "Central Processing Unit". It is generally the primary component of a computer that controls execution of the main program. It may not be the only processor within a system, however.

**CR1616:** Known as a button cell or coin battery. Has a 16mm diameter, a 1.6mm thickness, and a 3.0 voltage. Used in small electronic devices such as watches. Powers the real-time clocks in Game Boy Advance cartridges.

**CR2025:** Known as a button cell or coin battery. Has a 20mm diameter, a 2.5mm thickness, and a 3.0 voltage. Used in small electronic devices such as watches. Powers SRAM and/or real-time clocks in Game Boy cartridges.

**CR2032:** Known as a button cell or coin battery. Has a 20mm diameter, a 3.2mm thickness, and a 3.0 voltage. Used in small electronic devices such as watches. Powers SRAM and/or real-time clocks in Game Boy cartridges.

**Crystal Oscillator:** A type of oscillator that uses a crystal, such as quartz, to generate a given frequency. Used extensively in real-time clocks to provide accurate time-keeping.

**DMG:** Stands for "Dot-Matrix Game". Used as a shorthand to broadly reference the original monochromatic Game Boy, Game Boy Pocket, and Game Boy Light, along with all of their compatible games. Also used as part of a model number for individual Game Boy products in the form of DMG-xx where "xx" is a 2-digit number.

**DLC:** Stands for "Downloadable Content". Refers to content within a game that must be obtained or unlocked through external means. Typically this involves downloading data from a network such as the internet, but it can also be from other sources.

**DNS:** Stands for "Domain Name System". A key component of internet architecture and functionality. Best known for translating domain names such as *nintendo.com* into a specific IP address.

**DOL:** Stands for "Dolphin", the early codename for the GameCube. Typically used as part of a model number for individual GameCube products in the form of DOL-xxx, where "xxx" is a 3-digit number.

**EEPROM:** Stands for "Electrically Erasable Programmable Read-Only Memory". A type of non-volatile memory commonly used for saving small amounts of data. On the original Game Boy, EEPROM was used in a handful of cartridges, while the Game Boy Advance saw more widespread adoption. EEPROM does not require batteries to maintain its saved data.

**Firmware:** Software that provides low-level control for specific hardware and components, generally stored in non-volatile memory.

**Flash Cartridge:** A special type of video game cartridge that uses rewritable flash memory instead of a permanent ROM. Often used for personal homebrew projects, however, some official versions exist depending on the console.

**Flash Memory:** A type of non-volatile memory commonly used for saving data. Rarely appeared on the DMG and GBC, but became more widespread on the GBA. Data must be electrically erased and reprogrammed. Software often send various commands to flash controllers to handle the tasks of manipulating data. Flash memory does not require batteries to maintain its saved data.

**Force-feedback:** Also known as haptic feedback, another name for rumble features in video games. Games that support force-feedback often vibrate or shake when played thanks to special hardware.

**FRAM:** Stands for "Ferroelectric Random Access Memory". A type of non-volatile memory commonly used for saving data. It appeared in GBA cartridges, quickly replaced SRAM, and became a common method of backing up cartridge data. FRAM does not require batteries to maintain its saved data.

**Gachapon:** A type of hand-cranked vending-machine that dispenses toys in plastic capsules. Alternatively spelled as "Gashapon".

**Game Pak:** Another name for game cartridge. Generally specific to Nintendo terminology.

**GBA:** Stands for "Game Boy Advance", Nintendo's successor to the Game Boy Color. Launched on March 21, 2001.

**GBC:** Stands for "Game Boy Color", Nintendo's successor to the original Game Boy. Launched on October 21, 1998.

**GCN:** Stands for "GameCube Nintendo", Nintendo's official abbreviation for the GameCube.

**Gyroscope:** A device used to measure orientation as well as angular velocity. In the context of video games, it is often used as input for motion controls.

**HTTP:** Stands for "Hypertext Transfer Protocol". One of the primary protocols for transmitting and receiving data over websites and servers.

**Infrared:** Electromagnetic radiation with longer wavelengths than visible light but shorter than radio waves. It cannot be detected by the human eye. Used to transmit signals at a distance.

**Interrupt:** A request from hardware or software that prompts a processor to halt execution of the main program and handle whatever activity initially triggered the interrupt.

**ISP:** Stands for "Internet Service Provider". Usually a company, organization, entity, or group that provides people with access to the internet.

**LED:** Stands for "Light Emitting Diode", a type of semiconductor that produces light when a current is run through it.

**Mapper:** A term that refers to different Memory Bank Controllers on the Game Boy. A mapper controls how the game accesses ROM, cartridge RAM, and any additional hardware that may also be present. The game software often has the Game Boy's CPU read/write data to certain memory locations, which triggers the mapper to take certain actions depending on how it was designed.

**MBC:** Stands for "Memory Bank Controller", Nintendo's official name for mappers on the Game Boy. Used to identify a series of mapper variants, such as the MBC1, MBC2, MBC3, MBC5, MBC6, and MBC7.

**MCU:** Stands for "Microcontroller Unit", a miniature computer with its own CPU, memory, and programmable input and output.

**MGB:** Possibly stands for "Miniature Game Boy", typically used as part of a model number for individual Game Boy Pocket products in the form of MGB-xxx, where "xxx" is a 3-digit number.

**MultiBoot:** Refers to the process of sending small apps to the Game Boy Advance while its BIOS waits. Does not require a cartridge.

**Officially Licensed:** In the context of this book, any product that Nintendo approved for use with their Game Boy hardware. It does not imply that Nintendo was the creator or maker in each case, however.

**OXY:** Typically used as part of a model number for individual Game Boy Micro products in the form of OXY-xxx, where "xxx" is a 3-digit number.

**PCB:** Stands for "Printed Circuit Board". This is the material to which electronic components are affixed. Typically comes in a variety of colors, most commonly green, blue, red, and black.

**Peripheral:** General term for any hardware not directly integrated with a video game console. Ranges from simple devices such as controllers and memory cards to more comprehensive products such as internet adapters. In this book, the term is synonymous with words such as "add-on" and "accessory".

**POP3:** Stands for "Post Office Protocol Version 3". An internet protocol used to retrieve e-mail messages.

**Protocol:** Regarding communication, a structured way in which multiple sides send and receive information.

**Prototype:** Typically a piece of hardware or software that was used to design, develop, or debug a product. May be experimental in many regards, and the associated product may never have been released.

**QWERTY:** A ubiquitous keyboard layout for Latin-script alphabets.

**RAM:** Stands for "Random Access Memory", a type of volatile memory. Commonly used by the CPU and other components as a temporary holding area for data used when executing the main program. If a console is turned off, the contents of RAM are erased.

**Real-Time Clock:** A clock that more or less moves forward at a rate of one second per second. In gaming, it is generally independent from other components like the CPU to keep track of time. Instead, it often uses crystal oscillators to provide a constant and consistent pace. The main feature for gaming is that they can run even while the console itself is turned off. Requires some sort of battery to act as a source of power, however.

**ROM:** Stands for "Read-Only Memory", a type of non-volatile memory used to store data. In the context of the Game Boy, this refers to the mask ROM integrated circuits found in the cartridges. These are used to store the game's code and data. The information stored in ROM cannot be changed electrically.

**RPG:** Stands for Role-Playing Game, a type of game where players assume the role of characters in a fictional world. Often utilizes such mechanics as leveling, hit points, and other character attributes.

**SDK:** Stands for "Software Developer Kit", a development framework given to third-parties to create applications for a platform.

**SD:** Stands for "Secure Digital", a type of flash memory intended to store large amounts of data on a card-like medium. Created by the SD Association in 1999. Eventually replaced other formats such as CompactFlash and SmartMedia, becoming the current dominant technology in this field. Used in everything from cameras, smartphones, PCs, and even video game consoles.

**Serial Port:** The port where the Game Boy receives the Link Cable. Data is transferred one bit at a time.

**SmartMedia:** A type of flash memory intended to store large amounts of data on a card-like medium. Created by Toshiba around 1995. Used primarily in digital cameras. Offered a copy-protection feature based on hardwired IDs.

**SMTP:** Stands for "Simple Mail Transfer Protocol". An internet protocol for transmitting e-mail.

**SRAM:** Stands for "Static Random Access Memory". A type of volatile memory commonly used for saving data. On the Game Boy, SRAM was used in nearly all DMG and CGB games that had saves, with few exceptions. Some early GBA titles used SRAM before moving onto FRAM. SRAM requires a battery to maintain its data.

**TCP:** Stands for "Transmission Control Protocol". A transport-layer protocol for the internet. Guarantees reliable transmissions with error-checking.

367

**Toys-To-Life:** A category of video games that use physical collectible items such as figurines to interact with the game. Most items contain data within them or cause a separate device to generate the data. It is distinct from barcode scanning, which ordinarily relies on cards.

**Transceiver:** A device capable of both sending and receiving something, often in the context of signals or data transmissions.

**UDP:** Stands for "User Datagram Protocol". A transport-layer protocol for the internet. Does not rely on handshakes, therefore, transmissions across a network are not guaranteed.

**URL:** Stands for "Uniform Resource Locator". It is effectively a specific address to a given file in the context of web servers.

**Volatile:** In computing, a type of memory that only retains data as long as power is supplied. Once the power source is removed, the data is erased.

**VRAM:** Stands for "Video Random Access Memory". A type of volatile memory used for storing raw graphics and color palettes in video game consoles.

# References

**General Information**

"AGB/AGS/OXY: Game Boy Advance", *Nintendo HardwareNumber*,
 https://maru-chang.com/hard/agb/english.htm
"DMG/MGB/CGB: Game Boy Series", *Nintendo HardwareNumber*,
 https://maru-chang.com/hard/gb/english.htm
"DOL: Nintendo Game Cube", *Nintendo HardwareNumber*,
 https://maru-chang.com/hard/dol/english.htm
"Edge of Emulation" by Daniel Baxter, *Shonumi's Things and Stuff*,
 https://shonumi.github.io/articles.html
"Más que juegos: Nintendo Game Boy Advance" by ClawGrip, *Jungle Hunt via Internet
 Archive*, March 28, 2008, https://web.archive.org/web/20080524041533/
 http://junglehunt.blogspot.com/2008/03/m-que-juegos-nintendo-game-boy-
 advance.html

**Game Link Cable — 1st & 2nd Generation**

"Accessory [アクセサリー]" by Nintendo of Japan,
 https://www.nintendo.co.jp/n02/dmg/hardware/option/acce.html
"Game Boy Link Ports & Cables & Peripherals" by Great Hierophant, *Nerdy Pleasures*,
 April 24, 2021, http://nerdlypleasures.blogspot.com/2021/04/game-boy-link-
 ports-cables.html
"Serial Data Transfer", *Pan Docs*,
 https://gbdev.io/pandocs/Serial_Data_Transfer_(Link_Cable).html

**4-Player Adapter**

"Beyond Donkey Kong" by Ken Horowitz, Chapter: 'Nintendo "VS." the World.',
 McFarland & Company, Inc., 2020
"DMG-07 4-Player Adapter" by Daniel Baxter, *Dan Docs*,
 https://shonumi.github.io/dandocs.html#dmg07
"F-1 Race Instruction Booklet" by Nintendo of America, 1990
"FaceBall 2000 Instruction Manual" by Bullet-Proof Software, 1991
"Interview with: Robert Champagne" by Don Komarechka, *Internet Archive*,
 January 11, 2005, https://web.archive.org/web/20100509163809/
 http://fb2k.retro-spect.ca/rchampagne.html

**Barcode Boy**

"Barcode Boy" by ClawGrip, *Jungle Hunt*, February 16, 2014,
 http://junglehunt.blogspot.com/2014/02/barcode-boy.html
"Barcode Boy" by Daniel Baxter, *Dan Docs*, https://shonumi.github.io/dandocs.html#bcb
"Barcode Boy Cards", *Internet Archive*, June 7, 2018,
 https://archive.org/details/BCBCards

**HuC-1 | HuC-3 | GB KISS LINK**

"Cartridges by mappers: HuC-1" by Gekkio and contributors, *Game Boy hardware
 database*, https://gbhwdb.gekkio.fi/cartridges/huc1.html
"Cartridges by mappers: HuC-3" by Gekkio and contributors, *Game Boy hardware
 database*, https://gbhwdb.gekkio.fi/cartridges/huc3.html
"Comunicaciones por infrarrojos en consolas portátiles de Nintendo" by Clawgrip, *Jungle
 Hunt*, July 2, 2010, http://junglehunt.blogspot.com/2010/07/comunicaciones-
 por-infrarrojos-en.html
"Game Boy Software Review", http://www.asahi-net.or.jp/~ua4s-njm/gb_soft/gbrev.html
"GB KISS & GB KISS LINK MODEM FAQ" by Esteban, *Base Nectaris*,
 https://nectaris.tg-16.com/GB-KISS-LINK-FAQ-hudson-gameboy-nectaris.html
"HuC1", *Pan Docs*, https://gbdev.io/pandocs/HuC1.html

369

"HuC-3", *Pan Docs*, https://gbdev.io/pandocs/HuC3.html

"Pocket Family GB [ポケットファミリーGB]" by Hudson, *Internet Archive*,
 https://web.archive.org/web/20021118082740/http://www.hudson.co.jp
 /gamenavi/gamedb/softinfo/family/kissfamily.html

**MBC3 Real-Time Clock**

"BlueLeaff comments Looking for a List of Game Boy and GBA Games that can't be
 Emulated due to Extra Hardware in the Cart" by BlueLeaff, *Reddit*, August 9,
 2015, https://www.reddit.com/r/Gameboy/comments/3gd77s/
 looking_for_a_list_of_game_boy_and_gba_games_that/ctx9dqv/

"MBC3", *Pan Docs*, https://gbdev.io/pandocs/MBC3.html

"RTC / Second Counter", *Pokemon-Mini.net*,
 https://www.pokemon-mini.net/documentation/rtc-second-counter/

**TAMA5**

"Cartridges by mapper: TAMA5" by Gekkio and contributors, *Game Boy hardware
 database*, https://gbhwdb.gekkio.fi/cartridges/tama5.html

"Game de Hakken!! Tamagotchi Osucchi to Mesucchi Instruction Manual [ゲー
 ムで発見!たまごっち オスっちとメスっち取扱説明書]" by Bandai, 1997

"TAMA5 (WIP)" by endrift, *Game Boy Development Forum*, August 9, 2022,
 https://gbdev.gg8.se/forums/viewtopic.php?id=469

**Game Boy Camera**

"Game Boy Camera", *Pan Docs*, https://gbdev.io/pandocs/Gameboy_Camera.html

"Game Boy Camera Instruction Booklet" by Nintendo of America, 1998

"Game Boy Camera Technical Information v1.1.1" by Antonio Niño Díaz, March 2015,
 https://github.com/AntonioND/gbcam-rev-engineer/raw/master/doc/
 gb_camera_doc_v1_1_1.pdf

**Game Boy Printer**

"Game Boy Printer", *Pan Docs*, https://gbdev.io/pandocs/Gameboy_Printer.html

"Game Boy Printer Instruction Booklet" by Nintendo of America, 1998

"Gameboy Printer Paper Simulation" by Raphaël Boichot and Brian Khuu, June 6, 2022,
 https://github.com/Raphael-Boichot/GameboyPrinterPaperSimulation

"GB Printer Interface Specification" by anonymous, December 1, 2001,
 https://www.mikrocontroller.net/attachment/34801/gb-printer.txt

**Pocket Sonar**

"Curiosidades sobre 'Pocket Sonar' (ポケットソナー) de Bandai" by ClawGrip, *Jungle
 Hunt*, December 30, 2013, http://junglehunt.blogspot.com/2013/12/curiosidades-
 sobre-pocket-sonar-de.html

"Gyogun Tanchiki: Pocket Sonar" by Daniel Baxter, *Dan Docs*,
 https://shonumi.github.io/dandocs.html#ps

"Gyugun Tanchiki Pocket Sonar Instruction Manual [魚群探知機ポケットソナー取扱
 説明書]" by Bandai, 1998

"Mr. Wizard Predict Future for Fish Finders", *Recreational Boat Building Industry*,
 September 24, 1998, https://www.rbbi.com/wizard/wizfish/wizfish.htm

"Pocket Sonar: Find Fish With a Game Boy" by Norman Caruso, *Gaming Historian*,
 October 8, 2019, https://www.youtube.com/watch?v=5mHSHmk_UU4

**GBC Infrared**

"GBC Infrared" by Daniel Baxter, *Dan Docs*, https://shonumi.github.io/dandocs.html#ir

"Infrared", *Bulbapedia*, https://bulbapedia.bulbagarden.net/wiki/Infrared

"Nintendo Handhelds and Infrared: A History" by Daniel, *Random Blog*, January 23, 2018, http://blogo77.blogspot.com/2018/01/nintendo-handhelds-and-infrared-history.html

"Sakura Taisen GB Geki Hanagumi Nyuutai! Instruction Manual [サクラ大戦GB檄・花組入隊! 取扱説明書]" by Media Factory, 2000

"The Switch Joy-Con's Infrared Sensor Is Cooler Than We Thought" by Stephen Totilo, *Kotaku*, February 2, 2018, https://kotaku.com/the-switch-joy-con-s-infrared-sensor-is-cooler-than-we-1822669059

"Unlock Your Ubi" by IGN Staff, *IGN*, April 3, 2000, https://www.ign.com/articles/2000/04/03/unlock-your-ubi

## Barcode Taisen Bardigun

"Barcode Taisen Bardigun [バーコード対戦バーディガン]", *Tsutaya*, http://shop.tsutaya.co.jp/game/product/4990324040188/

"Barcode Taisen Bardigun Instruction Manual [バーコード対戦バーディガン取扱説明書]" by TAM, 1998

"Barcode Taisen Bardigun Scanner" by Daniel Baxter, *Dan Docs*, https://shonumi.github.io/dandocs.html#btb

## MBC5 Rumble

"DS Rumble Pak compatible games complete list" by Gyron, *GBAtemp Forums*, April 7, 2015, https://gbatemp.net/threads/ds-rumble-pak-compatible-games-complete-list.386149/

"GBA Game Boy Player" by Martin Korth, *GBATEK*, August 20, 2021, https://problemkaputt.de/gbatek.htm#gbagameboyplayer

"MBC5", *Pan Docs*, https://gbdev.io/pandocs/MBC5.html

"New Colors! Game Boy Color", *Nintendo Power #120*, Page 118, May 1999

"PlayStation analog and rumble support list", *RetroArch Database Issues*, January 1, 2016, https://github.com/libretro/libretro-database/issues/64

"Rumble Pak guide" by Martin Watts, *N64 Today*, February 27, 2019, https://n64today.com/2019/02/27/rumble-pak-guide/#list

## GB Memory Cartridge

"Game Boy Memory Cartridge", *Niwanetwork*, https://niwanetwork.org/wiki/Game_Boy_Memory_Cartridge

"How to program a NINTENDO POWER Cartridge?", *NesDev Forums*, https://forums.nesdev.org/viewtopic.php?t=11453

"Nintendo Magazine Cover No. 27 [任天堂マガジン表紙 No. 27]" by Nintendo of Japan, *Nintendo Online Magazine*, November 2000, https://www.nintendo.co.jp/nom/0011/index.html

"The Nintendo Power Flash Cartridge - Game Boy" by Kelsey Lewin, December 18, 2016, https://www.youtube.com/watch?v=uv7fmUFOGDo

## Sewing Machines

"The Game Boy Sewing Machine(s)! Sewing and Embroidery for the Game Boy Color" by Kelsey Lewin, July 11, 2018, https://www.youtube.com/watch?v=ykRmzS-FYSQ

"Izek Instruction Manual Model 1500" by Singer Corporation, 2000

"Nuotto [ヌオット]" by Jaguar Internation Corporation, https://www.jaguar-net.co.jp/products/oldproducts/jn-2000/index.html

"nu ・yell" by Jaguar International Corporation, https://www.jaguar-net.co.jp/products/oldproducts/jn-100/index.html

"Sewing Machines" by Daniel Baxter, *Dan Docs*,
    https://shonumi.github.io/dandocs.html#sew
"Sewing up a younger generation" by Jura Koncius, *Washington Post*, January 21, 2001
"Singer Quantum Futura CE 200", *Carnegie Mellon Textiles Lab*,
    https://github.com/textiles-lab/singer-quantum-futura-ce-200

**Turbo File GB**
"RPG Tsukuru Advance [RPG ツクール アドバンス]" by Enterbrain, *Internet Archive*,
    https://web.archive.org/web/20030618083733/http://enterbrain.co.jp/digifami/
    products/rpggba/index.html
"SNES Add-On Turbo File" by Martin Korth, *Fullsnes*,
    https://problemkaputt.de/fullsnes.htm#snesaddonturbofileexternal
    backupmemoryforstoringgamepositions
"Storage Turbo File" by Martin Korth, *Everynes*,
    https://problemkaputt.de/everynes.htm#storageturbofile
"Turbo File Advance" by Daniel Baxter, *Dan Docs,*
    https://shonumi.github.io/dandocs.html#tbfa
"Turbo File GB" by Daniel Baxter, *Dan Docs*,
    https://shonumi.github.io/dandocs.html#tbgb
"Turbo File Twin" by Jonny, *SNES Central*, https://snescentral.com/article.php?id=0908

**Full Changer**
"Game Boy Color Motion Controls (Zok Zok Heroes)" by Retro Ali, *Today in Retro*,
    February 1, 2019,   https://www.youtube.com/watch?v=LYYB99JnYEs
"Zok Zok Heroes Full Changer" by Daniel Baxter, *Dan Docs*,
    https://shonumi.github.io/dandocs.html#zzh
"Zok Zok Heroes Instruction Manual [ぞくぞく "ヒ ローズ取扱説明書]" by Media
    Factory,   2000

**MBC7**
"MBC7" by endrift, *Game Boy Development Forum*, May 29, 2017,
    https://gbdev.gg8.se/forums/viewtopic.php?id=448
"MBC7", *Pan Docs*, https://gbdev.io/pandocs/MBC7.html
"Cartridges by mappers: MBC7" by Gekkio and contributors, *Game Boy hardware
    database,* https://gbhwdb.gekkio.fi/cartridges/mbc7.html

**Power Antenna**
"Bug Sensor [バグセンサー]" by Smilesoft Co.,Ltd., *Internet Archive*, 2001,
    https://web.archive.org/web/20030828113512/http://rocketcompany.co.jp/
    bugsite/bug090.html
"Power Antenna + Bug Sensor" by Daniel Baxter, *Dan Docs*,
    https://shonumi.github.io/dandocs.html#pabs
"Power Antenna Advance [パワーアンテナ アドバンス]" by Smilesoft Co.,Ltd.,
    *Internet Archive*, 2002,
    https://web.archive.org/web/20161023103746/http://www.rocketcompany.co.jp/
    t2/t2_007.html
"Telefang Antenna [テレ ファング・アンテナ]" by Smilesoft Co.,Ltd.,
    *Internet Archive*, 2000,
    https://web.archive.org/web/20030904192758/http://rocketcompany.co.jp/
    telefang/tele060.html

**Mobile Adapter GB**

"Developing the Famicom Modem" by Masaharu Takano, *Internet Archive*, October 8, 2010, https://web.archive.org/web/20120120170645/ http://trendy.nikkeibp.co.jp/article/special/20081006/1019522/

"A Look Back at Mobile System GB, Pokémon Crystal's Online Service" by Jake, *PokéCommunity Daily*, January 19, 2018, https://daily.pokecommunity.com/2018/01/19/pokemon-crystals-online-service/

"Low Numbers for Mobile Adapter GB" by Craig Harris, *IGN via Archive.today*, March 29, 2001, https://archive.ph/baaR7

"Nintendo Magazine Cover No. 29 [任天堂マガジン表紙 No. 29]" by Nintendo of Japan, *Nintendo Online Magazine*, January 2001, https://www.nintendo.co.jp/nom/0101/index.html

"Mobile Adapter GB" by REON Team, *Dan Docs*, https://shonumi.github.io/dandocs.html#magb

"Mobile Adapter GB Delayed" by GameSpot Staff, *GameSpot via Archive.today*, October 30, 2000, https://archive.ph/PghDy

"Mobile Adapter GB Instruction Manual [モバイルシステムＧＢ取扱説明書]" by Nintendo of Japan, 2001

"Mobile Trainer Instruction Manual [モーバイル・トレーナー取扱説明書]" by Nintendo of Japan, 2001

"Online w/ Game Boy Color & Game Boy Advance | Mobile Adapter GB" by Danny Bivens, *The Famicast,* May 29, 2020, https://www.thefamicast.com/2020/05/online-w-game-boy-color-advance -mobile.html

**MBC6**

"Cartridges by mappers: MBC6" by Gekkio and contributors, *Game Boy hardware database*, https://gbhwdb.gekkio.fi/cartridges/mbc6.html

"MBC6 Flash Operation" by Daniel Baxter, *Dan Docs*, https://shonumi.github.io/dandocs.html#ndg_fla

"MBC6 research" by endrift, *Game Boy Development Forum*, September 1, 2019, https://gbdev.gg8.se/forums/viewtopic.php?id=544

**Game Link Cable ― 3rd & 4th Generation**

"Communication Ports" by Martin Korth, *GBATEK*, August 20, 2021, https://problemkaputt.de/gbatek.htm#gbacommunicationports

**e-Reader**

"e-Reader Instruction Booklet" by Nintendo of America, 2002

"GBA Cart e-Reader" by Martin Korth, *GBATEK*, August 20, 2021, https://problemkaputt.de/gbatek.htm#gbacartereader

"List of e-Reader applications", *Niwanetwork*, https://niwanetwork.org/wiki/List_of_e-Reader_applications

**GBA Tilt Cartridge**

"GBA Cart Tilt Sensor" by Martin Korth, *GBATEK*, August 20, 2021, https://www.problemkaputt.de/gbatek.htm#gbacarttiltsensor

"Motion Sensor [動きセンサー]" by Nintendo of Japan, https://www.nintendo.co.jp/n08/khpj/ugoki/index.html

"Space World 2001: Game Boy Advance to GameCube Connectivity" by Craig Harris, *IGN*, August 22, 2001, https://www.ign.com/articles/2001/08/22/space-world- 2001-game-boy-advance-to-gamecube-connectivity

"Yoshi's Great Power [ヨッシーのすっごいちから]" by Nintendo of Japan,
https://www.nintendo.co.jp/n08/kygj/power/index.html

**GBA Music Recorder**
"2908 - Music Recorder", *No Intro Dat-o-Matic*,
https://datomatic.no-intro.org/index.php?page=show_record&s=23&n=2908
"Gamester GBA Jukebox By Radica (Game Boy Advance)" by Just Some Retro Gamer,
*Retro Game Tech*, July 2, 2021,
https://www.youtube.com/watch?v=FHg3fgEAGGo
"GBA Jukebox" by M. Wiley, *IGN*, November 6, 2003,
https://www.ign.com/articles/2003/11/06/gba-jukebox
"Music Recorder" by Daniel Baxter, *Dan Docs*,
https://shonumi.github.io/dandocs.html#mus

**GBA Real-Time Clock**
"GBA Cart Real-Time Clock (RTC)" by Martin Korth, *GBATEK*, August 20, 2021,
https://www.problemkaputt.de/gbatek.htm#gbacartrealtimeclockrtc

**Joy Carry Cartridge**
"Experience the interlocking of the GC and GBA! [ＧＣとＧＢＡの連動を体験！]",
February 18, 2003, https://www.1101.com/nintendo/puzzle/index.html
"Experience the latest games at the store! Let's play with Joy Carry! [店頭で最新ゲーム
を体験！ジョイキャリーで遊ぼう！]" by Nintendo of Japan, *Nintendo
Online Magazine No. 57*, April 2003,
https://www.nintendo.co.jp/nom/0304/2/index.html
"Hikaru no Go 3 Instruction Manual [ヒカルの碁３取扱説明書] by Konami Computer
Entertainment Japan, 2003
"Joy Carry Cartridge" by Daniel Baxter, *Dan Docs*,
https://shonumi.github.io/dandocs.html#jcc
"Utilization of the Joy Carry (8M DACS) [ジョイキャリー(8M DACS)の活用]",
*Optimize*, https://optimize.ath.cx/bootcable/joycarry.html

**Multi Plust On System**
"Juguetes en los videojuegos Pluster World (冒険遊記プラスターワールド) para Game
Boy Advance" by ClawGrip, *Jungle Hunt via Internet Archive*, December 2,
2012, https://web.archive.org/web/20130507084947/
http://junglehunt.blogspot.com/
"Multi Plust On System" by Daniel Baxter, *Dan Docs*,
https://shonumi.github.io/dandocs.html#mpos
"Pluster World figure explanation (provisional) [プラスターワールドのフィギュア説
明（仮）]", February 18, 2004, http://wolf.tank.jp/plust/

**Solar Sensor**
"GBA Cart Solar Sensor" by Martin Korth, *GBATEK*, August 20, 2021,
https://www.problemkaputt.de/gbatek.htm#gbacartsolarsensor
"Kojima's GBA experiment—and the sunny island childhood it changed forever" by Jean-
Karlo Lemus, *Ars Technica*, March 27, 2020,
https://arstechnica.com/gaming/2020/03/kojimas-gba-experiment-and-the-
sunny-island-childhood-it-changed-forever/
"La serie Boktai de Konami para Game Boy Advance" by ClawGrip, *Jungle Hunt*,
October 30, 2011, http://junglehunt.blogspot.com/2011/10/la-serie-boktai-de-
konami-para-game-boy.html

"Overheating", *TaiyouWiki*, https://boktai.fandom.com/wiki/Overheating

**Game Boy Advance Infrared Adapter**

"AGS-006" by Daniel Baxter, *Dan Docs*, https://shonumi.github.io/dandocs.html#agb006

"Cyber Drive Zoids Instruction Manual [サイバードライブゾイド機獣の戦士ヒュウ 取扱説明書]" by TOMY, 2003

**Virtureal Racing System**

"Carrera GO Formula 1 Cup - 20805" by Carrera, http://www.carrera-go.de/set/20805.htm

"Carrera meets Gameboy", March 22, 2002, *Computer Woche*, https://www.computerwoche.de/a/carrera-meets-gameboy,1060825

"Carrera Power Slide Instruction Booklet" by Stadlbauer Marketing and Vertrieb GmbH, 2002

"Virtureal Racing System" by Daniel Baxter, *Dan Docs*, https://shonumi.github.io/dandocs.html#vrs

"VRS – The Carrera track on the Gameboy [V.R.S. – Die Carrerabahn am Gameboy]", *Joe's Carrera GO!!! fan page*, https://www.go143.de/v-r-s/

**Advance Movie Adapter**

"Advance DS Movie" by AM3, *Internet Archive*, https://web.archive.org/web/20090203040506/http://am3.co.jp/index.html

"Advance Movie Adapter" by Daniel Baxter, *Dan Docs*, https://shonumi.github.io/dandocs.html#ama

"'Advance Movie' to play animation on Game Boy Advance will be released on November 20th - the first one is 'Detective Conan' [ゲームボーイアドバンスでアニメ を再生する'アドバンスムービー'を11月20日に発売――第1弾は'名探 偵コナン']" by Yasuhito Sakuma, *ASCII.jp*, October 24, 2003, https://ascii.jp/elem/000/000/340/340253/

"GBA movie vending machine to hit Japan", by Hirohiko Niizumi, *Game Spot*, July 6, 2004, https://www.gamespot.com/articles/gba-movie-vending-machine-to-hit-japan/1100-6101943/

"Japanese Anime For Gameboy Advance - AM3 Smart Media Player", *Anime Link*, December 13, 2019, https://animelinkrevista.blogspot.com/2019/12/japanese-anime-for-gameboy-advance-am3.html

**Magical Watch**

"Leftovers from the past [以前からの残り物]" by bdashmura, https://bdashmura.exblog.jp/4303388/

"Magical Watch" by Daniel Baxter, *Dan Docs*, https://shonumi.github.io/dandocs.html#maw

"Wagamama Fairy: Mirumo de Pon! Hachinin no Toki no Yousei Instruction Manual [わ がままフェアリーミルモでポン！8人の時の妖精取扱説明書]" by Konami Computer Entertainment Japan, 2003

**Battle Chip Gate**

"BattleChip Gate", *The Rockman EXE Zone*, https://www.therockmanexezone.com/wiki/BattleChip_Gate

"Battle Chip Gate" by Daniel Baxter, *Dan Docs*, https://shonumi.github.io/dandocs.html#bcg

"Beast Link Gate", *The Rockman EXE Zone*, https://www.therockmanexezone.com/wiki/Beast_Link_Gate

"Operation Battle (MMBN4)", *The Rockman EXE Zone*,
https://www.therockmanexezone.com/wiki/Operation_Battle_(MMBN4)

"Operation Battle (MMBN5)", *The Rockman EXE Zone*,
https://www.therockmanexezone.com/wiki/Operation_Battle_(MMBN5)

"Progress Chip Gate", *The Rockman EXE Zone*,
https://www.therockmanexezone.com/wiki/Progress_Chip_Gate

## Wireless Adapter

"GBA Wireless Adapter" by Martin Korth, *GBATEK*, August 20, 2021,
https://problemkaputt.de/gbatek.htm#gbawirelessadapter

"Information on the Launch of the Joyspot Service [ジョイスポットサービス開始のご
案内]" by Nintendo of Japan, March 11, 2004,
https://www.nintendo.co.jp/corporate/release/2004/040311.html

"Majesco Wireless Link compatibility" by pasc, *GBAtemp Forums*, January 2, 2019,
https://gbatemp.net/threads/majesco-wireless-link-compatiblity-thread.527820/

"The much-talked-about new service! JoySpot experience report [話題の新サービス！
ジョイスポット体験レポート]" by Nintendo of Japan, *Nintendo Online
Magazine No. 69*, April 2004,
https://www.nintendo.co.jp/nom/0404/pokemon/index.html

"A new service is now available on JoySpot! [ジョイスポットに新しいサービスが登
場！]", *Inside Games*, April 23, 2004,
https://www.inside-games.jp/article/2004/04/23/13612.html

"Nintendo Wireless Adapter Specification" by denopqrihg, June 23, 2005

## Soul Doll Adapter

"Legendz Soul Dolls: from a time before Amiibos" by Kei, *DeJapan*, December 17, 2018,
http://blog.dejapan.com/2018/12/otaku-life/legendz-soul-dolls-amiibos-
nintendo-gba/

"Soul Doll Adapter" by Daniel Baxter, *Dan Docs*,
https://shonumi.github.io/dandocs.html#sda

## Campho Advance

"Campho Advance Instruction Manual [キャムフォアドバーンス取扱説明書]" by
Digital Act, 2004

"Concerning the end of the 'Campho Advance' [「カムフォアドバンス」の行末を案じ
てみる]" by Shinobu Enmacho [忍之閻魔帳],
https://blog.goo.ne.jp/ipod_mini/e/4e7af937cf94412c7355106e70f10b7e

"Game Boy Advance to Videophone! Campho" by Digital Act, *Campho Home Page via
Internet Archive*, https://web.archive.org/web/20050216014628fw_/
http://www.campho.jp/index.html

"GBA becomes a videophone! Peripheral device 'Campho Advance' released on 7/30
[GBAがテレビ電話に変身！周辺機器「カムフォアドバンス」7月30日
に発売]", *Dengeki Online*, July 8, 2004, https://dengekionline.com/data/news/
2004/7/8/8374ad5b86df7d54c8dce0b89e795a7e.html

"Peripheral device that turns GBA into a videophone, released from 30th [GBAがテレビ
電話になる周辺機器，30日から発売]", Softbank Games, *Softbank
Publishing*, July 8, 2004,
https://nlab.itmedia.co.jp/games/gsnews/0407/08/news14.html

## Wario Ware Twisted

"CG-L43 Datasheet" by NEC TOKIN Corporation, March 27, 2002

"GBA Cart Gyro Sensor" by Martin Korth, *GBATEK*, August 20, 2021,
    https://problemkaputt.de/gbatek.htm#gbacartgyrosensor
"NEC TOKIN's Piezoelectric Devices" by NEC TOKIN Corporation, *NEK TOKIN
    Product Page via Archive.today*, https://archive.ph/6NeU
"Rotating Made In Wario 'What is Spinning?' Page [まわるメイドインワリオ 「まわ
    るってなんだ」のページ]" by Nintendo of Japan,
    https://www.nintendo.co.jp/n08/rzwj/mawaru/index.html
"Shake Up. When Games Go Wild" by George Sinfield, *Nintendo Power #193*, Page 101,
    July 2005

## Play-Yan

"iQue MP4 Manual" by iQue, *Internet Archive*, 2005,
    https://archive.org/details/iQueMP4Manual
"Play-Yan" by Daniel Baxter, *Dan Docs*, https://shonumi.github.io/dandocs.html#pyn
"Play-Yan [プレイやん]" by Nintendo of Japan, https://www.nintendo.co.jp/n08/playan/
"Play-Yan - List of SD memory cards whose operation has been confirmed [プレイやん -
    動作確認済ＳＤメモリーカード一覧]" by Nintendo of Japan,
    https://www.nintendo.co.jp/n08/playan/subwin2/index.html
"PLAY-YAN micro" by Nintendo of Japan,
    https://www.nintendo.co.jp/n08/play_yan_micro/index.html
"Play-Yan Micro: The Little Media Player That Could" by AK Family Home,
    September 10, 2018,
    https://www.youtube.com/watch?v=75zeuauUq38
"Play Yan - The Retro Graveyard" by Dead Horse Gaming, *The Retro Grave Yard*, Jun 13,
    2016, https://www.youtube.com/watch?v=Lkj8BTq7zqM

## Drill Dozer

"Drill Dozer Instruction Booklet" by Nintendo of America, 2005
"GBA Cart Rumble" by Martin Korth, *GBATEK*, August 20, 2021,
    https://problemkaputt.de/gbatek.htm#gbacartrumble

## GlucoBoy

"Glucoboy: a glucose meter for gameboy" by Nicolas Nova, *Pasta&Vinegar via Internet
    Archive*, December 6, 2005, https://web.archive.org/web/20080409090306/
    http://liftlab.com:80/think/nova/2005/12/06/glucoboy-a-glucose-meter-for-
    gameboy/
"GlucoBoy brings blood sugar monitoring to GameBoy" by Joshua Fruhlinger, *Engadget*,
    October 26, 2004, https://www.engadget.com/2004-10-26-glucoboy-brings-
    blood-sugar-monitoring-to-gameboy.html
"GLUCOBOY: Game Boy glucose meter" by Christopher Grant, *Engadget*, December 6,
    2005, https://www.engadget.com/2005-12-06-glucoboy-game-boy-glucose-
    meter.html
"GLUCOBOY MOVES CLOSER TO REALITY", *Diabetes In Control via Internet
    Archive*, https://web.archive.org/web/20080708202327/
    http://www.diabetesincontrol.com/issue173/np.shtml
"GlucoBoy turns diabetes blood-testing into a game" by Scott Jon Siegel, *Engadget*,
    December 6, 2007, https://www.engadget.com/2007-12-06-glucoboy-turns-
    diabetes- blood-testing-into-a-game.html
"Littlest gamers play with blood" by Kate Benson, *The Sydney Morning Herald*,
    November 14, 2007, https://www.smh.com.au/national/littlest-gamers-play-with-
    blood-20071114-gdrl9s.html

"Nintendo Meets Diabetes Care: The History of the Glucoboy and Didget Blood Glucose Monitors" by Kelsey Lewin, October 25, 2018, https://www.youtube.com/watch?v=8iO_0nKk7vk
"United States Patent No. US 6,494,830 B1", December 17, 2002

**Vaus Controller**
"Vaus-like controller planned for Alleyway?", NesDev Forums, January 24, 2019, https://forums.nesdev.org/viewtopic.php?t=18348

**Daisy-Chain Link Cable Connector**
"Faceball 2000 - The 3D First Person Shooter for the original Game Boy that supported 16 players!", *Reddit*, September 6, 2022,https://www.reddit.com/r/Gameboy /comments/x6y87z/faceball_2000_the_3d_first_person_shooter_for_the/

**WorkBoy**
"Workboy", *Nintendo Power #36*, Pages 56-57, May 1992
"WorkBoy: Lost Game Boy Add-on FOUND After 28 Years" by Liam Robertson, *DidYouKnowGaming?*, December 26, 2020, https://www.youtube.com/watch?v=SZcrPM-jDqY

**Game Boy Printer Color**
"Reverse enginnering the unreleased GameBoy Printer COLOR" by LuigiBlood, *LuigiBlood's Blog via Tumblr,* August 29, 2019

**PageBoy**
"PageBoy: Nintendo's LOST Game Boy Add-on" by Liam Robertson, *DidYouKnowGaming?*, December 26, 2021, https://www.youtube.com/watch?v=Eg6an-Tyxsw
"United States Patent No. US 8,961,320 B2", February 24, 2015

**Sakura Taisen TV Adapter**
"Sakura Taisen GB: Geki Hanagumi Nyuutai!", *The Cutting Room Floor*, https://tcrf.net/Sakura_Taisen_GB:_Geki_Hanagumi_Nyuutai!#TV_Adapter

**Game Eye**
"E3 2002: Game Eye Revealed" by Craig Harris, *IGN via Internet Archive*, May 22, 2002, https://web.archive.org/web/20020602202336/http://pocket.ign.com/articles/ 360/360492p1.html
"Nintendo unveils GameEye" by Shane Satterfield, *GameSpot*, May 17, 2006, https://www.gamespot.com/articles/nintendo-unveils-gameeye/1100-2868152/
"Stage Debut", *Lost Media Wiki*, https://lostmediawiki.com/Stage_Debut_ (lost_build_of_cancelled_Nintendo_GameCube_game;_2002-2004)
"United States Patent No. US 7,713,129 B2", May 11, 2010
"Zelda's Study: The unreleased Nintendo GameEye" by Reece Heather, Zelda Universe, June 18, 2019, https://zeldauniverse.net/2019/06/18/zeldas-study-the-unreleased-nintendo-gameeye/

**NetCard**
"GBA NetCard - New Viewer Menu Mockup" by LuigiBlood, October 19, 2020, https://www.youtube.com/watch?v=HzxckF585lk
"NetCard", *Niwanetwork*, https://niwanetwork.org/wiki/NetCard
"Okay, let's talk about GBA Netcard a bit." by LuigiBlood, *Twitter*, October 4, 2020, https://twitter.com/luigiblood/status/1312822638989971456

www.ingramcontent.com/pod-product-compliance
Lightning Source LLC
LaVergne TN
LVHW041202050326
832903LV00020B/422